ANIMA AND AFRICA

C. G. Jung understood the anima in a wide variety of ways but especially as a multifaceted archetype and as a field of energy. In *Anima and Africa: Jungian Essays on Psyche, Land, and Literature*, Matthew A. Fike uses these principles to analyze male characters in well-known British, American, and African fiction.

Jung wrote frequently about the Kore (maiden, matron, crone) and the "stages of eroticism" (Eve, Mary, Helen, Sophia). The feminine principle's many aspects resonate throughout the study and are emphasized in the opening chapters on Ernest Hemingway, Henry Rider Haggard, and Olive Schreiner. The anima-as-field can be "tapped" just as the collective unconscious can be reached through *nekyia* or descent. These processes are discussed in the middle chapters on novels by Laurens van der Post, Doris Lessing, and J. M. Coetzee. The final chapters emphasize the anima's role in political/colonial dysfunction in novels by Barbara Kingsolver, Chinua Achebe/Nadine Gordimer, and Aphra Behn.

Anima and Africa applies Jung's African journeys to literary texts, explores his interest in Haggard, and provides fresh insights into van der Post's late novels. The study discovers Lessing's use of Jung's autobiography, deepens the scholarship on Coetzee's use of *Faust*, and explores the anima's relationship to the personal and collective shadow. It will be essential reading for academics and scholars of Jungian and post-Jungian studies, literary studies, and postcolonial studies, and will also appeal to analytical psychologists and Jungian psychotherapists in practice and in training.

Matthew A. Fike, Ph.D., is a Professor of English at Winthrop University in Rock Hill, South Carolina, where he teaches courses in critical thinking, Shakespeare, and Renaissance literature. He is the author of *The One Mind: C. G. Jung and the Future of Literary Criticism* (Routledge).

ANIMA AND AFRICA

Jungian Essays on Psyche, Land, and Literature

Matthew A. Fike

Routledge
Taylor & Francis Group

LONDON AND NEW YORK

First published 2017
by Routledge
2 Park Square, Milton Park, Abingdon, Oxon OX14 4RN

and by Routledge
711 Third Avenue, New York, NY 10017

Routledge is an imprint of the Taylor & Francis Group, an informa business

British Library Cataloguing in Publication Data
A catalogue record for this book is available from the British Library.

Library of Congress Cataloging in Publication Data
Names: Fike, Matthew, author.
Title: Anima and Africa : Jungian essays on psyche, land, and
literature / Matthew A. Fike.
Description: Abingdon, Oxon ; New York, NY : Routledge, 2017. |
Includes bibliographical references.
Identifiers: LCCN 2016054667 | ISBN 9780415786836 (hardback :
alk. paper) | ISBN 9780415786850 (pbk. : alk. paper) |
ISBN 9781315226668 (ebook)
Subjects: | MESH: Psychiatry in Literature | Jungian Theory | Africa
Classification: LCC BF109.J8 | NLM WM 49 |
DDC 155.2/644—dc23
LC record available at https://lccn.loc.gov/2016054667

ISBN: 978-0-415-78683-6 (hbk)
ISBN: 978-0-415-78685-0 (pbk)
ISBN: 978-1-315-22666-8 (ebk)

Typeset in Bembo
by Keystroke, Neville Lodge, Tettenhall, Wolverhampton

FOR MY SISTER

Some portions of *Anima and Africa* were previously published in the following journals:

- Chapter 1: "Hemingway's Francis Macomber in 'God's Country,'" *Journal of Jungian Scholarly Studies* 9.5 (2014): 1–23.
- Chapter 2: "Encountering the Anima in Africa: H. Rider Haggard's *She*," *Journal of Jungian Scholarly Studies* 10.1 (2015): 1–18.
- Chapter 3: "Anima and Psychic Fragmentation in Olive Schreiner's *The Story of an African Farm*," *English in Africa* 42.1 (2015): 77–101.
- Chapter 4: "'The Reality of the Singular': Anima and *Unus Mundus* in Laurens van der Post's *A Story Like the Wind* and *A Far-Off Place*," *English in Africa* 43.1 (2016): 57–86.
- Chapter 5: "C. G. Jung's *Memories, Dreams, Reflections* as a Source for Doris Lessing's *Briefing for a Descent into Hell*," *Journal of Jungian Scholarly Studies* 11.1 (2016): 15–25.
- Chapter 9: "Shadow Dynamics in Aphra Behn's *Oroonoko*." *Journal of Jungian Scholarly Studies* 4.2 (2009): 1–12.

CONTENTS

ACKNOWLEDGEMENTS

I wish to thank the Jungian Society for Scholarly Studies for many opportunities to present and publish my work and Winthrop University for financial support that enabled me to travel to the JSSS and other conferences. I deeply appreciate the support and encouragement of my department chairs: Gregg Hecimovich, Robert Prickett, and Casey Cothran. Great thanks also go to the staff of the Dacus Library, especially Nancy White in circulation and Phillip Hays in interlibrary loan. Family members helped out as well—Francis Fike proofread some of the chapters, and Deborah Brower suggested topics for two of the chapters. Finally, I am grateful to the staff at Routledge: Susannah Frearson, for her encouragement and guidance as this book took shape; and Rebecca Hogg for her assistance in the early stages of the publication process.

A NOTE ON THE TEXT

Anima and Africa is prepared according to the *MLA Handbook*, 7th edition, with the following exceptions: all ellipses are my insertions unless otherwise indicated; omissions at the start or end of quotations are not marked by ellipses; all emphases are in the original quotations unless otherwise indicated; double quotation marks are used only when required for clarity; and all items on the Works Cited list are assumed to be print sources unless otherwise indicated. References to *The Collected Works of C. G. Jung* include volume and paragraph numbers. For example, a reference to paragraph 460 in volume 5 appears as follows: (*CW* 5, par. 460). Shakespeare quotations are taken from David Bevington's *The Complete Works of Shakespeare*, 4th edition. Biblical quotations are taken from the *Harper Study Bible: Revised Standard Version*. *MDR* refers to Jung's *Memories, Dreams, Reflections* and BPE to his Bugishu Psychological Expedition.

INTRODUCTION

"Wood for you. Hurry up. Approach cautiously," reads a sign outside the hut where Charlie Marlow discovers Towson's *An Inquiry into some Points of Seamanship* in *Heart of Darkness* (52). These seven words are good advice not only for Joseph Conrad's character, who needs fuel for his boiler and fears being attacked by natives, but also for anyone who attempts to apply Jungian theory to literary works with African settings and characters.

Jung's writings must be weighed frankly if one is to make use of his helpful insights without perpetuating his less helpful assumptions. To begin with, there is much value in Jung's positions, as Michael Vannoy Adams points out in *The Multicultural Imagination*:

> Like Freud, Jung was a universalist, who believed that there is a fundamental unity to the human psyche, independent of time and place—and, I would emphasize, independent of "race." According to Jung, at bottom, we are all archetypally identical, typically human. Jung also believed, however, that there is a diversity to the psyche—that we are not only archetypally the same but also historically, culturally, and ethnically different. History, culture, and ethnicity are circumstances that condition human nature and differentiate us.
>
> (49)

That is, archetypal similarity and human difference are in the same relationship as archetype and archetypal image: inherited potential versus its cultural or artistic activation. However, when Jung strays into "biological reductionism" his theory becomes "psychological racism" (Adams 131). Sound theory and racism mingle, for example, in the relationship between the "archaic," which characterizes the human psyche across races and ethnicities, and the "primitive," a category associated with the assumed characteristics of indigenous peoples, whom Jung compares to children and animals and whom he considers unreflective and emotional, though vital in a way that Europeans are not (*MDR* 244–45, 269). Such thinking illustrates the binaries that Abdul R. JanMohamed calls "a manichean allegory of white and black, good and evil, salvation and damnation, civilization and savagery, superiority and inferiority, intelligence and emotion, self and other, subject and object" (*Manichean* 4). Jung's essentialist assumptions about African natives also anticipate Edward Said's concept of Orientalism: "The Oriental is irrational, depraved (fallen), childlike, 'different'; thus the European is rational, virtuous, mature, 'normal'" (40). Michael Ortiz Hill gets to the heart of Jung's attitude by arguing that his Eurocentric advocacy of the Great Chain of Being relates to his "greatest illumination" in Africa, the discovery of "the Horus principle among the Elgonyi," which concerns the birth of light/consciousness. The 1925–1926 Bugishu Psychological Expedition (BPE) convinced Jung that humans had evolved from "the darkness [unconsciousness] of prehistoric times" to the consciousness of native Africans to the higher consciousness that characterizes civilized culture, with European hegemony as the logical implication (quotations are from *MDR* 274; Hill 131).

Also troubling is Jung's position on "going black," originally a British expression that Adams defines as going back in time and space; it is the embrace of "black-primitive-instinctive" over "white-civilized-rational" (51–53). Jung states that those who travel to places like Africa that are not "overgrown by civilization" may experience the shadow as "a relapse into barbarism" and prehistory (*MDR* 246). Of his own experience, for example, he writes, "The deeper we penetrated into the Sahara, the more time slowed down for me; it even threatened to move backwards" (*MDR* 240). Similarly, Marlow's journey up the river is "like traveling back to the earliest beginnings of the world" (48), and there "on a prehistoric earth" he considers the loud gyrations of "prehistoric man" on the river bank to constitute a "wild and passionate uproar" (50–51). A visitor to Africa not only projects the shadow when witnessing such scenes but may also experience changes within his own psyche. He may go native, according to Jung, through loss of Western identity, reversion to the instinctive, and involvement with native women. Following a dream of having his hair kinked by an African American barber, Jung drew back for fear of straying too far from his European identity. In contrast, Kurtz has gone fully native through improper methods of harvesting ivory, murder, and relationship with "a wild and gorgeous apparition of a woman" (Conrad 76). As Adams states, Kurtz "epitomizes the associations 'going black,' 'going primitive,' 'going instinctive,' and 'going insane'" (70).

Heart of Darkness sketches several alternative outcomes for the encounter with "the immensity" of the shadow in the jungle/unconscious (41).[1] The white-suited accountant is unaware that he stands near the abyss, Kurtz falls off the edge and experiences the unconscious at full force, and Marlow looks over the edge of the precipice but draws back. Jung achieved a fourth and more constructive type of encounter with the unconscious both in his mental breakdown in the 1910s and on his BPE.[2] In the former case, he consciously accessed the collective unconscious, whereas in Africa the primitive infected his psyche. Although his experiences there were colored by his essentialist assumptions, Jung genuinely attempted to understand the common humanity he shared with the natives he encountered, and he recorded his archetypal experiences and psychological discoveries. Jung also never lost his connection to the feminine. In Africa, for example, he enjoyed the company of a young English woman named Ruth Bailey during much of his expedition; her feminine complement to Jung and his two male companions (she made their triad a quaternity) was crucial to the success of the BPE.

Marlow, to his credit, tells the story of his journey and learns well the value of compassion and human solidarity, but the outcome is deficient with regard to the anima. The setting—he is with four male associates on a yacht anchored in the River Thames—signals that he remains out of touch with the women of his day and with an important aspect of himself. Marlow's deficiency with the anima is ironic because he is aware of the feminine throughout his journey. He considers the sea to be a "mistress" (19), benefits from the maternal solicitude of his aunt, notes the wisdom of one of the knitting women, watches the maternal bush take a tortured African man into its "bosom" (38), recognizes Kurtz's warrior-mistress as representative of Africa itself, and shows compassion to the Intended. Troublingly, many of these experiences reinforce his misogynistic biases about women and underscore the European notion that Africa is a female body to be penetrated by trade companies, steamboats, and projectiles from men-of-war and Winchester rifles. Marlow's antifeminism simply makes him a period-specific advocate of women's place in a sphere separate from men's and makes Africa a feminine Other.

Literary allusion furthers the understanding of Marlow's journey and Kurtz's situation. Like a descent into hell, the journey to the inner station is both physical and psychological. Shade at the outer station resembles "the gloomy circle of some Inferno"; Marlow imagines that he is "about to set off for the centre of the earth" (27); and Kurtz, like Dante's Satan, dwells at "the very bottom of there" (31, 33).[3] Marlow's trip upriver, then, is a descent or *nekyia* into the "region of the first ages" and down into the unconscious (64). However, he safely keeps his own potential for psychological regression in check—partly by projecting it onto the natives and partly, as Rinda West suggests, by shoring up his self-restraint with "a strong superego" and dedication to a *mission civilisatrice* (40). In contrast, Kurtz's Western self-restraint gives way to shadow possession so that the barbarity that he and his fellow modern Europeans associated with Africa's autochthonous culture comes fully to rest in his psyche. As his inability to leave the jungle indicates, shadow possession is like the underworld in Virgil's *Aeneid*, Book 6, which is easy to enter but difficult to escape. In the words of the Sibyl, "to recall your steps, to rise again / into the upper air: that is the labor; / that is the task" (Mandelbaum trans.; lines 178–80).[4]

Marlow's superego focuses, in particular, on his abiding concern with work in the physical world, which he calls "surface, the reality" as opposed to the "inner truth" of the unconscious (49). He is attracted to the darkness around him, but work is his saving grace, especially when duty keeps him from going "ashore for a howl and a dance" (51). Jung himself did not resist the desire to dance with the natives but put an end to the celebration with a rhinoceros whip and German curse words when the dancing natives became "a wild horde" (*MDR* 271). In any event, seamanship, efficiency, and mechanics keep Marlow's ego intact and enable him to resist the shadow possession that has ruined Kurtz. Rivets, Marlow's synecdoche for work, "were what really Mr. Kurtz wanted, if he had only known it" (Conrad 43). Ultimately, then, the novel's main question-at-issue concerns the shadow. What will happen when Marlow comes face to face with Kurtz who is "that Shadow—this wandering and tormented thing" and "a shadow darker than the shadow of the night" (81, 89)? Will Marlow's ego hold fast, will he succumb to shadow possession, or will he integrate the shadow and move toward individuation?

What invites the question is the unmistakable Marlow-Kurtz parallel. Indeed, as the brick-maker tells Marlow, "The same people who sent him [Kurtz] specially also recommended you" (40). Marlow's aunt has talked him up in her letters so that he appears to be "[s]omething like an emissary of light, something like a lower sort of apostle" (26), much as Kurtz, who has been considered a "prodigy," "an emissary of pity, and science, and progress," and "a universal genius" (40, 42), initially personifies enlightened civilization. Since "[a]ll Europe contributed to the making of Kurtz" (65), he attempted to bring European ideals to darkest Africa and believed his own rhetoric, for a while. When he realized the futility of his efforts (that is, failed to recognize his own shadow projection), he scrawled in his lofty manuscript: "Exterminate all the brutes" (66). Kenneth L. Golden accurately describes this shift of perspective as a Jungian *enantiodromia*, or swing to the opposite, which compensates for the repression of the shadow. Kurtz switches from seeing himself as a high-minded, Jove-like bringer of the light of civilization to the darkness of Africa to "taking a high seat amongst the devils of the land" (64). Being seduced by the darkness without, he is possessed by the shadow within and, through madness and genocide, incarnates colonial brutality. Ego does reassert itself on the downriver run when he focuses on concrete particulars ("My Intended, my station, my career, my ideas," Marlow summarizes [84]). After all, as Adams points out, Kurtz loses his soul, not his mind (70). But as his diseased body fails, he marks the unconscious (or hell itself) as it opens to consume him: "The horror! The horror!" (85). In contrast, Marlow stays anchored to the ego through work, rejects his aunt's inflationary rhetoric as "rot" (26), and escapes with a tropical disease and a tale whose lessons bring him little comfort. Consequently, neither character properly integrates the unconscious. It consumes and ruins Kurtz. By fending it off, Marlow remains essentially unchanged, though his body and psyche are somewhat the worse for wear. He clearly does make some progress with the shadow and the anima (shadow more than anima) but is far from fully individuated with regard to either. So as the journey ends and the novel opens, his psyche is characterized more by trauma than individuation.[5]

Anima and Africa makes occasional reference to *Heart of Darkness* but is primarily not about that novel or its main themes of colonialism and racism. Although most of the texts discussed in the following nine chapters reflect those concepts to varying degrees, the focus in this study is on the application of Jungian psychological concepts to male characters. The African continent facilitates access to the unconscious and thereby aids the individuation process. As Colleen Burke states, "Africa has become a topology of the mind . . . calling forth something lost in the psychology of the white European" (n.p.). Or as Said mentions, the Westerner projects "a sort of surrogate and even underground self" onto a non-Western "complementary opposite" (3, 58; cf. 95).[6] Although such binary thinking inhibits Marlow's individuation, he expresses an openness to the unconscious mind's far reaches when he states, "The mind of man is capable of anything—because everything is in it, all the past as well as all the future" (51). In other words, Conrad's description of Marlow's trip into the heart of Africa anticipates Jung's insights into the collective unconscious, which his BPE confirmed. *Anima and Africa* explores one waypoint in that massive sea—the anima, man's experience of his inner feminine principle—as portrayed in texts selected from British, American, and African literature.

Verena Kast balances Jung's period-specific limitations with the anima's range and possibilities. "It seems undeniable," she writes, "that Jung conflated the gender stereotypes of his time with the notion of anima and animus as archetypes" (116). She points out that anima qualities such as "vitality, creativity and flexibility," as well as *eros* and relationship, "are not gender specific—both can be constellated in men as well as women" (113, 126–27). Although this inclusiveness is a given in real life, fictional characters often illustrate binaries like *eros* and *Logos* so that the gender limitations of Jung's theory become useful tools, along with the anima's more gender-neutral principles. Kast notes, for example, the anima's compensatory relationship with the persona, males' projection of the anima onto females, the anima's function as a bridge to the unconscious, and its connection to the *anima mundi*.

A number of previous monographs provide scholarly context for *Anima and Africa*. Chapters 4 and 5 in Adams's *The Multicultural Imagination* deal with Jung's two trips to Africa (the first being to north Africa in 1920 when he was 45). Blake Burleson's *Jung in Africa* provides the authoritative version of the BPE, including helpful discussions of the "primitive" and "going black." Unlike these studies, which are not literary by design, West's *Out of the Shadow: Ecopsychology, Story, and Encounters with the Land* analyzes *Heart of Darkness* and another text under consideration here, Chinua Achebe's *Things Fall Apart*, arguing, for example, that Conrad depicts the "projection of shadow onto nature and natives" (33). Indeed, her study is primarily about the shadow rather than the anima, and it does not deal with the majority of authors selected for this study. JanMohamed's *Manichean Aesthetics: The Politics of Literature in Colonial Africa*, Said's *Orientalism*, and J. M. Coetzee's *White Writing: On the Culture and Letters of South Africa*—all literary studies to varying degrees—are not Jungian. Nor do these three books deal to a significant extent with any of the authors discussed below. In some cases, Jungian literary articles provide scholarly context, but in many cases there is scant Jungian commentary and sometimes none at all.

Anima and Africa contributes new insights into a unique collection of literary texts, many of which are well-known and frequently studied. All are accessible to Jungian psychological approaches; most are highly accessible. The following information attests to the high quality of the works under consideration. J. M. Coetzee, Nadine Gordimer, Ernest Hemingway, and Doris Lessing won the Nobel Prize in Literature. Aphra Behn was the first British woman to make a living as a professional writer. Olive Schreiner wrote the first South African novel to receive international attention. Henry Rider Haggard was C. G. Jung's favorite British novelist and is best known today as the author of *King Solomon's Mines*. Laurens van der Post was a World War II hero, an advisor to Prince Charles, the godfather of Prince William, a personal friend of Jung's, one of his biographers, a spokesman for Jungian psychology, and a Jungian novelist. Barbara Kingsolver's fiction received the National Humanities Medal in the United States. And Chinua Achebe wrote one of the most widely read African novels of all time. Joseph Conrad's *Heart of Darkness*, the ur-novel of the European encounter with Africa, is a touchstone throughout the study. Three of these authors are British (Behn, Conrad, Haggard); two are American (Hemingway, Kingsolver); four are South African (Schreiner, van der Post, Gordimer, Coetzee); one grew up in Southern Rhodesia, which is now Zimbabwe (Lessing); and one is Nigerian (Achebe).

Anima and Africa's examination of the individuation process is a triptych: application of basic principles about the anima (Chapters 1–3), its larger role as a sea of energy (Chapters 4–6), and its relevance to politics and colonialism (Chapters 7–9). First, Jung believes that a man must do shadow work before doing anima work and that the anima is multifaceted—the Kore (maiden, matron, crone) and the "stages of eroticism" (Eve, Mary, Helen, Sophia). The latter is used in two ways: Jung's way, with Eve as biological motherhood and Mary as spiritual motherhood; and a post-Jungian way, with Mary as mother and Eve as wife. The proper order of individuation and the anima's many faces resonate throughout the book but are emphasized in the chapters on Hemingway, Haggard, and Schreiner. Second, Jung also describes the anima as a field of energy even broader than the collective unconscious. Characters in works by van der Post, Lessing, and Coetzee tap into that larger field, sometimes through *nekyia* or descent into the unconscious. These middle chapters make new discoveries regarding Lessing's use of imagery from Jung's autobiography and Coetzee's use of motifs from Jung's favorite book, Goethe's *Faust*. Third, the chapters on Kingsolver, Achebe/ Gordimer, and Behn examine the role of the anima in fiction that depicts the oppressive effect that Western institutions have had on Africa's native peoples—an effect of which Jung was well aware.[7] In Achebe's words, Western institutions impose a version of the feminine in men that makes native cultures "fall apart."

Chapter 1 draws most heavily on Jung's autobiographical writings because his BPE journeyed through Kenya, the setting of Ernest Hemingway's "The Short Happy Life of Francis Macomber." Although the two authors went to Africa for vastly different reasons, Jung's insights into the personal and collective unconscious, along with the discoveries he made while there, provide a lens through which to complement previous Freudian and Lacanian studies of the story. Francis, a *puer aeternus* and introverted thinker, overcomes his initial mother complex by doing shadow work with his hunting guide, Robert Wilson. As the story progresses, Francis makes the unconscious more conscious through dreaming and then connects with the archaic/primordial man buried deeply below his modern civilized persona. The chapter thus resolves two long-standing critical cruxes: the title character makes genuine psychological progress; and his wife, whether she shoots at the buffalo or at him, targets primordial masculine strength.

Chapter 2 builds on the fact that Henry Rider Haggard's *She* was one of Jung's favorite novels and is frequently mentioned in the *The Collected Works*. Although his view that *She* depicts an encounter with the anima is a critical commonplace, his reasons for considering Ayesha, the title character, to be a classic anima figure have not been sufficiently explored. This chapter uses the anima's widely ranging nature—specifically, Jung's statements about the Kore and the stages of eroticism—to explain his interpretation and then to analyze Ayesha's effect on Ludwig Horace Holly, the main character and narrative voice. Holly's African journey is one of failed individuation: after repressing his anima in England, he projects his anima onto Ayesha in Africa, experiencing compensation and *enantiodromia* (a swing from misogyny to anima possession). In this fashion, *She* depicts the perils of directly confronting the anima archetype and the collective unconscious.

Chapter 3 argues that Schreiner's *The Story of an African Farm*, a novel based on autobiographical fragments, depicts an all-pervasive psychic fragmentation. In particular, the Kore and the stages of eroticism reveal the characters' psychic fragmentation as regards the anima. Among the novel's male characters, Waldo Farber and Gregory Nazianzen Rose receive detailed analysis, especially in terms of the anima's maternal aspect. Waldo is associated with the maternal through his creation over two nine-month periods of a sheep-shearing machine and a burial post. In addition, his attraction to the primitive and his shadow work with other men precede and enable his interest in marrying Lyndall. Gregory, though his relationship to the anima is complicated by cross-dressing, achieves a motherly Christ-like orientation as Lyndall's nurse. His name alludes to Saint Gregory Nazianzen, whose theological positions point affirmatively toward individuation, wholeness, and unity. But while both young men make some progress, neither properly overcomes his psychic fragmentation to achieve an ideal contrasexual relationship. As the novel closes, significant individuation remains a far-off destination.

Chapter 4, on Laurens van der Post's *A Story Like the Wind* and *A Far-Off Place*, includes a variety of Jungian themes and motifs but analyzes most thoroughly the ways in which the anima mediates between reason and other faculties necessary for wholeness. In Jung's writings, the anima is not only the contrasexual in men but also a unifier akin to the *unus mundus* or unitary world. In the two novels the anima bridges binaries such as reason and intuition and provides an antidote to the twentieth-century malaise arising from loss of the archaic. Although van der Post's work on Jung does not mention the *unus mundus*, *Wind* and *Place* depict not only various connections among matter, psyche, and spirit but also the main characters, François and Nonnie, as a necessary hybrid of European and native African qualities.

Doris Lessing was conversant in Jungian psychology, and her novel *Briefing for a Descent into Hell*, the subject of Chapter 5, includes more Jungian elements than previous critics have identified. In particular, it is likely that she borrowed from Jung's *Memories, Dreams, Reflections* when crafting her protagonist Charles Watkins's descent into madness and return to sanity. This chapter argues that the autobiography's Chapter 6, "Confrontation with the Unconscious," and Chapter 10, "Visions"—Jung's encounter with madness and his near-death experience—provided Lessing with not only a successful *nekyia* by which to evaluate Watkins's less successful inner journey but also a series of images that she reworked in the novel. Against this Jungian background, Watkins's shortcomings are considered in light of the novel's reminders of harmony, unity, and wholeness. These reminders include references to Africa, legendary sailors, and various images/motifs. The latter include the number twelve, mandalas, and quaternity as well as evolution, the *unus mundus*, and the quantum. All underscore the potential that is lost when Watkins regains his memory but, unlike Jung, forgets his vision of the collective unconscious.

Psychological studies of J. M. Coetzee's *Disgrace* have concentrated on the relationship between the main character, Professor David Lurie, and the concept of empathy as it relates to the Romantic poets whose works he teaches. Yet depth psychology permeates the novel. Chapter 6 pursues two lines of argument. First, it shows that the main character suffers from anima possession but that he does achieve some degree of individuation through a series of steps, which include shadow work, *abaissement du niveau mental*, *nigredo*, and *nekyia*. There are, for example, dreams and visionary moments in which unconscious content reaches conscious awareness. Lurie is not free of psychological problems as the novel concludes, but images of transformation mark his individuation with regard to the feminine. Second, Coetzee's allusions to the Faust legend—Arrigo Boito's *Mefistofele* and Johann Wolfgang von Goethe's *Faust*—further the sense that Lurie makes progress with the anima. Jung's comments in *The Collected Works* are particularly relevant here because the "stages of eroticism" arise from his study of *Faust*.

Unlike Doris Lessing's Charles Watkins and J. M. Coetzee's David Lurie, Kingsolver's missionary, the Reverend Nathan Price, is described in *The Poisonwood Bible* entirely from the points of view of his wife and four daughters. After discussing the novel's relationship to Conrad's *Heart of Darkness* in ways that complement the previous criticism, Chapter 7 argues that Nathan's experience with the collective shadow in World War II has permanently stunted his individuation. In his case, the anima is dissociated so that he illustrates many of the statements Jung makes about a man's dysfunctional relationship with the anima in "Anima and Animus," a chapter from *Two Essays in Analytical Psychology* (*CW* 7). As in Jung's reading of Goethe's character Faust, Nathan illustrates the split in the modern psyche between the rational/spiritual and humans' connection to the natural world and the unconscious. The split also applies to the West and Africa, with Africa being a static backdrop on which Westerners may etch their will.[8] Many other binaries contribute to Kingsolver's diagnosis, but she also offers a prescription for a middle ground of balance and cultural accommodation. Ultimately, her use of "eye" imagery suggests that the "eye" of Africa looking back at the Price family is also an "I," an acting subject with agency of its own.

Chapter 8 considers Chinua Achebe's *Things Fall Apart*, a novel about a colonial encounter in Nigeria, and Nadine Gordimer's *July's People*, a novel about the consequences of postcolonial upheaval in South Africa. In both cases, political strife is shown to thwart individuation, particularly work with the anima. Achebe's main character Okonkwo embraces hyper-masculinity via repression, projection, and displacement of his feminine side. The resulting lack of progress with the anima is evident in a strange episode involving the abduction of his daughter Ezinma by the priestess Chielo and in comments about *chi*, which has some similarities with the personal unconscious. Unlike the local missionaries who model individuation on the communal level by integrating the outcasts and appealing through emotion, Okonkwo becomes increasingly separated from the feminine through a series of offenses against mother earth and the anima such as the judicial murder of his "son" Ikemefuna. His counterparts in Gordimer's novel are Bam and Maureen Smales, whose manservant "July" saves them from violence in Johannesburg by taking them to his home village. There they find themselves in the bush, a symbol of the collective unconscious, but do no significant inner work. Helen, Mary, and especially Eve are relevant to the narration, but Sophia is notably absent. In neither novel, however, is mother really supreme because of gender- and race-related tensions. Finally, textuality underscores the characters' psychic disconnections. They are fictional to begin with, and numerous textual references imply that the Africa of Okonkwo's Umuofia or of July's village may one day be available only in books.

Chapter 9 serves as a conclusion by first summarizing the points that have emerged regarding Africa and Jungian psychology in the preceding sections. The chapter then provides a brief analysis of Aphra Behn's *Oroonoko*, which addresses both the abuses of slaves in Surinam and the psychological complexity of enslavement. Behn's portrayal of slavery illuminates the complementary processes that hold individuation at bay and thus propel the events toward tragedy: men's shadow projection manifests as brutality, especially against Oroonoko; and present women are objects of anima projection, while absent women symbolize the lack of men's anima integration. In addition, the narrator's frequent stress on female characters' tempering influence on men, which anticipates Jung's essentialism, is cultural accretion rather than psychological truth. The novel's essentialist position, however, deconstructs itself because of Imoinda's prowess in battle and the narrator's own unrealized complicity in slavery. Ultimately, by providing a compensatory voice, the novel critiques the culture of slavery that it reflects.

Thus, *Anima and Africa* provides Jungian readings of selected texts, but by necessity the study omits more than it encompasses. A companion volume could emphasize the anima in works by African writers, and a complementary study of animus in Africa would also be possible. What is not here may yet be accomplished, and in that respect this monograph is more of a beginning than a final destination.

Notes

1   The point is in sync with the archetypal approach advanced by Jadvyga Kruminiene and Arturas Cechanovicius. The authors suggest that Marlow, Kurtz, and the Russian illustrate the hero, the shadow, and the trickster, respectively. James Mellard analyzes the many parallels to the hero's journey articulated by Joseph Campbell in *The Hero with a Thousand Faces*. Colleen Burke argues that the novel anticipates "the Jungian concepts of the personal and the collective unconscious, as a journey of individuation, a meeting with the anima, an encounter with the shadow, and a descent into the mythic underworld" (n.p.). Nancy McNeal takes a similar approach with respect to the shadow in her article.

2   For similarities between Jung's African expedition and Conrad's voyage up the Congo River, see Gloria L. Young.

3   For a fuller articulation of the comparison to the *Inferno*, see Robert O. Evans.

4   Lillian Feder notes this comparison (285) and many other parallels to the journey into Hades.

5   As Rinda West states, he encounters the shadow but does not confront it (45); as Golden maintains, Marlow gains "at least a modicum of self-knowledge about the possibilities for evil even in the 'good' man but [does] not *consciously* realize the oppositional nature of what resided within his psyche" (36); or as Mellard asserts, Marlow gains only "a knowledge of the world which reaffirms Kurtz's final message ['The horror!']" (13). McNeal accurately states that Marlow's psyche, in his quest for unity and wholeness, "is not affected by the jungle" (4), but she proposes, less convincingly, that he "represents an individual who achieves balance and integration" (8). Kruminiene and Cechanovicius are off the mark in stating that "his return to Europe is symbolically viewed as that of an individuated Self, liberated and renewed—a complete man having reached the wholeness of his psyche" (118).

6   Adams, in his Chapter 9, discusses this projection process in connection with Laurens van der Post's writings about Africa.

7   Jung writes: "What we from our point of view call colonization, missions to the heathen, spread of civilization, etc., has another face—the face of a bird of prey seeking with cruel intentness for distant quarry—a face worthy of a race of pirates and highwaymen. All the eagles and other predatory creatures that adorn our coats of arms seem to me apt psychological representatives of our true nature" (*MDR* 248–49).

8   For Africa as a backdrop, see Chinua Achebe's "An Image of Africa: Racism in Conrad's *Heart of Darkness*" (12).

1

ERNEST HEMINGWAY'S FRANCIS MACOMBER IN "GOD'S COUNTRY"

In *Death in the Afternoon*, Ernest Hemingway states: "If a writer of prose knows enough about what he is writing about he may omit things that he knows and the reader, if the writer is writing truly enough, will have a feeling of those things as strongly as though the writer had stated them. The dignity of movement of an ice-berg is due to only one-eighth of it being above water" (192).[1] "The Short Happy Life of Francis Macomber," one of two stories that arose from Hemingway's African safari, is a fine illustration of the "ice-berg" principle. Since what lies beneath its action and dialogue are the characters' psychological dynamics, C. G. Jung's insights into the personal and collective unconscious, along with the discoveries he made while himself in Africa, are especially relevant. In the two previous decades, studies by Michael Vannoy Adams, Anthony Stevens (*Two Million*), and Blake Burleson have identified Jung's African expedition as the provenance of many assumptions within his model of the psyche, but the trip-theory nexus has relevance to Jungian literary criticism as well. Like most studies of "Francis Macomber," Chapter 1 is "traditional" rather than postmodern, though it *is* post-Jungian in acknowledging the essentialism and misogyny of Jung's statements about the feminine, along with the racism of his view of the primitive. Jung is useful in many respects, including his theories' participation in some of the problematic cultural assumptions that animate Hemingway's story.

The Jungian rubric, however, is surprisingly absent from previous psychological approaches to "Francis Macomber" that sound much of the submerged seven-eighths.[2] To begin with Horst Breuer's view, Francis plays the role of the child who rejects "mother-imago" Margot and embraces father-figure Wilson (193–94). Joseph DeFalco also sees Wilson as "not unlike an authority-father figure" (203), and Richard B. Hovey views him as a surrogate father (126). Kenneth W. Harrow tracks Francis's progress through Lacan's three stages of the Oedipus complex—desire for the mother, repression of desire because of fear of castration, and accession to paternal authority. In another Lacanian study, Bennett Kravitz sees "the Macombers' marriage as a symbiotic relationship" in which husband and wife fill each other's "void of 'ego incompleteness'" (84). Using Penelope Brown's concepts of polite linguistic discourse to analyze the dialogue's psychological significance, Donald E. Hardy suggests that Francis forsakes "not his rational faculties . . . but the control of his own positive face" (132). Finally, in the study most relevant to this chapter, Michelle Scalise Sugiyama uses evolutionary psychology to analyze the dynamics among the three central characters. Margot's "female reproductive value" (143), Wilson's prowess in hunting, and Francis's ability to make money come into conflict, generating infidelity, sexual jealousy, and possibly murder. Although Sugiyama does not mention Virgil Hutton's well-known study, her evolutionary approach to Margot—that she is trying to maximize her options—sensibly augments his claim that "being upset over her husband's display of weakness" means that Margot does not really wish "to be the dominating female" (248–49). Instead, she simply wishes to be well cared for by the fittest male.

Although Sugiyama generalizes about "the environment of evolutionary adaptiveness" (143), there is no mention that the African savanna, as Jung knew well, is the place where our species evolved. As Burleson notes in *Jung in Africa*, that continent is "the ancestral home of the human brain"; it is "an established fact of paleontology [that] *Homo sapiens* originated in East Africa. We now know that we are all Africans" (18, 62).[3] The story's description of "the parklike wooded rolling country on the far side" and "the untracked, parklike country" makes it clear that the setting is the savanna where humans evolved (21). Thus, Hemingway's modern characters enact ancient drives in the very place where evolution etched them permanently into the human psyche.

Along with complementing Freudian/Lacanian and evolutionary readings of "Francis Macomber," a Jungian psychological approach challenges the doubt that various scholars have expressed with regard to the title character's psychological state in the moments prior to his death. They believe that his change from cowardice to bravery is "much too improbable" (Gardner 188), that "the fate of Macomber's manhood [is] undecidable" (Strychacz 18), and that he "illustrates no dramatic change from boyish cowardice to heroic manhood" (Hutton 248), perhaps because his happiness is not "an integrative form of development, but [merely] an abrupt re-cathexis" (Breuer 195). The Jungian equivalent of these claims would be that Macomber's change is impermanent because he experiences *enantiodromia*, a swing between the opposites of negative inflation and positive inflation. DeFalco, however, correctly identifies Francis's experiences as "the journey toward individuation" (206), though the statement's Jungian resonance is left unexplored. For Jung, individuation means a movement toward psychic wholeness, or the Self, when the unconscious becomes conscious; in this fashion, greater psychic integration leads out of the inflationary cycle toward sustainable well-being. Hemingway hints that Francis's change is genuine and permanent, and this chapter will argue that his individuation becomes clearer if the story is read through a Jungian psychological lens. In brief, Francis, a *puer aeternus* and introverted thinker, overcomes his initial mother complex by doing shadow work with his hunting guide, Robert Wilson. As the story progresses, Francis makes the unconscious more conscious through dreaming and then connects with the archaic/primordial man buried deeply below his modern civilized persona. Like the reader who must infer the seven-eighths below the story's surface, Francis discovers psychic resources that lie below the veneer of his comfortable lifestyle, "the fairytale world of high society" (Gaillard 32).

Jung and Africa

It is hard to imagine two more diverse figures than Hemingway and Jung—the macho sportsman and the learned doctor; but both visited east Africa, though for vastly different reasons. Hemingway went on a three-month safari in the summer of 1933, published an account of the hunt in *Green Hills of Africa* in 1935, and used some of the book's details in "Francis Macomber," which appeared in the September 1936 issue of *Cosmopolitan*. Jung made two trips to Africa: the first was to Tunis and Algiers in 1920; then for five months in 1925–1926 his "Bugishu Psychological Expedition" (BPE) journeyed through Kenya, Uganda, Sudan, and Egypt. Although his main objective was to study Africans' dreams, the trip afforded him the opportunity to observe what happened to himself, a white European, in a remote third-world setting. The resulting experiences and insights provide a relevant lens through which fresh perspectives on "Francis Macomber" may be discovered.

Jung believes that consciousness is not original to our species but rather that consciousness emerged in prehistory and is still developing. In his autobiography, *Memories, Dreams, Reflections*, he identifies the "original state of twilight conscious-ness" in which humans "had existed from time immemorial" and from which they emerged "to become aware of their own existence," that is, to achieve conscious-ness as we know it (240). A lyrical passage in *The Archetypes and the Collective Unconscious* describes how that transformation may have occurred:

> I believe that, after thousands and millions of years, someone had to realize that this wonderful world of mountains and oceans, suns and moons, galaxies and nebulae, plants and animals, *exists*. From a low hill in the Athi plains of East Africa I once watched the vast herds of wild animals grazing in soundless stillness, as they had done from time immemorial, touched only by the breath of a primeval world. I felt then as if I were the first man, the first creature, to know that all this *is*. The entire world round me was still in its primeval state; it did not know that it *was*. And then, in that one moment in which I came to know, the world sprang into being; without that moment it would never have been. All Nature seeks this goal and finds it fulfilled in man, but only in the most highly developed and most fully conscious man. Every advance, even the smallest, along this path of conscious realization adds that much to the world.
>
> (*CW* 9i, par. 177)

Noting the contrast to the natural world, which "was still in its primeval state" and "did not know that it *was*," Jung, in an imaginative reverie, experiences the moment when consciousness emerged from primordial twilight. The last three sentences of his statement evince both the primitive's movement from twilight to consciousness (the world's spring into being) and the aware person's journey toward maximal consciousness. In other words, progress continues in the present within each conscious person. It is as if the evolution of human consciousness and the individual person's individuation are not separate achievements. Rather, one person's movement toward greater awareness mirrors the species' emergence from semi-consciousness.

Although Africa is the locale where consciousness emerged, Burleson notes that Jung understood the continent to represent the unconscious (200). It follows that the human awareness that Jung observed there diverges markedly from his own highly rational European way of thinking. Unfortunately, some of his further conclusions about the psychology of indigenous peoples are in sync with racist assumptions. He believes, for example, that Africans, like children or adolescents, are dominated by emotion—"these people live from their affects" (*MDR* 239–44). He also considers them child-like in their *participation mystique*, a term borrowed from Lucien Lévy-Bruhl.[4] In this magical mentality events are attributed to "so-called supernatural powers" rather than natural causes (*CW* 10, par. 113), and there is no distinction between the perceiving subject and the perceived object. Jung states: "For primitive man . . . the psychic and the objective coalesce in the external world. . . . Psychic happenings take place outside him in an objective way" (*CW* 10, par. 128). For Jung, whereas modern persons achieve psychic differentiation, "primitives" are less differentiated (*CW* 7, par. 156). Being "primitive" means projecting inner content onto the world and blurring the difference.[5]

Perhaps *participation mystique* fosters the ability to see the basic unity of all life rather than divisions like the one between hunter and hunted. Jung's experiences, reported in his *Visions* seminar, bear out the point. One morning he was astonished to discover that a lion that lived nearby had left tracks outside his tent. The natives told him, "It is not bad, it is *our* lion." Additional evidence came when Jung realized "the fact that leopards go hunting with you provided you carry your shotgun and not your big caliber gun; when you carry your big gun no leopard will appear." When his company shot a guinea fowl, the leopard made off with it before the hunters could reach it. The latter experience implies an almost intellectual process on the leopard's part, as well as partnership—human and big cat working together. Commenting on these episodes, Jung suggests, "It is quite possible that *participation mystique* with the non-ego means a certain change, not only in yourself, but also in the surrounding conditions" (qtd. in Burleson 135–36).[6] In other words, when one perceives the world in human terms, the observed animal returns the favor. A lion or leopard—dangerous prey—is no longer Other but brother. Of course, the main characters in "Francis Macomber" wish only to hunt and destroy great game, but the narrator does describe a wounded lion's agony from the animal's point of view. As Carey Voeller states, "The beast's humanized, dying moments function as the key factor in forging the connection of humankind with the animal world" (232). Although Hemingway went to Africa to take life and fancied himself a great white hunter, including the lion's point of view suggests that he may have developed some sense of life's overarching unity.

Participation mystique, however, is problematic when applied to an indigenous people because it implies a linkage between their race and their psychology.[7] A more fundamental, less controversial element of the primitive is that we as civilized persons have "those historical layers in ourselves" that link us to primitive times (Jung, *MDR* 244). In "Archaic Man," Jung states: "it is not only primitive man whose psychology is archaic. It is the psychology also of modern, civilized man, and not merely of individual 'throw-backs' in modern society. On the contrary, every civilized human being, however high his conscious development, is still an archaic man at the deeper levels of his psyche" (*CW* 10, par. 105). Burleson explains that when humans evolved out of "the ubiquitous unconscious," they carried with them "an undifferentiated layer of the human (and animal) psyche" (16). This layer can be observed, Jung believes, in the daily lives of modern-day primitives such as those he encountered on the BPE (*CW* 18, par. 18, 1288). But because the ancient wellspring is deeply buried, a modern civilized person like Francis suffers from malaise, psychic fragmentation, and a loss of vital wholeness.

In the decades when Jung's BPE and Hemingway's safari took place, journeying to Africa was considered therapeutic precisely because it threw the archaic in human psychology into bold relief. As Marianna Torgovnick states in her book *Primitive Passions*, "'The primitive' was widely valued as a way station or spa for men suffering from cultural alienation and psychic distress" (qtd. in Burleson 15).[8] She adds that André Gide, D. H. Lawrence, and others including Jung visited the continent. Jung emphasizes the continent's positive effect: "these seemingly alien and wholly different Arab surroundings awaken an archetypal memory of an only too well known prehistoric past which apparently we have entirely forgotten. We are remembering a potentiality of life which has been overgrown by civilization, but which in certain places is still existent" (*MDR* 245–46). As regards accessing the archaic in the civilized person, Jung biographer Barbara Hannah notes that encounters with indigenous peoples and animals mean that "in Africa you are in a way meeting those layers *outside*." Her sense that Africa "is the country of the Self, not of the ego" has particular significance in light of Jung's No. 1 and No. 2 personalities (172). Whereas No. 1 is "the ego-centered, time-bound person," No. 2 is "the Self-centered, timeless person of the collective unconscious" (Burleson 61). Jung went to Africa to seek relief from the stress of his clinical practice, the province of the ego, by researching the unconscious in others and by exploring its nether reaches in himself.

Such exploration of the deep unconscious can be perilous, as the Swahili word *shenzi* attests. In *Green Hills of Africa*, Hemingway translates the word as "a wild man" (180). Burleson states that it means "'uncivilized'" and identifies a series of English equivalents: "Going *shenzi* meant 'going black', 'going primitive', 'going native', 'going insane'" (188). In *Memories, Dreams, Reflections*, Jung states that "going black" means sleeping with black women (262). Cleary *shenzi* has racist undertones to the contemporary ear; but Adams, in his helpful study of race, understands that the term, which is British in origin, also means "to revert . . . to an earlier and lower state . . . [t]o go black is to 'go back'—in time and space" (51–52). For example, Jung interpreted his dream, in which his African American barber in Chattanooga, Tennessee, applied a curling iron to Jung's hair (in order to make it "kinky" like "Negro hair"), as a warning that his No. 1 personality was in danger of *shenzi* because his No. 2 personality was reverting to an earlier, more unconscious state by succumbing to *participation mystique* (*MDR* 272). Although a more positive interpretation of the dream can be advanced, it was not possible for Jung who pulled back, forewarned.

Francis Macomber's mother complex

While in Africa, Francis Macomber connects with the archaic psyche that is buried beneath his life as a socialite and sportsman. Before the trip and in its early stages, however, the ego dominates his superficial life. As Jung states, "The predominantly rationalistic European [or American] finds much that is human alien to him, and he prides himself on this [difference] without realizing that his rationality is won at the expense of his vitality, and that the primitive part of his personality is consequently condemned to a more or less underground existence" (*MDR* 245). The stated duality has some of its intellectual roots in Friedrich Schiller's *Letters on the Aesthetic Education of Man*, about which Jung comments in *Psychological Types*, Chapter 2 (*CW* 6, par. 101–222). Schiller argues that civilization has diminished creativity, feeling, imagination, instinct, intuition, matter, and the senses in favor of analysis, empiricism, intelligence, reason, societal control, speculation, spirit, and understanding. He suggests that beauty and the "instinct of play" (part 2, letter 14) can be instrumental in uniting the opposing sets of qualities; and he sounds like Jung in stating, "It will be quite possible, then, that in remote corners of the world humanity may be honoured in the person of the negro, while in Europe it may be degraded in the person of the thinker" (part 2, letter 7). Schiller's interest, however, lies in classical antiquity, the Golden Age of Greece and Rome, not in prehistory or archaic man. A more personal gloss may have greater relevance: Jung's own dream of a multi-story house in which each lower floor depicts an earlier age. A stone-age cave dwelling, "that is, the world of the primitive man within myself—a world which can scarcely be reached or illuminated by consciousness," lies beneath the cellar floor (*MDR* 160).

Francis's connections to the outer world through sports and other activities signal disconnection from this "underground existence," the archaic elements within the collective unconscious. The narrator enumerates these wide-ranging interests:

> he was thirty-five years old, kept himself very fit, and was good at court games, had a number of big-game fishing records. . . . He knew . . . about motor cycles [sic]—that was earliest—about motor cars, about

duck-shooting, about fishing, trout, salmon and big-sea, about sex in books, many books, too many books, about all court games, about dogs, not much about horses, about hanging on to his money, about most of the other things his world dealt in, and about his wife not leaving him.

(6, 18)

Ben Stoltzfus describes the statement about "court games" and other activities as summing up Francis's "essence before he goes to Africa" (220); and Carl P. Eby, who identifies guns as phallic symbols, "suspect[s] that Hemingway's guns were seldom *just* guns" (283–84 and n. 4). Similarly, Breuer views "sex in books" as signaling "phallic deficiency" (194). Jung too would see the canalization of sexual libido in Francis's hobbies: "In men, sexuality if not acted out directly, is frequently converted into a feverish professional activity or a passion for dangerous sports, etc., or into some learned hobby, such as a collecting mania," like saving money (*CW* 3, par. 105).[9] Not only do Francis's activities substitute for the inner work he needs to do; they also fall short of Jung's idea of American sports, which, being ruthless, brutal, savage, and gladiatorial, suggest "a glimpse of the Indian" and manifest, in spectators, "ancient instincts that are akin to bloodlust" (*CW* 10, par. 100, 977).

Although Francis is now thirty-five years old, his list of hobbies implies a sense of arrested development. Wilson underscores his client's status as a boy-man by calling him "laddybuck" (20) and by thinking that "his American face . . . would stay adolescent until it became middle-aged" (8). "It's that some of them stay little boys so long, Wilson thought. Sometimes all their lives. Their figures stay boyish when they're fifty. The great American boy-men" (25–26). Although Burleson is not writing about the story, he helpfully brings together Hemingway and Jung via a key concept that applies to the immaturity that Wilson recognizes in Francis: "There is exhilaration in living life on the thin line between life and death, and Africa, as Ernest Hemingway discovered, provided the perfect masculine playground for this edge. From a Jungian perspective, this phenomenon might best be understood as the problem of the *puer aeternus*" (32). Some of the characteristics of the eternal child that Jung's associate Marie-Louise von Franz enumerates fit Francis well. Such a person is between thirty and forty-five years of age, has a mother complex, and engages in dangerous sports in an attempt to separate from the mother (1). Flying is the example given, but big game hunting can be equally fatal.[10] Francis does engage in hunting and does have a mother-wife, but other characteristics of the *puer* do not fit him precisely. He does not fantasize ineffectually about future plans but merely knows that Margot will never leave him. Insofar as Jung understands that work is the cure for *puer aeternus* (5), Francis seems poised, despite his past attraction to "court games" and "sex in books," to make psychological progress toward greater maturity.

The passage's resonance with Jungian typology yields further insight into Francis's personality. Knowing about "sex in books," along with emphasis on many "books, too many books," implies that Francis, although "very tall, very well built . . . [and] considered handsome" (6), is not a man of deep sexual experience and that he would really rather just read. Being certain that Margot will not leave him suggests that she might want to, perhaps because of sexual inadequacy that motivates her frequent promiscuity. The narrator states, "If he had been better with women she would probably have started to worry about him getting another new, beautiful wife" (18). Francis's problem is at least, as Hovey suggests, "a timidity whose mark is lack of self-assertion" (124). Together, the information about "sex in books" and awkwardness with women suggests that Francis is an introverted thinker, which makes him easy prey for manipulation by extroverted Margot, whose beauty "had, five years before, commanded five thousand dollars as the price of endorsing, with photographs, a beauty product which she had never used" (6). Further evidence of her extroversion is that she kisses Wilson on the mouth in front of her husband, something an awkward introvert would be loath to do.

With proper caveats in place, an educated guess as to Francis's full personality type is possible: ISTP, which represents introverted, sensing, thinking, and perceiving. According to "Portrait of an ISTP," such a person has an adventuresome spirit, thrives on action, and is attracted to dangerous activities like riding motorcycles. ISTPs tend to be good athletes and have good hand-eye coordination ("kept himself very fit, and was good at court games"); follow through with a project, especially one that involves logical analysis ("hanging on to his money"), and are good at a variety of tasks (motor cars, duck-shooting, fishing, sports, dogs). ISTP is also loyal, trusting, and patient—qualities that the narrator implies at the end of the "sex in books" paragraph: "he had always a great *tolerance* which seemed the nicest thing about him if it were not the most sinister" (18; emphasis added). If Francis as ISTP is an educated guess, Margot's type is merely a guess—it is harder to pin down because the narrator comments on so little of her interior life; however, ENFJ (extraverted, intuitive, feeling, judging) captures some of her characteristics. ENFJs are people persons first and foremost, but "Portrait of an ENFJ" suggests a shadow side: they are manipulative and controlling and can easily get under people's skin; they can also be fussy and may judge too quickly. Although the two portraits seem to match Francis and Margot, an exact, reductive identification is neither possible nor desirable, for they are rounder characters than case study allows. The more important point is that they are mismatched and have married for the wrong reasons. Francis's money and Margot's beauty ("His wife had been a great beauty" [18]) bring them together, and significant friction is inevitable between a man and a woman who approach the world differently. Francis's interest in dangerous action brings him to Africa, and Margot dutifully accompanies him; but when inexperience results in an atypical failure to handle a crisis, consequences ensue: his wife becomes picky and judgmental; he in turn becomes over-stressed and angry.

Francis, an introverted *puer*, has arrived at chronological adulthood without achieving full manhood. Instead, sports and his other interests function as an avoidance mechanism—the American equivalent of failure to participate in tribal rites of passage. Jung knows that, in "primitive" societies, chronological age is an insufficient marker of adulthood. A male must also separate from the mother and abandon his childish ways while undergoing "initiation into the 'men's house' and ceremonies of rebirth"; afterwards a mother is sometimes not allowed to speak with her son (*CW* 7, par. 314; 18, par. 363). Here one may reprise the criticism of Robert Bly's promotion of "'male initiations' to wean boys from the dangerous contaminations of maternal influences" (Rowland, *Literary Theory* 17). In other words, Bly overlooks gender's cultural subjectivity in order to promote the essentialist idea that a man achieves the authentic Masculine by eschewing the authentic Maternal. Still, there is some value in tribal initiation rituals for modern men, and Jung predicts the consequences of improperly navigating the path to individuation.

> The modern civilized man has to forgo this primitive but nonetheless admirable system of education. The consequence is that the anima, in the form of the mother-imago, is transferred to the wife; and the man, as soon as he marries, becomes childish, sentimental, dependent, and subservient, or else truculent, tyrannical, hypersensitive, always thinking about the prestige of his superior masculinity.
>
> (*CW* 7, par. 316)

Marital dysfunction arises when the order of individuation is violated. For Jung, "If the encounter with the shadow is the 'apprentice-piece' in the individual's development, then that with the anima is the 'master-piece'" (*CW* 9i, par. 61). A tribal youth does his shadow work in the men's house and weds only after achieving full manhood. Otherwise, he is ill-equipped to deal with his mate. Perhaps with Circe in mind, Jung emphasizes the need for such preparedness in stating that "when animus and anima meet, the animus draws his sword of power and the anima ejects her poison of illusion and seduction" (*CW* 9ii, par. 30). The statement works if standard definitions of "animus" and "anima" are held in mind, but he appears to be referring simply to male strength and female seduction. Without the sword of masculine power, a man succumbs to feminine illusion, which in Francis's case involves a mother complex. Lacking the masculine strength of Odysseus, he has attempted the "master-piece" in marriage with Margot before laying the foundational "apprentice-piece" with other men. As a result, their marital interaction sounds at times like a whining son and a long-suffering mother.

> "You won't leave me."
> "No," she said. "I won't leave you and you'll behave your self."
> "Behave myself? That's a way to talk. Behave myself."
> "Yes. Behave yourself."
> "Why don't *you* try behaving?"
> "I've tried it so long. So very long."
>
> (20)

Hemingway modeled Margot after Jane Mason, with whom he had had an affair in Havana (Flora 76) and whom he considered the "worst bitch" (his words) he had ever known, though she possessed an admirable "eagerness to get laid" (Gardner 188). Jane is no doubt in the background when Wilson reflects on "American female cruelty": "They are, he thought, the hardest in the world; the hardest, the cruelest, the most predatory and the most attractive and their men have softened or gone to pieces nervously as they have hardened." He goes on: "She's damn cruel but they're all cruel. They govern, of course, and to govern one has to be cruel sometimes. Still, I've seen enough of their damn terrorism" (9–10). Hutton aptly points out "that Wilson criticizes Margaret [Margot] for what he himself practices on the native boys" (241). The guide's statements, therefore, are examples of projection. In addition, Hemingway/Wilson is not a solo voice; Jung, another adulterous man of his time, sounds the same misogynistic note that accompanies the story.

> I asked myself whether the growing masculinization of the white woman is not connected with the loss of her natural wholeness (*shamba*, children, livestock, house of her own, hearth fire); whether it is not a compensation for her impoverishment; and whether the feminizing of the white man is not a further consequence. The more rational the polity, the more blurred is the difference between the sexes.
>
> (*MDR* 263–64)[11]

The statement also illustrates Jung's essentialist position that there is a standard Feminine from which individual women deviate at their peril. That said, it is true that the Macombers are childless. Lacking children of her own, perhaps Margot treats her husband like one. In addition, the further away from the men's house a modern male strays, the more feminine he becomes. As humans become more "rational" (conscious) and more distant from the archaic layer, traditional gender roles become redefined. Although feminists would not necessarily favor such conclusions, misogynistic thinking does illuminate the dysfunctional Macombers to some degree. Jung's statement is relevant to Hemingway's story precisely because both men reflect the sexism of their time.

Hovey notes that Margot "is a Goneril-Regan in her bitchhood, more monster than woman" (126). Trouble arises when Lear makes his disrespectful daughters his surrogate mothers, and they mistreat him because doing so aligns with self-interest. Something similar happens in "Francis Macomber"; but this time, in Breuer's words, "mother and wife merge as 'bitch'" (196). The formulation *mother* + *wife* = *bitch* is a function of Francis's psychology as much as of Margot's. Their psycho-dynamics, however, involve not only Francis's mother complex but also Margot's animus possession. In describing the condition, Jung could not have been more accurate if he had had the Macombers—or Lear's elder daughters—in mind: "Turned towards the world, the anima is fickle, capricious, moody, uncontrolled and emotional, sometimes gifted with daemonic intuitions, ruthless, malicious, untruthful, bitchy, double-faced, and mystical. The animus is obstinate, harping on principles, laying down the law, dogmatic, world-reforming, theoretic, word-mongering, argumentative, and domineering" (*CW* 9i, par. 223).[12] Statements like this underlie Susan Rowland's critique of "Jung's erotic anima [as being] dangerous when substantiated into fantasies of female deviousness and power" (*Literary Theory* 17). As Richard Fantina speculates, "While the misogyny is unmistakable, perhaps Hemingway had more in mind than the portrait of a simply vicious woman" (157). Perhaps bitchery is to the tip of the iceberg as Margot's "animus possession" is to the submerged seven-eighths. Even worse, in terms of Jung's "stages of eroticism," Margot merges not only Mary (mother) and Eve (wife) but also Helen (whore).[13] DeFalco rightly calls Margot a "dangerous mother-temptress" (203). How can Francis as husband-son successfully relate to Margot as wife-mother, especially when she also plays the role of whore? The final feminine figure in Jung's quartet of stages, Sophia (wisdom), plays no part in the inner life of the story's lone female character, who appears not to be the sympathetic and "heroic" figure whose reputation Nina Baym tries to rehabilitate (118).

There are four types of women in Jung's stages of eroticism and four "persons" in his quaternity (Father, Son, Holy Spirit, and Satan). The number four is also central for Jung in a group setting that requires prolonged, purposeful action. He comments in *Memories, Dreams, Reflections* on "the archetype of the triad, which calls for the fourth to complete it, as we have seen again and again in the history of this archetype" (261). The BPE was originally conceived as a triad—Jung and his associates Peter Baynes and George Beckwith, a group that would probably have imploded if an English woman named Ruth Bailey had not joined the expedition. Francis, Margot, and Wilson—as a triad—have no fourth to round out the group and relieve the tensions that arise when Francis (son) disappoints Margot (mother) through cowardice, Wilson (father) fornicates with her, and Francis's values begin to shift toward Wilson's. In this Freudian interpretation of the story, Wilson functions as a father figure to Francis in order to help him separate from the mother-wife. Jungian theory, however, places greater emphasis on a male's accomplishment of the "apprentice-piece," shadow work with another man: Francis projects his shadow onto Wilson; as a result, his interaction with Wilson brings to consciousness an important aspect of himself.

Macomber's inner work

Vastly different though the two men may be (Francis, a boy-man; Wilson, a professional killer and probably a World War I veteran), they share a common typology: introverted thinking. As previously noted, Wilson thinks about Francis's boyishness and Margot's bitchery. Wilson also thinks about killing, a matter on which he "had his own standards" (21) so that, when Francis proposes allowing the lion to die on its own, Wilson "suddenly felt as though he had opened the wrong door in a hotel and seen something shameful" (15). The narrator registers the hunter's visceral reaction as an analogy because even when Wilson *feels*, he *thinks*. When Francis's act of cowardice sours relations with Margot, Wilson makes a decision that signals an introversion reminiscent of Francis's knowledge of "sex in books": "He would eat, then, by himself and could read a book with his meals" (8). Lack of feeling, which is implied by "his flat, blue, machine-gunner's eyes" (8), veers into cruelty as he thinks about the fornication with Margot: "Well, it was the poor sod's own bloody fault." She makes the same point with equal lack of feeling: "Yes, darling. That's the way I meant it to be [she had promised not to sleep with other men on the safari]. But the trip was spoiled yesterday [when Francis acted like a coward; therefore, her behavior is his own fault]" (19). Then, in a moment of twisted logic, Wilson justifies his behavior by thinking that "their standards were his standards as long as they were hiring him" (21). Since Francis is paying for the trip, his standard (no adultery) ought to be foremost in the guide's mind.[14]

Francis's panicked cowardice, his flight from a lion, is put in terms of another animal: "'I bolted like a rabbit,' Macomber said" (8). The image resonates with Margot's image a page later when she describes the eland he has killed: "'They're big cowy things that jump like hares, aren't they?' 'I suppose that describes them,' Wilson said." Macomber's rejoinder—that eland "are very good meat"—indicates that he does not grasp the parallelism of *bolted like a rabbit* and *jump like hares* or the implication of hunting prey that are "not dangerous" unless "they fall on you": namely, that he, in his cowardice, is a big cowy thing himself. The image of the fleeing rabbit takes on further significance in light of Hope B. Werness's statement that in art "the rabbit symbolized lust, and the image of a knight fleeing from a hare was a Medieval symbol of cowardice" (340). Francis's use of the rabbit image condenses the cowardice of his flight and the sexual desire that he feels for mother-Margot. What of the lion? In Jung's *Collected Works* the lion is indexed as a symbol of the Self, and it also "stands for the danger of being swallowed by the unconscious" (*CW* 9i, par. 315; 5, par. 277). The image of fleeing *like* a rabbit *from* a lion, then, suggests that Francis's initial response to the shadow work he must do with Wilson is to flee back to the comfort of the mother figure, followed by negative inflation (self-loathing).

Francis's lapse into cowardice is also a sign of a hyperactive imagination. Hemingway once stated, "Cowardice . . . is almost always simply a lack of ability to suspend the functioning of the imagination" (qtd. in P. Young 72). Overactive imagination may be the psychology behind "the Somali proverb that says a brave man is always frightened three times by a lion: when he first sees his track, when he first hears him roar and when he first confronts him" (11). Francis's panic simply illustrates the point. If lions frighten even brave men, his problem may be not that he is a despicable coward but that he is just a novice big game hunter, as the narrator suggests: "He was dressed in the same sort of safari clothes that Wilson wore except that his were new" (6). Even Jung, who went to Africa to explore the unconscious, panicked on two occasions. In one instance, fearing injury, he had to crack a whip and yell curses in German to get a group of dancing natives to end their festivities. In another that Adams calls "a paranoid delusion," he spent thirty minutes in the bush feeling as if unseen eyes were watching him (73). As Jung would agree, the point is that being frightened by a lion, dancing natives, or unseen eyes is not a badge of dishonor unless a man first pretends to be something he is not. As Hutton rightly states, "fear does not necessarily indicate cowardice" (247).

Whereas Francis's flight seems to indicate fear of the unconscious, he accomplishes some genuine inner work when he dreams "of the bloody-headed lion standing over him, and listening while his heart pounded" (18). To say merely that the "lion symbolizes death," as Stoltzfus does, is an oversimplification (221). In Hovey's view, the dream is part day residue and part a reaction to fear of being "killed or hurt by the father" (226, n. 16). For Bert Bender, the bloody lion is "an image not only of primitive suffering, courage and violence, but also of the red-faced Wilson who is at this moment 'standing over' Francis by cuckolding him" (96). Breuer considers the dreamer's subordinate vantage point to indicate a feminine position, and he notes that Francis awakens to discover a Freudian "primal scene" (194). A Jungian interpretation begins with the distinction Jung discovered on the BPE between Africans' big dreams and little dreams. Big dreams are significant for a whole clan; they are archetypal, collective, God-sent, mythological, numinous, and prophetic. Little dreams are significant merely to individual persons. Francis's dream is a little dream whose most important characteristic is its anticipatory quality. The bloody-headed lion harkens back to the events of the day (Wilson blew part of the charging lion's head off; Wilson has a red face), but it also looks ahead to the final scene in which Margot shoots Francis in the head. Jung is quite clear about "the aid of warning dreams" (*MDR* 245) and their role in both anticipating danger and identifying the need for inner work. Sometimes even a little dream can participate in the numinous:

> in normal people, archaic dream-products with their characteristic numinosity appear mainly in situations that somehow threaten the very foundations of the individual's existence, for instance in moments of mortal danger, before or after accidents, severe illnesses, operations, etc., or when psychic problems are developing which might give his life a catastrophic turn, or in the critical periods of life when a modification of his previous psychic attitude forces itself peremptorily upon him, or before during, and after radical changes in his immediate or his general surroundings.
>
> (*CW* 3, par. 566)[15]

Francis's lion dream, then, represents his fear of the lion (his pounding heart), Wilson's superiority in hunting and sex, and Francis's ultimate fate. But since the lion is a symbol of wholeness, the dream of a bloody-headed lion implies that blood sport will bring him closer to the Self and that he will end up a dead lion rather than a live rabbit—that his final moments will constitute a short, happy life.

Francis's dream also moves him closer to the archaic layer whose vitality is a crucial element of his brief happiness. The *East African Standard*, a Nairobi newspaper that reported on Jung's BPE, supports this archeological role of dreams: "The primitive man in the European has been found to become active when the individual is asleep" (qtd. in Burleson 142).[16] The dream nudges Francis's psyche in that deeper direction; but there is an intermediate step between dreaming and connecting with his hidden primordial strength: anger at Wilson for "topping" Margot (19). Breuer accurately describes Francis's transformation as "the repudiation of the mother, and an unqualified embracing of the father's mental world" (194–95). Of course, Francis is clearly not embracing father-Wilson (he refers to him as "red-faced swine" and "had no fear, only hatred of Wilson" [20, 22]); but Francis does shift to Wilson's "mental world" by setting aside thought and imagination in order to funnel his rage into the hunt, becoming at this moment a more complete man. When an introverted thinker embraces emotion (Jung's term is the "inferior function" because it is secondary to thinking), psychic progress is possible. As a result, the next time he shoots he "felt a drunken elation" and "had never felt so good" (23). The transformation is especially significant because he is hunting a "Cape buffalo, known in East Africa for its fierceness" (Oliver 331). After the admission that he was frightened during the pursuit, fear simply lifts: "For the first time in his life he really felt wholly without fear. Instead of fear he had a feeling of definite elation," "delight," "a wild unreasonable happiness," and "pure excitement" (24–25). Before, he canalized his sexual libido into sports and other activities; now, as he channels his rage at Wilson into the hunt, the strength of the deep unconscious, "the *primordial man*, the two million-year-old man within us all, the positive shadow," awakens (Stevens, qtd. in Burleson 61).[17] Now when he shoots at the second pig-eyed buffalo—as "he shot again at the wide nostrils and saw the horns jolt again and fragments fly" (27)—he is shooting not just to kill Wilson, the swine, but also to blow the cuckold's horns off himself. Several lines later, Margot's bullet hits the back of his head and blows his face off.[18]

Hemingway provides several hints that Francis's new mental state is not a temporary cathexis, positive inflation, or *enantiodromia* but instead a permanent condition. Wilson thinks of it this way: "More of a change than any loss of virginity. Fear gone like an operation. Something else grew in its place. Main thing a man had. Made him into a man. Women knew it too. No bloody fear" (26). For Francis, the experience is akin to "a dam bursting" (25). Surgical removal, loss of virginity, and a bursting dam are one-way trips that allow no going back. In place of fear there now grows "something else," a primordial strength that will brook no more infidelity. Margot knows genuine masculine strength when she sees it and is now "very afraid." When she comments on his bravery, "Macomber laughed, a very natural hearty laugh," which bespeaks self-esteem, well-being, and wholeness. When she asks if it is not "sort of late," and he replies, "Not for me," she knows that he may leave her; he will no longer tolerate her bitchery and infidelity because, presumably, he is now "better with women" (26, 18). The "apprentice-piece" is over. He has achieved a synthesis of what Jung calls the No. 1 and No. 2 personalities: the shadow, no longer an opponent, becomes a source of strength; modern ego melds with archetypal hunter. Hamlet (another introverted thinker with a mother complex), rejuvenated by his sea voyage, declares, "This is I, / Hamlet the Dane" (*Ham.* 5.1.257–58). Francis, had he lived, might have cried, "This is I, Francis the American!"

Macomber's death

Margot's shooting of Francis is the critical crux that has generated the most widely divergent opinions. On the positive side, it has been considered an accident (Baym 116) and an attempt to save his life (K. Lynn 436). Being shot in the head is a sign of "Francis' forsaking of his rational faculties" (Seydow, qtd. in Hardy 132), and the act signifies Margot's "inability to recognize the freedom of the husband-son figure" (DeFalco 206).[19] Perhaps the shooting is "a monumental 'Freudian slip'" in which she aims at the buffalo but shoots him accidentally on purpose (P. Young 73). "And what she cannot dominate, she must destroy" (Hovey 126). Nor are Hemingway's own statements helpful in reaching a definitive conclusion. In a 1953 interview with Jackson Burke, the author stated, "Francis' wife hates him because he's a coward. But when he gets his guts back, she fears him so much she has to kill him—shoots him in the back of the head" (qtd. in Myers 65). In 1959 he was more tentative: "I don't know whether she shot him on purpose any more than you do. I could find out if I asked myself because I invented it and I could go right on inventing. But you have to know when to stop" (qtd. in Flora 78–79). Of the possible interpretations, the most likely based on the evidence in the story is that Margot cannot tolerate the idea that her boy-husband has transformed into a man who might leave her, so she shoots not to save him from a wild animal but to save herself from divorce and poverty. The point is akin to James Gray Watson's conclusion that "her primary motive is neither to murder her husband nor to save him but to save herself" (qtd. in Sugiyama 148).[20] The imagery supports this reading. When he is under her thumb, she calls him "'Francis, my pearl'" (9). "The pearl is white, lily-livered, she implies" (Flora 77). After he attains his manhood and becomes, in Wilson's opinion, "a ruddy fire eater," Margot's face was white and she looked ill" (25). When Francis "felt a sudden white-hot, blinding flash explode inside his head and that was all he ever felt" (27), the transfer of whiteness back to him indicates Margot's lack of tolerance for his new vigor and her unwillingness to let Francis live except in his No. 1 personality. Having connected with the primordial hunter within him, Francis has incorporated an aspect of the No. 2 personality and can look forward to a life of sustained individuation. Insofar as the shooting denies him the opportunity to enjoy his progress and symbolically returns him to No. 1, the ego-centered boy-man, Margot's motherhood becomes predatorial.

An analogy to the concept of "bush-soul" may illuminate the shooting in an additional way. Jung states that the bush-soul is "a 'soul' that splits off completely and takes up its abode in a wild animal" (*CW* 10, par. 133). In a more extended comment, he gives examples of what happens when such an animal is slain:

> This projection of psychic happenings naturally gives rise to relations between men and men, or between men and animals or things, that to us are inconceivable. A white man shoots a crocodile. At once a crowd of people come running from the nearest village and excitedly demand compensation. They explain that the crocodile was a certain old woman

in their village who had died at the moment when the shot was fired. The crocodile was obviously her bush-soul. Another man shot a leopard that was lying in wait for his cattle. Just then a woman died in a neighbouring village. She and the leopard were identical.

(*CW* 10, par. 129)

Francis bears a similar relationship to the animals he hunts at the end of the story. First, his anger displaces his fear like a surgical removal. Then his happiness replaces his rage, which comes to rest in the buffalo, meaning that the buffalo and Francis are one-and-the-same. The first buffalo "bellowed in pig-eyed, roaring rage," and the second is "coming in a charge" at him (23, 27). Given this identification of man and prey, it no longer matters whether Margot shoots at Francis or at the charging beast; either way, the primordial strength of hunter and hunted, which would have seen her divorced, is the target. Of course, in a modern story, there is no primitive causality such as Jung observed in Africans' magical mentality—Francis dies because he is shot directly, not because his bush-soul departs. The key issue is not Margot's specific aim, which is impossible to discern despite the narrator's indication that "Mrs. Macomber . . . had shot at the buffalo" (28), but the more general effect, which is to destroy masculine strength.

Conclusion

Francis Macomber's temperament, childish pursuits, mother complex, and animus-possessed wife have conditioned him to panic during the lion hunt. Subsequently, through shadow work with Wilson, dream, and a connection with the ancient hunter within, he develops a more integrated psyche by forging a permanent connection to mankind's primordial vitality. Africa thus functions for Francis much as it did for Jung, who looked deeply into the collective unconscious during his BPE and enhanced the connection with his No. 2 personality. Neither the fictional character nor the famous psychologist fell prey to the type of tourism that Jung criticizes. "Jung saw the Westerner's obsession with world-travel to 'primitive' places, which for some meant 'going black' in Africa, as symptomatic of the culture's abiding illness. Travel was . . . a form of 'evasion'" (Burleson 225).[21] Travelers should not make a full-hearted transformation from a civilized Western mentality to *shenzi*, insanity, by falling prey to the unconscious, as Kurtz does in *Heart of Darkness*. Travel must instead be part of one's process of individuation, as it was for Jung on his BPE. His friend Laurens van der Post sums up Jung's achievement and his prescription to the modern masses: "The task of modern man was not to go primitive the African way but to discover and confront and live out his own first and primitive self in a truly twentieth-century way" (*Jung* 51). Macomber and Jung, however, approach this task in contrasting ways—violent blood sport versus conversation and psychological observation. Francis makes progress toward individuation the hard way, oblivious to the attitude Jung tried to cultivate, one of calm openness to what the unconscious may reveal. As an old Englishman advised Jung early in his journey, "'You know, mister, this here country is not man's, it's God's country. So if anything should happen, just sit down and don't worry'" (qtd. in Hayman 267).[22] If Francis had done so, he might have lived to enjoy the fruits of his inner work.

Notes

1 The passage is reprinted in John M. Howell's *Hemingway's African Stories* 51.
2 For an annotated bibliography of criticism on "Francis Macomber," see Kelli A. Larson, "On Safari with Hemingway: Tracking the Most Recent Scholarship." All of the important articles are anthologized in Jelena Krstovic's *Short Story Criticism* 90–237.
3 See also Anthony Stevens, *The Two Million-Year-Old Self*. Stevens states: "To him [Jung], the two million-year-old was a vivid metaphor for an age-old dynamic at the core of personal existence, there by virtue of the evolutionary heritage of our species" (3).
4 *CW* 6, par. 692 is also relevant to this discussion. Lévy-Bruhl uses the term "collective representations" to describe primitive people's "collective feeling-value" (Jung's words). However, the linkage of idea and affect is a more broadly human phenomenon, as the passage goes on to acknowledge: "Among civilized people, too, certain collective ideas— God, justice, fatherland, etc.—are bound up with collective feelings." The difference—a racist difference—is that, in primitives, the linkage is "mystical" (Lévy-Bruhl's word).
5 Michael Vannoy Adams, in *The Multicultural Imagination*, offers a helpful summary of the difference between "primitive" and "civilized." Being primitive involves "concrete percepts," attachment to sense perceptions, and emotion; it means being prelogical and mythical; it emphasizes the collective; and it involves the law of participation or subject-object unity. Being civilized means dealing with abstract concepts, detaching from sense impressions, and engaging the intellect; it is a logical, causal, and individual way of thinking that emphasizes the law of contradiction or subject-object duality (54).
6 See Jung's *Visions: Notes of the Seminar Given in 1930–1934 by C. G. Jung* 1.470–71.
7 I critique this shortcoming in *A Jungian Study of Shakespeare* 89–98. See also Adams, *Multicultural*, chapter 4.
8 See Marianna Torgovnick, *Primitive Passions: Men, Women, and the Quest for Ecstasy* 23.
9 In an *Explicator* note, Cecil D. Eby rightly states that Francis must make a definitive transition to manhood through hunting dangerous prey. But Eby is probably incorrect to identify him as a varsity letterman. Of the mentioned activities, only "court games" are varsity sports; it is unlikely that Francis lettered in four of them. "Four-letter man" is a euphemism for various pejorative four-letter words, as Hemingway's own use of the phrase in *Green Hills of Africa* indicates (84, 95).
10 Burleson uses Alan Cobham as an example of *puer aeternus* probably because von Franz's example is Antoine de Saint-Exupéry's *The Little Prince*, in which flying is an important motif. Cobham was attempting the first trans-African flight when Jung encountered him (182).
11 A nearly identical statement appears in *CW* 5, par. 272.
12 Jung also states: "A woman possessed by the animus is always in danger of losing her femininity, her adapted feminine persona, just as a man in the circumstances runs the risk of effeminacy. These psychic changes of sex are due entirely to the fact that a function which belongs inside has been turned outside. The reason for this perversion is clearly the failure to give adequate recognition to an inner world which stands autonomously opposed to the outer world, and makes just as serious demands on our capacity for adaption" (*CW* 7, par. 337).
13 As Jung observes, "The whore (*meretrix*) is a well-known figure in alchemy. She characterizes the arcane substance in its initial, 'chaotic,' maternal state" (*CW* 14, par. 415). Jung comments on the "stages of eroticism" in *CW* 16, par. 361.
14 A view of Wilson as a thinker is in sync with previous comments on the character. Flora states, "He is an incomplete man—unable to merge his life successfully with that of

another person" (80). Also, George Cheatham notes in Wilson "an inadequacy, an incompleteness, suggested by his incomplete tan. Significantly, moreover, it's the top of his head that's missing, the distinctively humanizing part, a detail underscored by Wilson's clipped, fragmented, unratiocinative speech." Cheatham concludes: "Wilson, in short, lacks full humanity" (113). Hutton's statement about Wilson's eyes begins with the right formulation but veers into caricature: the eyes "suggest the deficiency of human warmth one finds in the technicolor movie stereotype of a specialist in torture" (239). Wilson's speech is not so much "unratiocinative" as introverted and unfeeling. Yet Wilson is not wholly without feeling, as the narrator indicates after Wilson shares his Shakespearean motto: "He was very embarrassed, having brought out this thing he had lived by, but he had seen men come of age before and it always moved him" (25). Feeling is simply his inferior function.

15 Adams adumbrates the five types of Jungian dream interpretation: phenomenological, amplificatory, compensatory, subjective, and prospective (77).

16 See "What Dreams Reveal" 5.

17 See Stevens, *Private Myths* 122.

18 When Wilson says to Margot, "'I wouldn't turn him over,'" he is implying that Francis's face is missing. Wilson then "knelt down, took a handkerchief from his pocket, and spread it over Francis Macomber's crew-*cropped* head where it lay" (28; emphasis added). The language echoes Prince Hal's words to Hotspur: "And all the budding honors on thy crest / I'll *crop* to make a garland for my head" (*1 Henry IV* 5.4.72–73; emphasis added). The detail is overlooked in two previous studies of Hemingway's use of Shakespeare by John J. McKenna and Marvin V. Peterson, and Gary Harrington. Harrington does note "Hal's using his 'favors' to 'hide [Hotspur's] mangled face' (*1 Henry IV* 5.4.96)" (153). The word "favors" appears in Hal's promise to "wear a garment all of blood / And stain my favors in a bloody mask" (3.2.135–36). Hutton also does good reading of the Shakespearean motto, but his unawareness of the motto's personal significance to Hemingway weakens the critique (243–44). As P. Young notes, a British officer taught Hemingway the motto in 1917 (73). My reading also diverges from Hutton's sense that "Macomber's moment of 'heroism' resembles that of the soldier who temporarily goes berserk in battle" (248).

19 See John J. Seydow 40.

20 See James Gray Watson 216.

21 Burleson is quoting Jung's words to Laurens van der Post, as reported in *Jung and the Story of Our Time* 53.

22 When Hannah states (above) that Africa "is the country of the Self, not of the ego" (172), she is interpreting the old man's words to Jung.

2

THE ANIMA'S MANY FACES IN HENRY RIDER HAGGARD'S *SHE*

In *The Archetypes and the Collective Unconscious*, C. G. Jung writes: "The anima . . . has not escaped the attentions of the poets. There are excellent descriptions of her, which at the same time tell us about the symbolic context in which the archetype is usually embedded. I give first place to Rider Haggard's novels *She*, *The Return of She* [sic], and *Wisdom's Daughter*" (*CW* 9i, par. 145). Similarly, in his "Foreword to Brunner," he notes, "The motif of the anima is developed in its purest and most naïve form in Rider Haggard. True to his name, he remained her faithful knight throughout his literary life and never wearied of his conversation with her." For Jung, "Rider Haggard is without doubt the classic exponent of the anima motif" (*CW* 18, par. 1279–80). Jung's take on *She*, however, runs more deeply than these opening quotations suggest: it is one of the few literary texts on which he offers significant commentary, which makes the task in Chapter 2 partly metacritical. He mentions Haggard's fiction repeatedly in *The Collected Works*; in fact, as Sonu Shamdasani notices, there are more references to Haggard than to Shakespeare (144). Further discussion appears in *Analytical Psychology: Notes of the Seminar Given in 1925 by C. G. Jung* and *Visions: Notes of the Seminar Given in 1930–1934 by C. G. Jung*.[1] Coincidentally, the 1925 seminar took place just months before his Bugishu Psychological Expedition set out for Africa. Not surprisingly, Blake W. Burleson, author of *Jung in Africa*, notes that *She* "was one of Jung's favorite novels" (30).

Although Jung's view that *She* depicts an encounter with the anima is a critical commonplace, his reasons for considering Ayesha (pronounced Assha [149n]), the She of the book's title, to be an anima figure have not been sufficiently explored.[2] The most helpful concepts for this purpose—the Kore and the stages of eroticism—have been virtually ignored.[3] This chapter, which uses these tools to examine Jung's claim in connection with the anima's effect on Ludwig Horace Holly, the main character and narrative voice, coalesces around the theme of Holly's failed individuation. After showing that Ayesha closely matches Jung's understanding of the anima, we will turn to her effect on Holly. In brief, he represses his anima in England and later projects it onto Ayesha in Africa, experiencing compensation and *enantiodromia* (a swing from inveterate misogyny to anima possession). Sadly, his encounter with Ayesha repeats the relational failure that he experienced a quarter century before: her preference for Leo, the emptier but more attractive vessel, over the erudite but ugly Holly reenacts the situation that sparked his initial repression. Insofar as Holly projects the anima and fails to achieve individuation, Haggard presents the African journey as a psychological encounter in the spirit of Jung's famous statement: "The psychological rule says that when an inner situation is not made conscious, it appears outside, as fate" (*CW* 9ii, par. 126).

Ayesha as a "classic" anima figure

In *The Archetypes and the Collective Unconscious*, Jung associates the anima with wisdom, the historical aspect, "a superior knowledge of life's laws," and the quality of being outside of time (*CW* 9i, par. 64). All of these qualities directly characterize Ayesha; but in Norman Etherington's words, "if Ayesha is meant to personify an unattainable dream of femininity, how are her less endearing traits to be explained?" (*Rider Haggard* 87). Jung's comment in his 1925 seminar provides the seed of an answer: "Her [Ayesha's] potency lies in large measure in the duality of her nature" (112). The anima is not only bipolar but multi-faceted, as Jung makes clear in his comments on the Kore and the stages of eroticism; both help to explain his sense that Ayesha is an anima figure.

The Kôr/Kore pun has been surprisingly overlooked in the criticism, though "Kôr" has been helpfully glossed, and a connection between Ayesha and the goddess has been noted. On the one hand, Elaine Showalter mentions "the core, Kôr, *coeur*, or heart of darkness which is a blank place on the map" (81); and Barri J. Gold says that Kôr represents "the very core of a giant female body" (314). Ayesha refers to the pillar of fire as "the very Fountain and Heart of Life" (257; ch. 15).[4] On the other, Alan Pickrell states that Ayesha "presents all three faces of the goddess in one personage: the maiden, the matron, and the crone" (20). But no one, not even Jung himself, has put together *kore* (Gk., girl), Haggard's Kôr, and the Kore. This nexus implies that Kôr is a fitting locale for Holly to do anima work with a female who represents all three facets of the Kore.[5] Ayesha is the virgin mother of her people, has lived for over twenty-two centuries, and through a devolutionary aging process in the pillar of fire becomes a shriveled old hag reminiscent of Gagool in *King Solomon's Mines*.

Jung claims in "The Psychological Aspects of the Kore" that the Kore corresponds to "the *self* or *supraordinate personality* on the one hand, and the *anima* on the other" (*CW* 9i, par. 306; cf. par. 314–15). Although Ayesha, a stumbling block to male individuation, hardly represents the Self, the Kore-Ayesha-anima nexus is highly relevant in terms of bipolarity. The description in the following quotation would fit Ayesha almost perfectly if one substituted "murderer" for "whore."

The anima is bipolar and can therefore appear positive one moment and negative the next; now young, now old; now mother, now maiden; now a good fairy, now a witch; now a saint, now a whore. Besides this ambivalence, the anima also has "occult" connections with "mysteries," with the world of darkness in general, and for that reason she often has a religious tinge. Whenever she emerges with some degree of clarity, she always has a peculiar relationship to *time*: as a rule she is more or less immortal, because outside time. Writers who have tried their hand at this figure have never failed to stress the anima's peculiarity in this respect. I would refer to the classic description in Rider Haggard's *She*.

(*CW* 9i, par. 356)[6]

In "Mind and Earth," however, Jung underestimates Ayesha's maternal aspect: "The most striking feature about the anima-type is that the maternal element is entirely lacking. She [anima] is the companion and friend in her favourable aspect[;] in her unfavourable aspect she is the courtesan. Often these types are described very accurately, with all their human and daemonic qualities, in fantastic romances, such as Rider Haggard's *She*" (*CW* 10, par. 75).

Part of Ayesha's maternal quality is her association with the anima via a connection between snake imagery and the life force. In a paragraph that ends with another reference to "the novels of Rider Haggard," Jung comments on the snake-anima connection. The snake's color, green, is "the life-colour"; and the anima is "the *archetype of life itself*." Snake symbolism suggests that the anima not only has "the attribute of 'spirit'" but also "personifies the total unconscious" (*CW* 5, par. 678). In Apuleius's *The Golden Ass*, Isis (the mother of Horus and a mother figure to her people) is associated with snakes (Cott 20); and since Ayesha is an anima figure and a priestess of Isis, a theriomorphic description makes good sense. She moves and hisses like a snake, has "a certain serpent-like grace" (153; ch. 13), and wears a double-headed "snaky belt" (260; ch. 26) around "her snaky zone" (211; ch. 20). Thus, Haggard's snake imagery signifies both the danger of this particular woman and an archetypal dimension, the maternal life force.

Whereas the Kore suggests the anima's bipolarity, the "stages of eroticism" (Mary, Helen, Eve, and Sophia) show the anima more properly as multifaceted (*CW* 16, par. 61). Jung suggests that Eve is mother and that Mary represents religious feeling, an interpretation that Daryl Sharp echoes in his *Jung Lexicon* (20–21). The following articulates the reinterpretation suggested in Chapter 1, the *stages* through which a male progresses with his anima: Mary, mother; Helen, girlfriend, mistress, whore; Eve, wife, murderer; and Sophia, wisdom.[7] Considered this way, the stages align nicely with Ayesha who is a mother or Isis figure to her people; a siren who incites masculine desire with her unearthly beauty; a prospective wife for Kallikrates whom she slew in ancient times and for Leo, to whom her kiss proves fatal in the sequel; and a source of wisdom (like Isis) as well as a living fount of knowledge regarding ancient history and nature's secrets.

Haggard's descriptions of Ayesha reinforce these connections, particularly with Sophia and Helen. Ayesha claims that her wisdom is ten times greater than Solomon's

(149; ch. 8) and later strikes Holly as "more like an inspired Sibyl than a woman" (218; ch. 21). Although Holly is deeply learned, his wisdom is insignificant compared with hers, as his footnote makes clear: "Now the oldest man upon the earth was but a babe compared to Ayesha, and the wisest man upon the earth was not one-third as wise. And the fruit of her wisdom was this, that there was but one thing worth living for, and that was Love in its highest sense" (221n; ch. 21). Of course, She does not mean *agape*, and Helen-like associations give Ayesha's wisdom a dangerous edge: She considers herself more beautiful than Helen (149; ch. 8); radiates life like Aphrodite and beauty like Venus and Galatea (181, ch. 17; 212, ch. 20); and, as "a virgin goddess" like Diana, warns Holly that his own passion (*eros*) may end him, much as the hounds tore Actaeon to pieces (154; ch. 13). Holly recognizes the threat by thinking of her as "this modern Circe" (157; ch. 14). Indeed, Ayesha has the potential to come between Holly and Leo, just as Circe separates Odysseus from his men. As Rebecca Stott observes, like the New Woman of Victorian England, Ayesha "will turn men into beasts, turn them against themselves and each other, infiltrate into and destroy the closed circle of the brotherhood" (*Fabrication* 117).

Ayesha's status as a dangerous woman and an Eve figure has not escaped the critics. Etherington believes that Haggard's women simultaneously suggest Eve and Satan (*Rider Haggard* 79). Evelyn J. Hinz calls her "a pagan Eve" (421), and Bruce Mazlish sees both Eve and Medusa in Ayesha's background (734). More remains to be said, however, about Ayesha's parallels to Eve. In the womb of the Earth, Ayesha stands naked "as Eve might have stood before Adam, clad in nothing but her abundant locks" (260; ch. 26), tempting Holly and Leo with knowledge and eternal life, for the fire combines the forbidden biblical trees' twin benefits, as Holly narrates.

> I know that I felt as though all the varied genius of which the human intellect is capable had descended upon me. I could have spoken in blank verse of Shakespearian beauty, all sorts of great ideas flashed through my mind, it was as though the bonds of my flesh had been loosened and left the spirit free to soar to the empyrean of its native power. The sensations that poured in upon me are indescribable. I seemed to live more keenly, to reach to a higher joy, and sip the goblet of a subtler thought than ever it had been my lot to do before. I was another and most glorified self, and all the avenues of the Possible were for a space laid open to the footsteps of the Real.
>
> (257–58; ch. 25)

In other words, Holly's temptation is to tap directly into the collective unconscious, the treasure trove of all human thought. The fire would enable him to keep his sanity and to have all the riches of human experience at his intellectual command—forever.

The anima as a Helen-like *femme fatale* is implied in Jung's statement that those "who have any psychological insight at all will know what Rider Haggard means by 'She-who-must-be-obeyed'" and that "they know at once the kind of woman who most readily embodies this mysterious factor [the anima]" (*CW* 7, par. 298).[8] Susan Rowland echoes this sentiment in stating that "Jung's erotic anima is dangerous when substantiated into fantasies of female deviousness and power" (*Literary Theory* 17). Jung himself speaks of something like the *femme fatale* in "Marriage as a Psychological Relationship."

> There are certain types of women who seem to be made by nature to attract anima projections; indeed one could almost speak of a definite "anima type." The so-called "sphinx-like" character is an indispensable part of their equipment, also an equivocalness, an intriguing elusiveness—not an indefinite blur that offers nothing, but an indefiniteness that seems full of promises, like the speaking silence of a Mona Lisa. A woman of this kind is both old and young, mother and daughter, of more than doubtful chastity, childlike, and yet endowed with a naïve cunning that is extremely disarming to men.

His footnote adds, "There are excellent descriptions of this type in H. Rider Haggard's *She*" (*CW* 17, par. 339 and n. 3). A Helen type is bad enough; but a woman like Ayesha, who appears multi-faceted to the male imagination, becomes the recipient, to some degree, of all four projected stages of eroticism. Such a woman is a cynosure who allows a man's imagination to latch on. Whatever his poison, his imagination finds some anchor for it in her persona. This process marks what Mazlish calls "the pubescent aspect of masculinity" in adult men (735), which views women as "everlastingly mysterious, dominating, immoral, terrifying, and fascinating, especially so in the Victorian period" (735).

Jung would underscore that the stages of eroticism depict man's experience of his inner feminine as it appears when projected on women. Like the Mona Lisa, a woman takes shape according to the machinery of the male psyche when he imagines her as he wishes. Like Galatea she springs to life as a reflection of a man's feminine ideal but has a separate identity apart from the wishes of the male projector. As such a female, Ayesha is devastatingly attractive, for She seems to embody the totality of the anima. Any man who has ever fallen in love with a waitress will agree that W. E. Henley accurately sums up this projection process: "With Ayesha, the heroic Barmaid—the Waitress in Apotheosis—numbers of intelligent men are in love, as the author himself appears to be" (qtd. in Cohen 215).

Always present in a male-female relationship is the possibility that the dynamics of the anima will overwhelm and consume the masculine—that the anima (or the unconscious in general) will swallow the masculine rather than becoming properly integrated into the Self. The threat is most pronounced when a man fixates on a woman who, in his mind's eye, is a *femme fatale*. A woman like Ayesha—youthfully ancient, sweetly powerful, coldly alluring—is a fitting repository of male fear and desire because She invites projection so powerful and permanent that it leads to anima possession rather than to individuation through the anima work that Jung calls the "master-piece" (*CW* 9i, par. 61). Ayesha, a *femme fatale*, is Jung's image of the anima because the most powerful figure of the projected anima leads to the most damaging psychological dysfunction. Such a woman disrupts the brotherhood of men (the shadow work or "apprentice-piece" that they are supposed to do first with each other), as when Holly "is rent by mad and furious jealousy" because Ayesha prefers Leo, the younger, more attractive man (212; ch. 20).

Holly, projection, and compensation

As the novel's central character, Holly is like the hub of a bicycle wheel, with projections radiating like spokes to all of the following: misogyny (Billali, Job); the wise old man (Billali); conventionality (Job); gentlemanly qualities (Leo); the intellect (Cambridge colleagues); instinct (the goose); savage rage (the Amahagger); and the anima (Ayesha, Ustane, Truth). Jung and his colleagues note many of these projections in their 1925 seminar. A more convincing theory of the psyche relates to his sense that "a compensatory relationship exists between persona and anima" (CW 7, par. 304). "The anima, being of feminine gender," Jung writes, "is exclusively a figure that compensates the masculine consciousness" (CW 7, par. 328). Here is the model that he develops around a central core of ego/consciousness:

External reality
Persona
EGO
Anima
The unconscious

The persona mediates between ego and the external world, just as the anima bridges ego and the unconscious. Persona and anima are in a compensatory relationship so that a man's "ideal persona is responsible for his anything but ideal anima" (CW 7, par. 310). A female-resistant persona yields a more powerful anima, which "likewise is a personality" (CW 7, par. 314). Jung might as well be describing Holly's misogyny in stating, "If the soul-image is not projected, a thoroughly morbid relation to the unconscious gradually develops" (CW 6, par. 811). Jung states, "If the persona is intellectual [like a Cambridge don's], the anima will quite certainly be sentimental," meaning subject to powerful anima projection (CW 6, par. 804).[9] Libido "gets dammed up and explodes in an outburst of affect" (CW 6, par. 808): Holly's powerful misogyny leads to powerful projection. In other words, it is the anima's job to remind him that he is not, at his core, a hater of women and that he is still capable of love and lust.

That Holly has emphasized his intellect and repressed his interest in women is beyond doubt. As Hinz states, Holly is Western culture's "intellectual offspring—a skeptical, individualistic, scientifically-oriented academic with a firm belief in the moral and political British constitution" (426). He is, however, an academic in the Socratic mode—learned but ugly. Women loathe his appearance, so he projects his anima on one who pretends to like him for mercenary purposes.

Women hated the sight of me. Only a week before I had heard one call
me a "monster" when she thought I was out of hearing, and say that I had
converted her to Darwin's theory. Once, indeed, a woman pretended to
care for me, and I lavished all the pent-up affection of my nature upon her.
Then money that was to have come to me went elsewhere, and she
discarded me. I pleaded with her as I have never pleaded with any living
creature before or since.

(41; ch. 1)

From this devastating experience misogyny results, as the faux-editor notices:

I remember being rather amused because of the change in the expression
of the elder man, whose name I discovered was Holly, when he saw the
ladies advancing. He suddenly stopped short in his talk, cast a reproachful
look at his companion [Leo], and, with an abrupt nod to myself, turned
and marched off alone across the street. I heard afterwards that he was
popularly supposed to be as much afraid of a woman as most people are of
a mad dog, which accounted for his precipitate retreat.

(36; introduction)

In believing that men and women shrink from him, Holly creates a cycle of
repression and isolation. He even hires Job, a man servant, instead of a female nurse,
lest a woman vie with him for Leo's affections (50; ch. 2).

Holly's libido (sexual and otherwise) is canalized into study and parenthood to
the point that he considers himself invulnerable to female beauty. To Ayesha he
demurs: "I fear not thy beauty. I have put my heart away from such vanities as
woman's loveliness that passes like a flower" (152; ch. 13). As Jung understood,
however, the more repression there is in the persona, the more strongly the anima
compensates. When Ayesha unveils herself, Holly's anima pounces, much as the
chthonic crocodile seizes the lion in the marshes. Now the scholar and inveterate
woman-hater falls in love with someone on whom he projects his feminine ideal.
In this respect, Jung is perhaps too general in his own comments on the novel's
relation to the projection process.

Rider Haggard's *She* gives some indication of the curious world of ideas
that underlies the anima projection. They are in essence spiritual contents,
often in erotic disguise, obvious fragments of a primitive mythological mentality that consists of archetypes, and whose totality constitutes
the collective unconscious. Accordingly, such a relationship is at bottom
collective and not individual.

(*CW* 17, par. 341)

The comment makes sense if one remembers Jung's emphasis on Haggard as an
exemplar of the visionary mode, which means that the fictional material comes

through a writer from the collective unconscious (*CW* 15, par. 157). In another remark better suited to Holly the character, Jung states that "a man, in his love choice, is strongly tempted to win the woman who best corresponds to his own unconscious femininity—a woman, in short, who can unhesitatingly receive the projection of his soul" (*CW* 7, par. 297). Here Andrew Libby's summary of Ayesha's qualities is instructive, for all of them are tailored to appeal to Holly: She "is an inquisitive intellectual, a learned philosopher, a talented chemist, a penetrating psychic, and on top of all that, a ravishing beauty" (9). Ayesha, who rivals Helen for loveliness, acknowledges his basic goodness despite his ugliness, and can discuss ancient history in multiple foreign languages, is a disappointed academic man's dream come true.

Numerous passages make it clear that, when Holly's anima surges forth in response to Ayesha unveiled, his psyche is in a state of anima possession. All that he once repressed becomes anchored in the ancient woman. He is attracted and horrified by her eyes' diabolically attractive force. He imagines that he will spend the rest of his life sick at heart now that She has set eyes on him. He is filled with passion and jealousy, worships her, and begs her to marry him. He and Leo, "like confirmed opium-eaters," would not return to Cambridge in an instant even if they could (221; ch. 21). Imagining that her face will be before him always, he grows weary of a life filled with "the bitterness of unsatisfied love" and a broken heart (230; ch. 22). Such anima possession, Holly knows, is "a very bad state of mind for a man on the wrong side of middle age to fall into" (268; ch. 26). In other words, encountering Ayesha does not enable him to make progress in his relationship with the anima; Ayesha is a rather more compelling version of the greedy English woman who earlier rejected him. Leo too is possessed by the anima but against his will: he vows never to consider another woman, and Holly recognizes that they "both loved her now and for always, she was stamped and carven on our hearts, and no other woman could ever raze that splendid die" (267; ch. 26). For Leo, the possession is so severe that, unlike Odysseus who draws his sword and rushes at Circe, he cannot even draw his knife. He instead confesses to Ayesha, his wife Ustane's murderer, "I am in thy power, and a very slave to thee" (231; ch. 22).

Possession suggests that *She* is the story of Holly's encounter in Africa with what he has repressed in England—the feminine, his sexual libido, and the anima that links the ego and the unconscious. Now various details suggest additional compensation by the unconscious. Geography is the first piece of this process: Africa is depicted as a woman's body. As Showalter points out, Holly's dream of being buried alive relates to engulfment in the dreaded female body (86; Haggard 98, ch. 7). Jung would add that if the anima "is regarded as the feminine and chthonic part of the soul" (*CW* 9i, par. 119), then journeying into a geographical underworld is emblematic of encountering the inner feminine. More specifically, the setting of the climactic scene reflects the female reproductive system. In order to reach the core of the volcano, the company must traverse a bottomless chasm between a rocky spur and a quivering boulder, objects that Lindy Stiebel considers phallic and clitoral, respectively (86). Lest the reader miss the sexual implication, Holly describes the rocky outcropping as like "the spur upon the leg of a cock in shape" (244; ch. 24). The group then moves single file through a Tartarus-like "funnel" or "low and narrow" passage like a birth canal in order to arrive, in Ayesha's words, at "the very womb of the Earth, wherein she doth conceive the Life that ye see brought forth in man and beast—ay, and in every tree and flower" (256; ch. 25). In a perfect blending of masculine and feminine images, Holly and company now encounter the phallic pillar of fire in a feminine cavern. Thus, having eschewed women and sexuality in England, he penetrates the very heart of that particular darkness: the sexuality he once resisted now confronts him writ large in the geography of the African underworld. The trouble with these details of the landscape, however, is that encountering externals does not mean that internals are engaged. Fearing death, Holly and Leo do not bathe in the pillar of fire but instead draw back from what it represents psychologically, an unfiltered encounter with the collective unconscious. Even so, they barely escape with their lives and their sanity. Africa does compensate for England, but it does so in the spirit of *enantiodromia*, a swing to an opposite alternative that does not engender a resolution/*coniunctio*.

The statue of Truth—a blindfolded and winged woman holding a torch and standing on the world, encountered earlier in the final journey—represents the same human reluctance to experience the deep unconscious without filters. Sandra M. Gilbert's sense that Truth represents "the contradictions between power (the torch) and powerlessness (the blindfold)" is largely beside the point (46). If the veil represents the barrier between the ego and the unconscious, casting aside the veil means encountering the unconscious without the mediating agency of the anima. That is why Ayesha's translation of the statue's inscription sounds a cautionary note.

> "*Is there no man that will draw my veil and look upon my face, for it is very fair? Unto him who draws my veil shall I be, and peace will I give him, and sweet children of knowledge and good works.*
>
> "*And a voice said, Though all those who seek after thee desire thee, behold, Virgin art thou, and Virgin shalt thou go till Time be done. No man is there born of woman who may draw thy veil and live, nor shall be. In death only can thy veil be drawn, oh Truth.*"
>
> (240, ch. 23)

The inscription begins with a stated ideal—seeing the face of truth (achieving full individuation). But Truth will remain a virgin (is not procreative, has limits) because no man can draw back Truth's veil on this side of another veil, death. One cannot encounter the unfiltered unconscious and survive any more than one could survive a flight into the sun. Insanity would be the result, as it nearly is for Holly when Ayesha unveils. With both Truth and Ayesha, the veil's purpose is to keep consciousness out, just as the miles of quagmire, crocodiles, snakes, and mosquitoes exist to keep Europeans from penetrating the heart of Africa. The image of veiled Truth, then, builds on Ayesha's veil, anticipates the withdrawal of Holly and Leo from the womb of the Earth without bathing in the fire, and suggests that individuation (in this life at least) is a journey without an ultimate destination.

There is also a connection between the veil image and the Romantic quest poem.[10] Showalter sounds an appropriate note—"above all, the quest romances are allegorized journeys into the self" (82). In addition, the obvious connection between Ayesha and John Keats's "La Belle Dame Sans Merci" has been discussed by critics such as Gilbert (43) and Robert O'Connor (43–44). Still unnoticed is a remarkable parallel to the veil image in Percy Bysshe Shelley's "Alastor; or the Spirit of Solitude" (1815), which provides a helpful gloss on the projection process in *She*. A poet traveling in a Coleridgean landscape complete with a volcano encounters "an Arab maiden" (line 129) who loves him deeply. The poet dreams, however, of "a veiled maid" whose "voice was like the voice of his own soul / Heard in the calm of thought" and who speaks to him of matters dear to his own heart (lines 151, 153–54).

> Knowledge and truth and virtue were her theme
> And lofty hopes of divine liberty,
> Thoughts the most dear to him, and poesy,
> Herself a poet.
>
> (lines 158–61)

She parts her lips in a sexually provocative way, and then the poet "Folded his frame in her dissolving arms" (line 187). The Wordsworthian narrator comments, "The spirit of sweet human love has sent / A vision to the sleep of him who spurned / Her choicest gifts" (lines 203–05). Now the poet tragically pursues the visionary maid in the physical world, ignoring "youthful maidens" who express interest (line 266). Eventually, he dies alone and unfulfilled.

In "Alastor," the poet rejects a mortal woman like Ustane in order to seek a projection of his own anima like Ayesha—devastatingly beautiful but ultimately unattainable. In *She*, Holly and Leo, like the poet, are haunted by memories of a veiled maid whom they have lost. Inspired by Leo's psychic dream, they pursue her again in the sequel, *Ayesha, the Return of She*. Whereas the unfulfilled quest kills the poet, achieving the object of the quest kills Leo when he fails to withstand her potent kiss. "Alastor" and *She* are both stories about the tragedy that ensues when love of an attainable woman is rejected or denied, and instead the anima is projected onto an unobtainable other. The moral, it seems, is to know oneself well enough to desire a partner whose presence facilitates individuation rather than deepening one's disconnections with the world.

Conclusion

This chapter has argued that the anima's multi-faceted nature is fundamental to Jung's interpretation of Ayesha as an anima figure and that Holly succumbs, through compensation and *enantiodromia*, to anima possession, which steers him away from individuation and *coniunctio*. Her power to enchant and overwhelm mortal men also lies in her being a unity of archetype and archetypal image. As an image, Ayesha is a flesh-and-blood character with whom Holly and Leo can interact; but as an archetype She unveils a nonverbal realm capable of inducing possession and insanity. It is not necessarily, as Claudia Crawford argues, that "the unveiling of She, of woman herself, leads to the impossibility of language" and accounts for Holly's failure to describe her adequately (86). That failure, expressed in statements such as "The man does not live whose pen could convey a sense of what I saw" (153; ch. 13) and She "surpasses my powers of description" (160; ch. 14), may bear little relationship to Ayesha-as-woman and much more to Ayesha-as-archetype. The description fails because anima transcends language: Holly cannot adequately capture the woman's image in words because She represents what words can never capture. Describing the anima is as impossible for Holly as fully summing her up is for Haggard in his dozens of novels. Since anima cannot be circumscribed, characters must simply experience her. As Jung knew well, Haggard's simple yarn proves to be a fitting vehicle for that encounter.

Notes

1 For this chapter I used Andrew M. Stauffer's edition of *She: A History of Adventure*. Another fine edition is Norman Etherington's *The Annotated "She": A Critical Edition of H. Rider Haggard's Victorian Romance*. My work on Haggard includes two previous publications: "Visionary and Psychological: Jung's 1925 Seminar and H. Rider Haggard's *She*" and "Time is Not an Arrow: Anima and History in H. Rider Haggard's *She*" (see Works Cited). Here is further evidence of the novel's accessibility to Jungian interpretation. The chest that Leo inherits contains various artifacts, including a "scarab" or gem cut in the shape of a beetle. Although Jung does not comment on it, the image surely resonated with him. In 1913, he had a vision that included the image of "a gigantic black scarab" (*MDR* 179). Similarly, in *Synchronicity: An Acausal Connecting Principle*, he recounts how a scarabaeid beetle knocked on the window as a female client was telling him about "a dream in which she was given a golden scarab" (*CW* 8, par. 843). In this synchronicity and in *She*, the scarab image suggests movement in the unconscious.

2 Regarding Ayesha's name, Evelyn J. Hinz notes, "The Greek name for the cosmic order is 'Aisa,' the Persian 'Asha'" (421).

3 Some sense of the anima and anima projection runs through much of the previous criticism, though usually minus the Jungian terminology. To begin with, the feminine informs the two major strands of criticism of *She*: the Victorian "New Woman" (Showalter 85; Heller 62–63, 86) and colonialism/imperialism (Libby 3–4; Stott, "'Scaping"; Stiebel). For other studies of imperialism, see Brantlinger and Katz. The novel's non-Jungian critics offer some relevant insights into the journey's psychological implications (Hallock, par. 26; Mazlish), but Patricia Murphy's Freudian approach has definite limitations (61). Haggard's critics have mentioned the process of projecting a man's ideal feminine image (Cohen 112–13; Ellis 117–18; Etherington, *Rider Haggard* 77, 87; Moss 28). Also, the psychological and the transpersonal are both present in *She* (Cohen 112). The novel is explored in a chapter of one Jungian doctoral dissertation (Kates) and in an extended explication by an acquaintance of Jung's (Brunner). More recently, Ayesha has been related to the "Goddess archetype" and Haggard's interest in such figures to his relationships with women so that writing *She* is a compensatory act (Pickrell 18, 24). In particular, Ayesha's nickname, She-who-must-be-obeyed, reflects a rag doll by the same name, which Haggard's nurse used to enforce his bedtime (Whelan, par. 3). Here Jung's comment

resonates meaningfully: "Those of my readers who know Rider Haggard's description of 'She-who-must-be-obeyed' will surely recall the magical power of this personality. 'She' is a mana-personality, a being full of some occult and bewitching quality (*mana*), endowed with magical knowledge and power" (*CW* 7, par. 375). Jung did not know about the rag doll, but his projection-related description of Ayesha seems relevant to Haggard's childhood experience. Finally, Ayesha is often considered to be a *femme fatale* (Gilbert 42; Hallock, par. 3; Libby 8; Rodgers 36; and Stott, "'Scaping" 151 as well as *Fabrication*, ch. 4). For *femme fatale*, see also n. 8 below.

4 The pillar of fire must have resonated powerfully with Jung because of a dream that he had had as a very young boy. "In the dream I went down into the hole in the earth and found something very different on a golden throne, something non-human and otherworldly [a giant phallus], which gazed fixedly upward and fed on human flesh" (*MDR* 14). Jung's explication stresses the dream's religious antecedents; however, a giant phallus within the earth is also a pairing of masculine and feminine images, much like Haggard's pillar of fire in the womb of the earth.

5 Regarding the goddess's tripartite nature, see Adam McLean's *The Triple Goddess*.

6 It appears that Haggard's biographer, Morton Cohen, may have this passage in mind when he sums up "the traditional ideal qualities of womanhood" (113).

7 C. S. Lewis states in *A Preface to* Paradise Lost that Eve is the first murderer (124).

8 In the criticism, Ayesha is widely considered to be a *femme fatale*. Sandra M. Gilbert considers her "absolutely identical with the Byronic *femme fatale* who haunted nineteenth-century writers" (42); Hallock calls her Haggard's "most famous fictional femme fatale" (par. 3); and Libby sees her as "a femme fatale motivated by a toxic combination of love, jealousy, and ambition who disrupts rational thinking, threatens male homosocial friendship, and endangers British political stability" (8). For Terence Rodgers, Ayesha as *femme fatale* is "a magnetic figure of male longing but also fear, who threatens the integrity of empire, manliness and brotherhood" (36). For Stott, Africa itself is the *femme fatale*, "dangerously seductive, potentially violent, unpredictable, all knowing" ("'Scaping" 151). See also Stott's *Fabrication*, ch. 4. Clinical psychologist Sue Austin uses a gender studies approach to compare Ayesha to another *femme fatale* about whom Jung had much to say—Salome.

9 See also *CW* 10, par. 79: "Self-control is a typically masculine ideal, to be achieved by the repression of feeling. Feeling is a specifically feminine virtue, and because a man in trying to attain his ideal of manhood represses all feminine traits—which are really part of him, just as masculine traits are part of a woman's psychology—he also represses certain emotions as womanish weakness. In so doing he piles up effeminacy or sentimentality in the unconscious, and this, when it breaks out, betrays in him the existence of a feminine being. As we know, it is just the 'he-men' [or intellectual men] who are most at the mercy of their feminine feelings."

10 Critics have found varied significance in Ayesha's veil. Gold, not very helpfully, remarks on the nineteenth-century figure of nature unveiling before science (313). Terence Rodgers sees the veil as an erotic invitation to the Oriental sexuality of harem girls (41, 44). Showalter, in a comment that Jung would scoff at, recalls Freud's interpretation of looking at Medusa: fear of female sexual organs and castration anxiety (145). She also considers the veil to represent feminine chastity and modesty versus sexuality and exoticism (144–45).

3

THE ANIMA AND PSYCHIC FRAGMENTATION IN OLIVE SCHREINER'S *THE STORY OF AN AFRICAN FARM*

Olive Schreiner's *The Story of an African Farm* is "the first distinctly 'feminist' fiction in English" (Bristow viii) and the first South African novel to attract international attention. Shortly after its publication in England in 1883, Henry Norman commented on the author's achievement: "She has the right word to say about almost all. Orthodox Christianity, Unitarian Christianity, woman suffrage, marriage, Malthusianism, immortality—they all arise over the horizon of this African farm" (qtd. in Bristow vii). To this list we could add agnosticism, colonialism, feminism, political economy, sexuality, social Darwinism, and Transcendentalism. It is obvious, however, that Schreiner saw the whole work as emblematic of women's experience because after its original title, *Mirage*, she added as a motto the metaphor, "Life is a series of abortions" (qtd. in Bristow xxv). But *African Farm* also has things to say about the female side, or anima, of its various male characters, particularly Waldo Farber and Gregory Nazianzen Rose. Although there are some previous psychological studies in the Freudian vein, the novel's Jungian dimension, especially its treatment of the anima, has yet to be explored.[1] Sounding remarkably Jungian, Lyndall quite rightly states that "all things are in all men, and one soul is the model of all" (164; pt. 2, ch. 4), but the characters do not achieve what the narrator calls the "redemption [that] is from within . . . wrought out by the soul itself, with suffering and through time" (209; pt. 2, ch. 9). Chapter 3 argues that Schreiner emphasizes the anima's maternal aspect but that "fragmentation"—the distribution of positive qualities among various male characters rather than their unity in a single character—obviates the possibility that any one of them can achieve significant individuation (a process in which greater wholeness results from making the unconscious conscious).[2] As for Waldo and Gregory, that lack of inner work qualifies previous assertions that they are Victorian "New Men."

Autobiographical fragments and *African Farm's* composition

Not only does fragmentation determine the limits of the characters' individuation, but the word "fragments" also relates to the author's compositional method, which may be approached by comparison with Henry Rider Haggard's *She* (1886). Haggard considered *African Farm* one of the most significant Victorian novels (Showalter 48, 84; Murphy 189). Lyndall may even be a "prototype" of Haggard's Ayesha, the She of the title (Gilbert and Gubar 60), just as the allegory of the hunt for Truth may be a precursor of Haggard's statue of Truth. Although neither novel depicts successful individuation, Schreiner's narrative technique diverges markedly from Haggard's. For example, besides employing a "multiple protagonist structure" (Clayton, *Olive* 42) rather than a participatory narrator, she departs from the adventure story at which he would excel. She writes in the Preface:

> It has been suggested by a kind critic that he would better have liked the little book if it had been a history of wild adventure; of cattle driven into inaccessible "kranzes" [walls of encircling rock] by Bushmen; "of encounters with ravening lions, and hair-breadth escapes." This could not be. Such works are best written in Piccadilly or in the Strand: there the gifts of the creative imagination, untrammelled by contact with any fact, may spread their wings.
>
> (xxxix–xl)

Rather than setting down "those brilliant phases and shapes which the imagination sees in far-off lands" (lx), as Haggard would do in *She*, Schreiner paints with a palette of fragments—facts and scenes from her own personal experience. The difference between the two authors, though, is not as black-and-white as Jung's distinction between the visionary and psychological modes would suggest: fragments of Haggard's life colored the tale that swept into him from the collective unconscious, and Schreiner's imagination obviously had an effect on the fragmentary personal details that contributed an autobiographical stamp to *African Farm*. Names are but one example of such personal detail. Lyndall is the maiden name of Schreiner's mother; Schreiner was called by her middle name, Emilie, until the age of twelve; and Otto's name is contained within Gottlob, the first name of the author's father. The names Waldo and Em honour Ralph Waldo Emerson, who had great influence on Schreiner. Emerson's essay "Self-Reliance," which states, "Trust thyself: every heart vibrates to that iron string," probably inspired Schreiner's pseudonym, Ralph Iron; and in German *Schreiner* means cabinetmaker, which links to Waldo's creation of "a small carved box" (163; pt. 2, ch. 4).[3]

The epigraph from Alexis de Tocqueville's *Democracy in America* also reinforces the sense that *African Farm* is written in the psychological/autobiographical mode: what Schreiner depicts has its roots in fragmentary childhood experiences—both the main characters' and her own.

> We must see the first images which the external world casts upon the dark mirror of his mind; or must hear the first words which awaken the sleeping

powers of thought, and stand by his earliest efforts, if we would understand the prejudices, the habits, and the passions that will rule his life. The entire man is, so to speak, to be found in the cradle of the child.[4]

Whereas de Tocqueville considers the statement an analogy for the growth of nations, Schreiner sees it as straightforwardly relevant to her main characters, Waldo and Lyndall, whose childhood is the foundation of their young adulthood. Much as William Wordsworth in "My Heart Leaps Up" says that "The Child is the father of the Man" (line 7), Schreiner asserts: "Not what we are taught, but what we see, makes us, and the child gathers the food on which the adult feeds to the end" (28; pt. 1, ch. 4); and "The first six years of our life makes us; all that is added later is veneer" (160; pt. 2, ch. 4). Just as the characters' later years rest upon their childhood, the novel itself includes "facts" drawn from Schreiner's own younger life in Africa. Her childhood memories are the fragmentary building blocks of her autobiographical fiction. Carol Barash notes, for example, that the novel's religious dimension reflects the author's mother's dogmatic religiosity and that the various "strangers" who visit the farm have real-life counterparts in Schreiner's childhood experience (Introduction 5–6). Someone once even gave her a copy of Herbert Spencer's *First Principles*, the book that Waldo receives from a stranger (Brandon 71).

Schreiner weaves such fragments into a story whose characters are subject to psychological fragmentation, a point that subtly emerges when she compares "the stage method" of fiction writing to "the method of the life we all lead" (xxxix). There is a connection between this distinction in the Preface and the dying Lyndall's interest in reading. After having Gregory throw a book she dislikes out into the street, she picks up a large volume. "This was Shakespeare—it must mean something" (244). What it means bears upon the issue of fragmentation. As Shakespeare's Jaques famously states in *As You Like It*, "All the world's a stage, / And all the men and women merely players" (2.7.138–39).[5] Jaques then narrates the seven ages of man, which are predictable and symmetrical, though slightly cynical—a typical, if not ideal, life in line with Schreiner's stage method. "According to that [method]," she writes, "each character is duly marshalled at first, and ticketed; we know with an immutable certainty that at the right crises each one will reappear and act his part, and, when the curtain falls, all will stand before it bowing. There is a sense of satisfaction in this, and of completeness." The implication is that a plot, whether comic or tragic, unfolds on stage according to viewers' assumptions regarding traditional dramatic formulae. *African Farm*, however, follows "the method of the life we all lead"—a life that violates such dramatic expectations through irony or psychological disunity. Malvern van Wyk Smith helpfully suggests that the novel actually contains both methods and that part one, the stage method, is Victorian in nature, whereas part two illustrates the more verisimilar Modernist method (151–52). The latter type's disruption and disappointment have the final word when potential and integrity die with Waldo and Lyndall, who are survived by the sturdy but marginal Tant' Sannie, Em, and Gregory. Therefore, insofar as Shakespeare illustrates the stage method of composition, Lyndall's final act of reading ironically underscores the fullness that she has not achieved when she dies prematurely without having made much progress in her individuation. As her childhood self presciently observes, "it is only the made-up stories that end nicely [satisfyingly]; the true ones all end so," that is, unhappily, unsatisfactorily, and with characters in a static state of psychic fragmentation (14; pt. 1, ch. 2).

Fragmentation and the unconscious

The story told in *African Farm* depicts the unconscious in ways that illuminate the issue of fragmentation. As the novel opens, moonlight bathes the main characters. The fact that they are asleep signals an interest in the unconscious, as do a number of dreams (some of them precognitive) later on. In addition, the moon—Gerald Monsman calls it "the dreaming feminine moon" (104)—establishes the maternal and the feminine as key psychic factors that characters, both male and female, will have to negotiate in their waking lives. Later on, Lyndall even says, "Men are like the earth and we [women] are the moon; we turn always one side to them, and they think there is no other, because they don't see it—but there is" (165–66; pt. 2, ch. 4). In other words, the opening scene suggests that inscape will be as important as landscape and that the feminine will play an important role as the characters attempt to make the unconscious conscious by moving away from psychic fragmentation and toward the Self.

Roberta Mazzanti argues that the attic scenes also signify the unconscious, as if climbing up in the barn signals delving down into the psyche (131–32). Characters who visit the attic receive a sort of inner revelation: Waldo discovers the joy of reading, Gregory his appreciation of women's clothing, and Tant' Sannie her fiancé's infidelity. That Blenkins and Em do not visit the attic signifies, Mazzanti suggests, a reluctance to look within (131). In the narrator's words, Blenkins "liked to know what was in all locked-up places and out-of-the-way corners, but he was afraid to climb the ladder" (75; pt. 1, ch. 11).[6] Visiting "the attic of the unconscious," as Mazzanti calls it (132), is a step in their individuation process; characters who do not go there are more static. What remains static, one might add, is the fragmentary psyche; and "the year of the great drought" (10; pt. 1, ch. 2) suggests that in the Karoo, which is parched by the relentless masculine sun, the inner work of individuation will be challenging and incremental at best. The setting's harshness and remoteness make it especially difficult for male characters to achieve progress with the anima.

In contrast, the moonlit sea, which Waldo visits on a Christmas vacation from his job at a wholesale store (where wholeness ironically eludes him), hints at the inner work he evidently achieves in his overall travels. In fact, his unfinished letter to Lyndall describes the sea as one might describe the unconscious:

> "Of all the things I have ever seen, only the sea is like a human being; the sky is not, nor the earth. But the sea is always moving, always something deep in itself is stirring it. It never rests; it is always wanting, wanting,

wanting. It hurries on; and then it creeps back slowly without having reached, moaning. It is always asking a question, and it never gets the answer. I can hear it in the day and in the night; the white foam breakers are saying that which I think."

(227; pt. 2, ch. 11)[7]

Stephen Gray's comment, "The sea is symbolic merely of Waldo's own perpetually confused mumblings; it is no gateway, no exit" (140), is clearly unsatisfactory in a psychological context. Not only does Waldo anthropomorphize the sea by suggesting that it is always alive with desire; but the passage's suggestion of unity among earth, sea, sky, and psyche—versus fragmentation and incompleteness—also parallels Spencer's emphasis on the unity of evolutionary life in *First Principles* (537), as well as the novel's concluding assertion of "Universal Unity," "the Universal Whole," and "Universal Life" (259–60; pt. 2, ch. 13). Wholeness and unity resonate with Jungian psychology in two significant ways: first, as an analogue to the wholeness of the Self, which is the goal of individuation; and second, as the equivalent of Jung's term *unus mundus*, a comprehensive field that includes matter, psyche, and spirit. It is not that Waldo becomes a significantly individuated character. Rather, if his description of the seascape participates in inscape, then he does make some progress in the right direction.

Fragmentation and the anima

So far we have defined fragments as personal experiences that shape characters' lives or an author's fictional product, whereas fragmentation signifies the opposite of individuation—lack of wholeness resulting from the failure to bring unconscious content up to conscious awareness. There is a causal relationship between the two concepts: fragmentation characterizes a psychic life based on fragments. Since this chapter's main interest lies in the male characters' relationship with the inner feminine principle, we turn now to the female characters who are the object of anima projection. Here some Jungian tools—the Kore and the stages of eroticism— will illuminate the fragmentary nature of psyche in *African Farm*.

Mazzanti makes the following helpful comment, though she does not specifically reference Jung or use the word "Kore": "Because of [Lyndall's] descent from the Moon, we may foretell that in the course of the novel the child will reveal the archetypal attributes of the moon-goddess, in her three incarnations as Virgin, Mother and Witch [crone]" (123). Lyndall, the critic suggests, is doomed to be either a virgin or a spinster, like the hen that sits on eggs that will never hatch and unlike various images of more successful motherhood—the black woman and her child (banished by Tant' Sannie), a sow suckling piglets, a hen and her chicks, a red cow that feeds a white cow's orphaned heifer, and the maternal functions described in "Hours and Seasons." This excellent reading of the Kore would be even stronger if Mazzanti had noticed that the word "crone" actually appears in the novel. After returning to the farm, Lyndall no longer dresses in pinafores (a sign of her former virginity), announces her dislike of "the crying of babies" (motherhood), finds it strange that "the candle standing on the dressing-table still cast the shadow of an old crone's head in the corner beyond the clothes-horse," and seems fixated on "the old crone's face" (149–51; pt. 2, ch. 4). The candle's crone-like shadow eerily prefigures her childless fate. She will not enjoy the state of motherhood, which Schreiner in *Woman and Labour* calls "that crowning beatitude of the woman's existence, which, and which alone, fully compensates her for the organic sufferings of womanhood" (127). In other words, Lyndall's womanhood is destined to be a series of fragments rather than a successful, temporally appropriate, and unitary progression from maiden to mother to old woman.

Ironically, Tant' Sannie is a crone who manages to have a healthy baby; but she is, more specifically, what Jung calls a Terrible Mother. In a similar vein, she strikes Monsman as akin to Chaucer's Wife of Bath who has also had multiple husbands (65), Gilbert and Gubar as "the Old Woman" (60), and Nancy L. Paxton as "a caricature of the 'natural' and 'instinctive' Wordsworthian mother idealized by Victorian novelists and normalized by social Darwinists" (569). Here Mazzanti misses an opportunity, seeing in Lyndall and Waldo's relationship an element of fairy tale but overlooking the fairy tale's treatment of the Terrible Mother. A statement in Schreiner's *Woman and Labour* provides the missing linkage between Tant' Sannie and fairy tale: "the two terms signifying intimate human relationships which in almost all human languages bear the most sinister and antisocial significance are both terms which have as their root the term 'mother,' and denote feminine relationships—the words 'mother-in-law' and 'step-mother'" (171). Both terms signify motherhood corrupted by cruelty. Set against Tant' Sannie as crone-mother are suggestions of a more desirable state—Schreiner's "wish for both sexual and maternal love" (Burdett 35) and Waldo's compensatory story of "the African farm as a divine mother" (Gilbert and Gubar 62). But in the verisimilar mode, sex leads to the birth of a child who lives only one day: motherhood obviates sex and brings death. Moreover, as the drought and the Farber men's deaths suggest, the farm may be a killing field rather than a nourishing mother. In other words, the novel's portrayal of the Kore shows that its parts are dysfunctional and that there are fractures among them—not an ideal life but a realistic one.

Similar to the three aspects of the Kore, all four of Jung's stages of eroticism illuminate aspects of the fragmentary feminine in *African Farm*. He writes, "Four stages of eroticism were known in the late classical period: Hawweh (Eve), Helen (of Troy), the Virgin Mary, and Sophia" (*CW* 16, par. 361). These figures correspond, Jung explains, to the purely biological mother, *eros*, religious devotion or spiritual motherhood, and Sapientia/wisdom/truth. Tant' Sannie's fertility, the black woman with her child, Lyndall's pregnancy, Em's impulse to feed others, and images of female animals with their offspring all suggest Eve, the biological mother, versus the opening's absence of any real mothers. Helen (*eros*) figures include Lyndall (a version of the Victorian *femme fatale*) and the daughter of Human-Nature and Excess in the hunter allegory that the stranger relates to Waldo. The daughter is one of two Sensuality twins, brother and sister, who like sirens tempt the seeker of Truth

(Sophia) to follow them and to believe that "Truth is a shadow" (129; pt. 2, ch. 2). The allegory, of course, is the stranger's accurate interpretation of the carvings on the burial post. The carving suggests that, for Waldo at this stage of the novel, love and truth are a binary; his psychic progress lies in work, not in woman or God. Jung's stages, which should lead in a complementary fashion toward unity and wholeness, are instead discrete and mutually exclusive.

Moreover, the characters' inability to embrace fully one or more stages of eroticism signals fragmentation. The novel opens, for example, with the longing for spiritual motherhood (Mary). Waldo feels anxiety about death and salvation; when he sacrifices a mutton chop on an altar and God does not light the fire through supernatural means, the boy considers himself a Cain figure and confesses that he loves Jesus but hates God. Regarding the Christian faith, Waldo and his father, old Otto, illustrate problematic opposites. Whereas Waldo becomes a seeker of Truth (Sophia) apart from a faith in which he cannot believe, Otto credulously accepts any statement, biblical or otherwise, regardless of its veracity, simply because someone makes it. When Lyndall asks how one can be sure that Blenkins is telling the truth, Otto responds angrily:

> "How do you know that anything is true? Because you are told so. If we begin to question everything—proof, proof, proof, what will we have to believe left? How do you know the angel opened the prison door for Peter, except that Peter said so? How do you know that God talked to Moses, except that Moses wrote it? That is what I hate!"
>
> (28; pt. 1, ch. 4)

The opposition of belief and proof, of course, directly reflects evolution's challenge to Christianity in Victorian England where Lyndall later studies. In such weighty matters as science and faith, her own prescription offers a sensible middle ground: "Books do not tell everything" (14; pt. 1, ch. 2). One must develop an intellectual life and a critical intelligence, as she does in England; otherwise, one can fall prey to lies, as Otto falls to Blenkins's machinations, realizing too late that saying something does not guarantee its truthfulness. Blenkins crushes the old man just as surely as he destroys Waldo's sheep-shearing machine by stamping it into fragments. The fact that Waldo spent nine months creating the machine and nine carving the post signifies *African Farm*'s concern with male characters' relationship to biological and spiritual motherhood. The futility of the effort to create the machine and the brutality of the opposing force are summed up in the image of Doss, Waldo's dog, who, a few lines after Blenkins's destructive act, interrupts a dung beetle at work: "The beetle was hard at work trying to roll home a great ball of dung it had been collecting all the morning; but Doss broke the ball, and ate the beetle's hind legs, and then bit off its head. And it was all play, and no one could tell what it had lived and worked for. A striving, and a striving, and an ending in nothing" (74; pt. 1, ch. 10).

One may detect an echo of Gloucester's "As flies to wanton boys are we to th' gods; / They kill us for their sport" (*Lr.* 4.1.36–37) and Macbeth's idea that life "is a tale / Told by an idiot, full of sound and fury, / Signifying nothing" (*Mac.* 5.5.26–28). Both passages from Shakespeare imply that reality—fragmentary, malevolent, without purpose—begets fragmentation in the psyche.

If *African Farm* isolates *eros*, motherly anima, religious feeling, and truth from each other, then aspects of the anima work at counter purpose with each other to thwart the individuation process. Such fragmentation exists not only *within* characters like Otto and Waldo but also *among* the novel's various characters. Gilbert and Gubar rightly note that Otto and Blenkins may be "monsters of the psyche representing split halves of one self," and they correctly identify "a splintering" that presages their respective death and disappearance (55–56). This principle of fragmentation, which lies at the heart of the characters' psychological dysfunction, needs further exploration. Whereas each character, however base, manifests a characteristic of the ideal New Woman or New Man, no one achieves an individuated synergy of positive qualities. Among the female characters, for example, Em's emphasis on love as service is counterbalanced by passivity. Lyndall's intellectual curiosity withers under illness and lack of opportunity. If she is a New Woman, as Gilbert and Gubar assert (62), it is because Schreiner's purpose is to depict the challenges facing women who would explore traditionally male roles. Meanwhile, Tant' Sannie, the sole mother figure at the opening, possesses fortitude that rests on ignorance and hardens into cruelty when she and Blenkins torment Waldo over his discovery of J. S. Mill's *Political Economy* in the attic. Her obesity signifies her cunning boldness and gross materiality. If Tant' Sannie represents good fortune without grace or intellect, the black woman represents biological motherhood without material support. Thus, Tant' Sannie, Em, Lyndall, and the black woman encompass together the fertility, fortitude, intelligence, love, and service that characterize a complete person. The trouble is that each female character represents merely a fragment of the ideal, probably because of the "ancient archetypes" that still dictate female roles (Pratt, "Spinning" 154). Because positive qualities are distributed among the novel's females, not located in one person, all of the female figures are incomplete. Lyndall presents a particularly ambiguous portrait of the thwarted potential experienced by the Victorian New Woman, a portrait of potential sans opportunity. An ideal woman would not only have a measure of Em's humble service, Lyndall's analytical mind, Tant' Sannie's fortitude, and the black woman's fecundity. She would also enjoy constructive work beyond the home or the farm.

A very similar—indeed, verisimilar—fragmentation appears within the male characters; and, again, the ideal man would borrow a quality from each one. Although Waldo "embodies the listening virtues of the 'new man'" (Clayton, "Olive," par. 20), he is "not a hero of 'self-reliance'" (Gilbert and Gubar 63) despite his great physical strength. He has a religious impulse but no genuine faith, intellectual interest in art and science but not the tenacity to succeed in the world, and desire to marry Lyndall but no opportunity to ask for her hand.[8] Similarly, Otto's good-hearted generosity is qualified by a foolish literalism, Blenkins's cleverness by Napoleonic cruelty, and Piet's desire for marriage by submission to Tant' Sannie. Moreover, "R. R.," Lyndall's powerfully masculine lover and the father of her child, lacking responsibility, deserts her in her hour of need. Gregory's belief that motherly love-as-service requires cross-dressing is the sartorial equivalent of Otto's foolish belief that saying something makes it so. As these examples demonstrate, ideal male qualities are distributed among the characters and are further diminished by various shortcomings. Schreiner creates a raft of male characters who *together* suggest what the New Man would look like. But no male in the novel is a ruggedly masculine good listener who combines agile intellect, domesticity, and motherly attentiveness. Instead, they are all incomplete in their fragmentary approach to the anima. However, Waldo and Gregory, whom we shall now examine in greater detail, do make some progress with the inner feminine.

Waldo and the primitive

Crucial for Jung is the idea that the "apprentice-piece" (shadow work) must be a foundation for the "master-piece" with the anima (*CW* 9i, par. 61). It is important, therefore, to discuss ways in which Waldo makes headway with the shadow and its corollary, the primitive. Jung's understanding of the primitive (or archaic man) within the modern resonates with the novel in a way that implies fragmentation. Paintings by "these old wild Bushmen" (16; pt. 1, ch. 2); Waldo's own primitive carving on the burial post; the wild look in his eyes, which frightens Blenkins (an obvious trickster figure);[9] Waldo's assault on a man who borrows his horse and rides it to death; and the native Africans who are occasionally mentioned—all point toward the ancient primordial strength that lies latent within modern man. These hints, however, do not constitute a full-blown primordial awakening; Schreiner's purpose is not to depict the achievement of full masculine strength but to emphasize the way in which life's harshness impinges on individuation—how fragmentation abides despite hints of a deeper and personally beneficial dimension of psyche concealed in the unconscious. The problem is that Waldo and Lyndall are receiving objects more than they are acting subjects. In the verisimilar mode that the Preface discusses, life etches lines in the characters; characters do not bend life to their own will. As Waldo writes to Lyndall, "We are only the wood, the knife that carves on us is the circumstance" (225; pt. 2, ch. 11). A novel based on this principle uses a much lighter touch than Haggard does in *She*. In that novel, for example, whereas Ludwig Horace Holly and company descend into a literal volcano, the volcano within Mt. Etna merely serves as an analogy for fire and brimstone in Blenkins's sermon (37; pt. 1, ch. 5), much as "the lava-like earth chasms" yawn in the hunter allegory told by Waldo's stranger (130; pt. 2, ch. 2).[10] There is no volcano in *African Farm*; volcano references figure significantly only as images in texts that characters create. The same light touch appears in the novel's lack of full engagement with the primitive and Waldo's consequent inability to overcome his psychic fragmentation.

Although no male character in *African Farm* overcomes fragmentation to achieve full manhood, anima integration, and wholeness, Waldo comes the closest because he does do some work with the primitive and the shadow. The first indication of the primitive is his interest in the Bushmen's paintings, on which he comments to

Lyndall.[11] He believes "that the stones are really speaking—speaking of the old things, of the time when the strange fishes and animals lived that are turned into stone now, and the lakes were here," etc. He adds that "these old wild Bushmen," who hunted wild buck, wanted to make something, though lacking a clear understanding of why. Now they are all gone because the Boers have killed them, and even the wild buck have disappeared (15–16; pt. 1, ch. 2). In other words, economic forces have triumphed over something more psychologically fundamental and fulfilling. "Primitive" has even been emptied of its archaic significance and now, in Otto's usage, means merely "not very lofty" (19; pt. 1, ch. 3). What remains of that primitive era are rocks: some are fossils; others bear paintings. Both types suggest that the primitive within the psyche of the observer is latent, like Keats's "Cold Pastoral!" in "Ode on a Grecian Urn" (line 45)—present but frozen in time. The reader does see glimmers of ancient strength within Waldo, but it remains mostly petrified because of hard circumstances. For example, the potential for masculine strength is present even in the stranger's cynical view of "the clownish fellow at his feet . . . so coarse-clad and clownish" (121; pt. 2, ch. 2). Clownish means rural, but the word may echo Edmund Spenser's "Letter to Raleigh," which functions as a preface to *The Faerie Queene*. In the letter, the Redcrosse knight, a former farmer whose name, George, means "earth-tiller," is described as a "clownish person" (3). Since he is destined to become Saint George, the dragon slayer, the allusion signals the potential for successful growth toward masculine maturity and wholeness. As for Waldo, underneath his farmer's clothing slumbers an ancient hunter.

Waldo's interest in primitive art includes his own burial post whose figures, in the stranger's way of thinking, "were almost grotesque in their labored resemblance to nature," though they "bore signs of patient thought" (122; pt. 2, ch. 2). Upon receiving *First Principles*, Waldo gives him the post, so grateful to the stranger that he kisses the hoof marks that the man's horse leaves behind. Rachel Blau DuPlessis correctly notes that "Waldo's rejection of the quest is shown by the fate of his staff, carved to place on his father's grave" (25). The post is never placed above Otto's grave; it neither honours the father nor signifies that the son has taken his place. It instead ends up in the hands of the stranger, who probably discards it by the side of the road once he is out of sight. As the stranger intends, *First Principles* may indeed give Waldo "a centre round which to hang [his] ideas" (137; pt. 2, ch. 2). The trouble is that books not only compensate for the primitive but also prevent engagement with it. Intellection keeps the primitive in check and is the asbestos that separates Waldo from life. There is the same separation from the primitive in the stranger's case. Later in Waldo's travels, when he spends his nights reading "glorious books" (227; pt. 2, ch. 11), he presumably comes to understand that his reverence for the stranger is unjustified. One day, dressed in rural tancord, he finds the man sitting between fashionable ladies, one of whom tips him sixpence for picking up her whip. The stranger looks Italian and effete. Waldo feels ashamed of himself, probably projects his own lack of masculine engagement onto the stranger, does not engage him in conversation, and never seeks him out again.

There is no shadow work with the stranger, but there are moments besides the whipping by Blenkins when Waldo's interaction with other men helps him get in touch with the shadow. At times, primitive strength even seems to break through the surface. On his travels, for example, Waldo encounters evil men who take advantage of him or cheat him, including one who rides his beloved old horse to death. By hurling the offender halfway across the street, he succeeds in getting a modicum of respect from others, who stop calling him "Old Salvation," a nickname resulting from his refusal to adopt their disrespectful attitude toward women (and a reminder of his religious agony at the opening). A later episode also shows a possible connection with the primitive. After passing out drunk, Waldo awakens to meet a Hottentot boy (a member of the Khoikhoi, the first native tribe the Dutch encountered) who has pulled him out of the road and who now claims that the two are comrades. That nascent solidarity, however, quickly vanishes, like admiration for the stranger, when the boy chases after the brandy flask that Waldo hurls into the water, never to drink again.

Waldo's approach to the primitive is like a spark that does not light the tinder—it never fully becomes part of his consciousness. Perhaps the best support for this conclusion appears in "Gregory's Womanhood." Waldo, of course, is not present; the story of Lyndall's final days is Gregory's retrospective once he returns to the farm. In her sick room, she watches "the round streak of sunlight that came through the knot in the shutter, or the massive lion's paw on which the wardrobe rested" (242; pt. 2, ch. 12). Mazzanti states, "The metaphoric value of the lion's paw suggests to the reader a parallel between the Sphinx's riddles and Lyndall's unanswered questions about women's destiny, but at the same time it aptly stands for the mystery that this young woman represents to all the other characters in the novel" (133). The statement is good reading of the paw's significance for Lyndall, but the statement is troubling for its lack of masculine association. Whereas a live lion signifies primordial masculine strength (and, for Jung, the Self),[12] there is no lion in *African Farm*, only a severed body part that has become furniture in a way that mimics the petrific animals in the Bushmen's ancient paintings. Waldo never hears about the paw and never confronts an actual lion. Moreover, Lyndall's request that Gregory throw an unworthy book out into the street undercuts the masculine force Waldo uses to hurl the horse-killer into the street, much as Doss's slaying of the industrious dung beetle trivializes and parodies the sheep-shearing machine and Blenkins's act of crushing it. Altogether, these details imply that Waldo is at several removes from affirming primordial masculine strength. As the lion's severed paw suggests, such strength is present only as a psychic fragment.

Despite lack of full engagement with the primitive, Waldo does do some shadow work with other men. Along with this work or perhaps because of it, he is in touch with his maternal anima insofar as he spends nine months on both the post he gives to the stranger and the carved box he gives to Lyndall. As Jung points out, "Hollow objects such as ovens and cooking vessels are associated with the mother archetype, and, of course, the uterus, *yoni*, and anything of a like shape" (*CW* 9i, par. 156). Barash seems more on point, however, in noting that the nine-month period of creation signals a "desire for a union between male and female spheres" ("Virile" 273). More specifically, the carving is of a pyramid amid flowers, which suggests the coming together of masculine and feminine in the individuation process, as Waldo and Lyndall themselves might have done in a less realistic, less tragic story. The carved box also invites comparison to Em's sewing box, which she received from her late mother. Em's sewing box is a symbol of the wholeness of the Self but is appropriately empty, for individuation is a matter of regular effort over the sort of lifelong journey on which she is about to embark with Gregory as the novel closes. But as with Waldo, wholeness is a destination that the couple will probably never approach.

Gregory and the maternal anima

Like Waldo, Gregory makes some progress toward wholeness but remains fragmentary in his own way. To begin with, the Gregory-Lyndall relationship includes some significant autobiographical fragments. Lyndall, who idolizes Napoleon Bonaparte and who espouses greater freedom and opportunity for women, has a strong animus. Schreiner explains women's masculine strength as follows in *Woman and Labour*:

> We are the daughters of our fathers as well as of our mothers. In our dreams we still hear the clash of the shields of our forefathers as they struck them together before battle and raised the shout of "Freeedom!" In our dreams it is with us still, and when we wake it breaks from our own lips! We are the daughters of those men.
>
> (147)

Not surprisingly, the author preferred strong men (Kucich 100) yet thought of her husband, Samuel Cron Cronwright-Schreiner, in maternal terms. In one of her letters, she states, "Cron has been very good to me; he has stood by me as no man I think ever stood by a woman mentally and physically. If I am alive now I owe it to his care. Neither night nor day has he left my bedside for ten days except when he has been to fetch medicine or the doctor" (251). Insofar as Lyndall prefers strong men like "R. R." but ends up with the maternal, service-oriented Gregory, the ambivalent animus appears to be one of the novel's autobiographical elements. In fact, Gregory seems to embody a version of the ideal that Schreiner expresses in another letter: "My ideal is an equal care [that is] physical and mental from both father and mother. Not simply that the man provides the money and the woman gives the labour" (291). In nursing the dying Lyndall, Gregory fulfills both paternal and maternal roles. If that were all, critical opinion would be more uniformly positive regarding his actions. The trouble is that he shaves off his beard and puts on a dress, a detail reminiscent of Schreiner's own interest in cross-dressing.

On the positive side, a number of critics praise Gregory's devoted, loving service (Burdett 38) and his "passionate maternal behavior" (DuPlessis 28), claiming that he represents the New Man. He is thus an androgynous being (Monsman 74–75);

a figure of bisexuality (Murphy 221) or homosexuality (Bristow xxi); perhaps "Hagar, the Biblical embodiment of maternal solicitude"; and even the herald of "a new era in human relationships" (Parkin-Gounelas 105). The negative reading holds that the earlier Gregory is doltish and puerile, "insipid, sentimental, and fickle" (Berkman 228, 143), as well as "callow, narcissistic and romantically susceptible" (Burdett 36). The fact that he wants to *be* a woman (DuPlessis 28), much as Schreiner wished that she had been a man, mingles with homoerotic misogyny (Lane n.p.). He becomes Lyndall's "slave" (DuPlessis 103) and is "dog-like" in his devotion to her (K. Blake 216), a view that the presence of Doss at Lyndall's bedside reinforces. Ironically, since only the dog gets to lay its head between her breasts, Gregory does not live up to the potential in the anagram of his last name: *eros*.

Jung writes that "the [anima-possessed] patient will want to change himself into a woman through self-castration, or he is afraid that something of the sort will be done to him by force" (*CW* 9i, par. 82). It is possible that Gregory's cross-dressing is a symbolic form of self-castration, but the cross-dressing in *African Farm* is too superficial to constitute anima possession. Instead, his cross-dressing reflects a mother complex because the clothes that he tries on in the attic remind him of his mother's (212; pt. 2, ch. 10).[13] What occurs in Lyndall's sick room, then, constitutes *enantiodromia*, a swing from his male identity as a fiancé and farmer to a female identity as a motherly cross-dressed nurse. The shift does not make him a woman but does signal a complicated relationship with his anima. In the process, a sartorial version of active imagination enables the maternal anima to manifest, as Jung's January 10, 1929 letter to Kurt Plachte suggests: "I am indeed convinced that creative imagination is the only primordial phenomenon accessible to us, the real Ground of the psyche, the only immediate reality" (*Letters* 1.60). Nursing Lyndall connects him to his deeper psyche and true nature—not only the "fine nature" that he mentions in a letter to his sister, Jemima, but also his sense that he should have been a minister instead of allowing their father to make him a farmer (141; pt. 2, ch. 3). The most positive feature of Gregory's care of Lyndall is its Christ-like selflessness, which clearly reflects Em's "idea that love was only service" (146; pt. 2, ch. 3). He says to Lyndall, "I might but always be near you to serve you . . . to be of use to you" (199; pt. 2, ch. 8). Later she echoes this sentiment in stating that "happiness is a great love and much serving" (249; pt. 2, ch. 12). In terms of service, Gregory's cross-dressing makes him a thoroughly motherly man.

On the negative side, however, the issue of projection complicates the dynamics of the Gregory-Lyndall relationship as she nears the end of her life. Projection is a strong indicator of psychic fragmentation. Her fear of and desire for a strong man like "R. R." signal her ambivalent animus projection, much as Gregory ambivalently projects his anima on a helpless, anorexic teenager who is simultaneously a strong woman.[14] At one point in "Gregory's Womanhood," he even kisses her swollen feet in a show of affection, humility, and subservience. As a child, mother, crone, and *femme fatale*, she resembles Haggard's Ayesha in her ability to receive a variety of anima projections. That the characters are at cross-purposes should be obvious: Lyndall needs a rugged, masculine man with a maternal side (like Waldo) who will be a proper object of her projected animus; the more feminine Gregory seeks to be dominated and used and gets his wish when he becomes her nurse. The disguise guarantees that he will be even further removed from her romantic ideal. In other words, multiple and contradictory objects of projection signal that Lyndall's animus and Gregory's anima are both fragmented. Although Gregory's motherly solicitude is genuinely positive and worthy of emulation, the cross-dressing is more enigmatic. It suggests, by exaggeration, that the ideal New Man is individuated with respect to the anima but that individuation will be difficult to achieve because of gender's flexibility.

However complicated and ambivalent Gregory's anima projection may be, one thing is certain: nursing the dying Lyndall is an act of loving kindness that deepens his humanity. The point enables a re-visioning of his last name. "Rose" (like the flower), has been taken as a signal of effeminacy and masculine deficiency. With a name like Rose, it is little wonder that he puts on a dress. Absent from the criticism, however, is the fact that his last name is also a verb, which means that "Gregory Rose" is a complete sentence. Gregory Rose *rises* in his "womanhood" to a greater level of individuation through loving service. Something similar obtains with respect to his middle name, Nazianzen, an allusion to Saint Gregory Nazianzen, whose theological positions function as analogies to the unity of Jungian individuation, a process that provides an antidote for the state of psychic fragmentation.

John Henry Cardinal Newman's portrait of Saint Gregory (written in the 1830s) would have been available to Schreiner and may well have been her inspiration for Gregory Nazianzen Rose's middle name. Newman underscores Saint Gregory's contrast to his great but ultimately estranged friend, the more outgoing Basil; his affection, gentleness, kindness, tender-heartedness, warmth, and basic good nature, despite occasional irritability and imperfect control over his passions; and a personality mismatched with the role of preacher and church leader.[15] Newman writes:

> Gregory disliked the routine intercourse of society; he disliked ecclesiastical business, he disliked publicity, he disliked strife, he felt his own manifold imperfections, he feared to disgrace his profession, and to lose his hope; he loved the independence of solitude, the tranquility of private life; leisure for meditation, reflection, self-government, study, and literature.
>
> (75)

Monsman sums up Newman's chapter by stating: "Saint Gregory, according to Newman, had a gentle, feminine side not wholly free of irritability but affectionate and humble—all without sacrificing through a sex-role reversal his natural masculinity" (76). He also states that "the saint and his namesake both were victims of uncongenial roles, each forced to be what he in essence was not. . . . Gregory Rose is psychologically a woman but biologically a man" (75). The missing point, of course, is that Saint Gregory was a public ecclesiast who should have remained a private person, much as his namesake is a farmer who should have been a minister. Unlike the saint, however, Gregory Rose has no significant male friend with whom to do shadow work. In both respects—career and friendship—psychic fragmentation hinders his individuation.

Modern biographer John A. McGuckin identifies the heavy maternal influence in Saint Gregory's life, contrasting "his father's lack of spiritual sensitivity" with "his mother's deep-rooted visionary form of Christianity" (20, 35). It appears that she had some degree of psychic ability and that Gregory had some facility in interpreting her psychically acquired information. Consequently, "it seems that for Gregory it is the physical and spiritual tie to the mother that really matters . . . it was his mother who was the most significant power base he recognized" (18–19). In a Jungian vein, McGuckin notes "the significance of the Anima in Gregory Nazianzen's character," including gentleness, virginity, and the belief that spiritual inheritance came through the female line (6–7).

Although the maternal anima provides a strong connection between Saint Gregory and Gregory Rose, it is the saint's theological positions that suggest the individuation that eludes Schreiner's characters. Robbie McLaughlan notes that Saint Gregory espoused "apocatastasis" (141), which *The Cambridge Dictionary of Philosophy* defines as follows: "The restoration of all souls, including Satan's and his minions', in the kingdom of God. God's goodness will triumph over evil, and through a process of spiritual education souls will be brought to repentance and made fit for divine life" ("Apocatastasis" n.p.). Similarly, Saint Gregory opposed Arianism, the idea that Christ, rather than being truly divine, is a lesser person of the Trinity, inferior to the Father (McGuckin 9). In other words, Saint Gregory believed that Father and Son are co-equal, a unity rather than a hierarchy, much as he also believed that all souls will be one with God. So the divine loves all things, includes all things, and eventually draws them home to the Godhead—a perfect analogy for the way that the Self brings the fragmented parts of the psyche into wholeness. The point that Burdett makes about the saint's opposition to Arianism is equally true of apocatastasis: the name "'Gregory Nazianzen' thus names work of reconciliation and of unity" (37). There is, then, a noteworthy connection between the theological allusion in Gregory Nazianzen Rose's middle name and the universal life, unity, and wholeness that are Schreiner's Spencerian emphasis in the novel's penultimate chapter. As the narrator puts it in "Times and Seasons," existence is "Not a chance jumble; [but] a living thing, a *One*" (118; pt. 2, ch. 1).

It may be that, in nursing Lyndall, Gregory Nazianzen Rose "rises to the nobility of his name" (Berkman 228); but the differences between Rose and Nazianzen, though subtle, are significant. Whereas the saint retains his basic masculinity and seems to enjoy as much individuation as an introvert can achieve in public life, the fictional character cross-dresses in a show of just the opposite—a psychic fragmentation that pits different aspects of the anima against each other. As a result, Gregory Rose is a deeply ambiguous version of the New Man and the opposite of Waldo. Whereas Waldo is a masculine man with New Manly qualities like gentleness and intelligence but does not connect with Lyndall, Gregory connects with Lyndall but has to masquerade as a woman in order to do so. As she cynically says of him earlier, he is "a true woman—one born for the [separate] sphere that some women have to fill without being born for it" (164; pt. 2, ch. 4). But if he is living a lie, and if Lyndall hates lies,[16] there is no possibility of *coniunctio* here, no coming together of opposites in the spirit of the feminine flowers and masculine pyramid on Waldo's box. In the final analysis, Schreiner suggests that New Woman and New Man are elusive ideals that cannot be fully achieved because anima and animus are as fragmentary as the minerals that dot the landscape of the Karoo.

Conclusion

As McLaughlan notes, "For Jung and Conrad, Africa provided a partial means of reconnection with their primordial past, an atavistic landscape strewn with the archetypes of the collective unconscious; however, for Schreiner this expanse offers a site in which to experiment with, improvise around and transgress constricting gender roles" (141). In this respect, *African Farm* depicts psychic fragmentation as one of the symptoms of the essentialism that hindered the progress of the Victorian New Man and Woman and that would trouble Jung's writings in subsequent decades. But despite creating a world in which the prototypical New Woman and Man, Lyndall and Waldo, cannot survive and casting the other New Man, Gregory, in a dress, Schreiner emphasizes the maternal anima's impulse toward wholeness over the fragmentary lives within and among individual characters. As Lyndall reminds us, all things are in all persons, and the characters do make *some* progress toward individuation. Schreiner similarly incorporates many genres into the tale. As others have noted, the list includes allegorical tale, *Bildungsroman*, colonial Gothic, Dickensian farce, farm novel, naturalistic tragedy, New Woman fiction, satire of provincial manners, spiritual autobiography, neo-Transcendentalist novel of ideas, and Victorian melodrama (Esty 470). There are also dreams, letters, and even a parodic sermon (Shapple 97). The proliferation of genres mirrors the fragmentation within the characters; but these separate genres exist within a coherent whole, the novel itself. If generic variegation parallels the individuation process that begins to emerge from the main characters' psychic shards, then the novel analogically and rhetorically enacts a solution to the fragmentation it depicts. Since that progress is partial and the outcome disappointing, *African Farm* concludes squarely in the verisimilar mode that Schreiner outlines in her Preface.

Notes

1 Joseph Bristow's introduction to *African Farm* notes that Lyndall's "contradictory drives" (feminist independence vs. masochistic attraction to a dominant man) signal "the psychoanalytical unconscious" (xix). Carolyn Burdett sees Freudian fetishism in the disconnection between the Bushmen's primitive paintings and their physical absence in the present day (159). John Kucich explores the theme of masochism from a Freudian perspective, and Christopher Lane applies the Oedipus complex. Here is the only Jungian

comment on Schreiner's novel that could be located: "A significant number of women's novels (Olive Schreiner's *The Story of an African Farm*, Sylvia Plath's *The Bell Jar*) feature characters blocked in growth by a hatred of their bodies as well as an evil self-hate projected onto dismal lovers and horrible husbands" (Pratt, "Spinning" 162).

2 Daryl Sharp defines individuation as "a process of psychological differentiation, having for its goal the development of the individual personality. . . . Individuation is a process informed by the archetypal ideal of wholeness, which in turn depends on a vital relationship between ego and unconscious. The aim is not to overcome one's personal psychology, to become perfect, but to become familiar with it. Thus individuation involves an increasing awareness of one's unique psychological reality, including personal strengths and limitations, and at the same time a deeper appreciation of humanity in general. . . . The process of individuation, consciously pursued, leads to the realization of the self as a psychic reality greater than the ego. . . . In Jung's view, no one is ever completely individuated" (67–69).

3 See, for example, Bristow xxiv; Clayton, "Olive," par. 2, 3, and 16; and Monsman 67, 106. See also Monsman's connection to "Napoleon; Man of the World" in Emerson's *Representative Men*. Emerson quotes Napoleon as stating, "My hand of iron was not at the extremity of my arm, it was immediately connected with my head" (qtd. in Monsman 69). Monsman contrasts "the Napoleonic ethos of an iron will" with the weaknesses of Gregory Rose, adding, "Unlike Gregory's, Lyndall's is the Napoleonic 'hand of iron'" (72, 74). Ruth Parkin-Gounelas, however, states that "Ralph Iron" may come from that fact that during "the five years she wrote novels, her heart was 'like iron'" (92).

4 The quotation is from de Tocqueville's *Democracy in America*, volume 1, the beginning of chapter 2.

5 It is worth noting that Lyndall thinks that acting is the only profession for one such as herself (183; pt. 2, ch. 6). There may be a further connection to Shakespeare when Lyndall says, "I am a weak, selfish, erring woman" (247; pt. 2, ch. 12), which sounds like Hamlet's "frailty, thy name is woman!" (*Ham.* 1.2.146). In addition, her statement, "We are talking of to-morrow, and to-morrow" (185; pt. 2, ch. 6), as well as Waldo's stranger's statement, "to-morrow, and to-morrow, and to-morrow the hunter walked alone" (124; pt. 2, ch. 2), surely echoes Macbeth's "Tomorrow, and tomorrow, and tomorrow" (*Mac.* 5.5.19).

6 Ruth First and Ann Scott inaccurately claim that Blenkins is "an Irish entrepreneur" (94). Lyndall identifies him as an Englishman (13; pt. 1, ch. 2). Blenkins claims to be Irish but only after Otto tells him that Tant' Sannie hates the English (19; pt. 1, ch. 3).

7 Waldo's description of the sea resonates meaningfully with Matthew Arnold's "Dover Beach" (1867): "Listen! you can hear the grating roar / Of pebbles which the waves draw back, and fling, / At their return, up the high strand, / Begin, and cease, and then again begin, / With tremulous cadence slow, and bring / The eternal note of sadness in" (lines 9–14). In each case, the sea speaks what remains unspoken within the psyche. Also, both Waldo and the speaker of Arnold's dramatic monologue reflect the crisis of religious faith in the Victorian period.

8 There is also a slight implication that Waldo is more comfortable with female children than with an adult woman. For example, he stumbles verbally in his interaction with Lyndall upon her return to the farm, causing her to ask, "You liked the pinafores better?" (151; pt. 2, ch. 4). The narrator explains that his reaction relates mainly to fashion: "To Waldo she seemed superbly attired. She saw it." But there is also, in his unfinished letter to Lyndall, the story of his encounter with "a little girl" at the wholesale store. She likes his curly hair, and he lets her sit on his knee. Apparently, he projects the innocence of his anima onto her and, in general, is more comfortable with children than with adults. He comments in the letter: "If the world was all children I could like it; but men and women draw me so strangely, and then press me away, till I am in agony. I was not meant to live among people" (229; pt. 2, ch. 11). The world is not made for such introverts.

9 As Blenkins prepares to whip Waldo, the narrator notes: "He hardly liked the look in the fellow's eyes, though he stood there motionless. If he should spring on him!" After the beating, "There was a wild, fitful terror in the eyes. Bonaparte . . . himself was afraid

of that look" (91–92; pt. 1, ch. 12). Robbie McLaughlan aptly states, "When looking directly into Waldo's eyes, Blenkins locates a primal menace that fails to satisfy his 'narcissistic demand of colonial authority'" (140).

10 Schreiner's portrayal of Blenkins's religious hypocrisy illustrates the following statement by Jung: "Christian civilization has proved hollow to a terrifying degree: it is all veneer, but the inner man has remained untouched and therefore unchanged. . . . Inside reign the archaic gods, supreme as of old" (*CW* 12, par. 12).

11 D. L. Shapple deals extensively with the Bushmen's art in terms of colonialism but not its psychological significance for Waldo. Monsman notes that Waldo's last name, Farber, "links up with the analogue of the cave painter through its root meaning color or hue" (106). *Farber* is the German word for "dyer."

12 In Jung's *Collected Works* the lion is indexed as a symbol of the Self, and it also "stands for the danger of being swallowed by the unconscious" (*CW* 9i, par. 315; 5, par. 277).

13 See, for example, Jung's "The Mother Complex" (*CW* 9i, par. 161–71).

14 Lyndall's desire for a strong man perhaps echoes Desdemona's animus projection onto Othello, who is a trained killer.

15 Blenkins's sermon makes him a parody of Saint Gregory who was a great preacher.

16 See 239; pt. 2, ch. 12: Gregory tells the landlady that "he had come with the transport waggons [sic] that stood outside the town. He had walked in, and wanted lodgings for the night. It was a deliberate lie, glibly told; he would have told fifty, though the recording angel had stood in the next room with his pen dipped in the ink." For Lyndall's hatred of lies see 203; pt. 2, ch. 9.

4

"THE REALITY OF THE SINGULAR"

Anima and *Unus Mundus* in Laurens
van der Post's *A Story Like the Wind*
and *A Far-Off Place*

Much of Laurens van der Post's work following his first encounter with C. G. Jung in October 1949 (Jones 320) reflects Jung's influence, for "he was a kind of lighthouse" to van der Post (van der Post, *Walk* 39). The date of their first meeting is sometimes erroneously given as 1952, perhaps because it corresponds roughly to the publication date of *Venture to the Interior* (1951), the first of van der Post's Jungian works. There is also disagreement about the extent of Jung's transforming influence on van der Post's thought. Kenneth A. Robb notes a Jungian influence in all of van der Post's books after 1949, and he quotes Doris Lessing's observation that van der Post had "fallen under the spell of persuasive Papa Jung" (par. 10, 29). Christopher Smith asserts more credibly that Jung provided an "intellectual framework" that made van der Post's pre-existent ideas "more coherent" (881), and Frederic I. Carpenter suggests that van der Post's "reading of Jung's books merely strengthened the patterns of thought which he had already developed from personal experience and from literary sources" (62).

Some of the work that is relevant to the two novels under consideration, *A Story Like the Wind* and *A Far-Off Place*, examines van der Post's appropriation of background material. For example, Alan Barnard discusses van der Post's myth of the Bushmen in relation to anthropological texts; Edwin N. Wilmsen, van der Post's idea (in relation to Jung) that the Bushmen are direct descendants of the original humans; David Maughan Brown, the noble savage in colonial ideology; Dirk Klopper, two senses of the "primitive," as Other and as what "has been lost to the modern psyche" (38); and Marcia K. Farrell, the postcolonial framework as it relates to the François-Nonnie relationship. Only D. W. Lloyd reads the novels from a consistently Jungian point of view, stating that the "Jungian allegories, *A Story Like the Wind* and *A Far-Off Place*, constitute [van der Post's] fullest attempt to implement his Jungian insights in the dynamics of southern African life" (325). Lloyd focuses on the books' critique of reason, seeing both Ouwa's liberal rationality and the terrorists' revolutionary Marxism as flawed, for each assumes the reality of the Other. François embraces the Other by partnering with the Bushman Xhabbo and his anima by uniting with Nonnie. Her Catholicism softens and complements his Calvinism; they both achieve a combined "Bushman and Western sensibility" (327), which is grounded in "the unity of all creation" (328); and she will become his Sophia-like guide in the metropolitan world after the close of *A Far-Off Place*.[1]

Lloyd's reading is insightful so far as it goes, but more can be said. There is mention of Mopani but not of other wise old men—François's black African mentor 'Bamuthi and the witch-doctor uLangalibalela. There is also a conflation of Other and shadow despite a clear distinction between Xhabbo-as-Other and the books' proper shadow figures, the black African guerrillas who also manifest the collective shadow and suggest parallels to Nazi Germany and apartheid.[2] The progressive relationship between a male's shadow and anima is overlooked, the psychic phenomenon called "tapping" is not fully explicated, and the modified Lord's Prayer at the end of *A Far-Off Place* is erroneously attributed to François (it is rather van der Post's own inflationary sermon in the guise of Mopani's self-reflection). Finally, although the article links the idea of unity to synchronicity and "tapping," there is no connection made to Jung's *unus mundus* or its relationship to the anima.

That the *unus mundus* is also absent from *Jung and the Story of Our Time* illustrates biographer J. D. F. Jones's sense that van der Post "diminishes the sophistication and subtlety of Jung's immense scholarship" (325). Carpenter correctly notes, however, that van der Post's "mysticism" has to do with the unity of all things (155), a unity that corresponds to Jung's term *unus mundus*, the one world or unity world, which encompasses matter, psyche, and spirit. Even the vast collective unconscious is merely a subset of the *unus mundus*. James Hillman points out in *Anima: An Anatomy of a Personified Notion* that the anima in Jung is similarly all-inclusive: not only the contrasexual in men but also the archetype of life itself and many other things. Yet he does not mention the anima's strong resemblance to the *unus mundus*, though they are complementary principles of unity. Such overarching unity, this chapter argues, is the main theme and lesson of *A Story Like the Wind* and *A Far-Off Place*.

The first section examines their general and extensive debt to Jung. Section two augments Lloyd's work by probing more deeply into the problems that reason/*Logos* creates in modern civilization. Section three shows how the anima or feminine in *Wind* and *Place* includes not only the contrasexual principle in men but also a variety of other roles, including *mediatrix* between consciousness and the unconscious; François and Nonnie emerge here as a positive hybrid of European and native African ways of knowing.[3] The final section shows that the novels enact the overarching unity of Jung's *unus mundus*. Throughout what follows, the goal is to argue that van der Post critiques masculine reason to suggest that embracing the feminine (broadly defined) via archaic man's alternative ways of knowing provides an antidote to the ills of European civilization.

A note to the reader, however, is necessary before we proceed. Chapter 4 is not an endorsement of van der Postian myth-making or of Jungian assumptions about Africa or women—both men's writings are fraught with racism and essentialism—but rather a forthright attempt to view van der Post's novels as more thoroughly Jungian than anyone has previously recognized. If we understand "the primitive" to mean the psychologically archaic and separate it (as Jung often failed to do) from a context based on race, Jung has a point when he considers all persons to carry within them ancient psychic material, which Anthony Stevens calls *The Two Million-Year-Old Self*. In a post-Jungian spirit, this chapter offers a reading of van der Post that illuminates his intellectual context but frankly acknowledges his limitations.

Van der Post's common ground with Jung

Various details in the two novels illustrate van der Post's debt to Jung and Lloyd's sense that *Wind* and *Place* are Jungian allegory. Van der Post's allegorical sense is particularly direct in *Venture to the Interior*, and the theory that lies beneath is Jungian. Van der Post states, "For a voyage to a destination, wherever it may be, is also a voyage inside oneself" (51). The same principle animates the two novels, as the narrator explains: "World without and world within, after all, whether one knows it or not are expressions of one another; interdependent and ceaselessly in com-munication, serving something greater than the sum of themselves" (*Wind* 124; cf. *Place* 153). A dialectical relationship between matter and psyche echoes Jung's belief that the archetype is "psychoid," which means that it participates in both matter and psyche (matter has a psychological aspect, psyche a physical aspect). The quotation from *Wind* also illustrates the two novels' great flaw: the story is not merely told and the interpretation left to the reader. Rather than letting the tale speak for itself, the author intrudes to make sure that the correct meaning is apprehended. Still, the short passage does make a point that is perhaps the central truth in his work: inner parallels outer; as within, so without.

The psychoid factor lies at the heart of Jung's theory of synchronicities (meaningful coincidences), and it is plausible that van der Post knew of the psychoid factor because he frequently references synchronicities. Indeed, coincidences feature prominently in *Wind*, the most significant being the appearance of "a large praying mantis" in Mantis's Cave, which Xhabbo considers an actual visitation by the Bushman god (114). A bit later van der Post refers to "another of those *meaningful coincidences* which appeared to be such a speciality of their life in the bush" (125; emphasis added). Furthermore, just as the archetype unites inner and outer, van der Post's novels bridge the gap between Africa and Europe, ancient and modern, primitive and civilized, rural and metropolitan. If one cannot experience the "magic mirror" of Africa first-hand (*Dark Eye* 81), one may still read about such encounters in van der Post's novels and travel books. The phrase—evening "was always like a magic mirror on the walls of François's mind" (*Wind* 273)—signals not mere reflection but something akin to Samuel Taylor Coleridge's "secondary imagination," a magical or recreative interchange between setting and psyche (567; ch. 13).

There also appear to be four categories in which van der Post borrowed from Jung or at least had him squarely in mind. The first is the witch-doctor uLangalibalela who is a Jung-like figure. "'Bamuthi noticed François's amazement [upon reaching uLangalibalela's camp] and remarked: 'You can tell the greatness of a prophet by the number of women who gather round him'" (*Wind* 177). Jung too was surrounded by women, as van der Post knew well because his second wife, Ingaret Giffard, studied with Jung's associate Toni Wolff and because van der Post lectured at the C. G. Jung Institute and the Psychological Club of Zurich. In *Jung and the Story of Our Time*, van der Post notes "the [great] numbers of women around and working with and for Jung" and credits "this impressive circle of women colleagues and friends" to Jung's effort to embrace "the feminine in life" (228). Also like the witch-doctor, Jung "healed those who were 'thin' in heart and mind" (*Wind* 175); and he was open to "a kind of knowledge which, at any moment, could go far beyond any rational limits" (181). Notably, the principle that one must be in a state of humility and receptivity (not "heat" or inflation) when encountering uLangalibalela (179) illuminates Jung's statement that van der Post was well-adjusted and not in need of analysis. As a friend who was a Jungian analyst charitably said after van der Post's death, "Laurens had an extremely fluent ego-structure and Jung had the sense that it wouldn't change" (qtd. in Jones 322). Perhaps van der Post, whom Jones considers a mythomane, never underwent analysis because he lacked its most fundamental prerequisite, a humble acknowledgement of his own true story.

Other details in van der Post's books seem sufficiently similar to Jung's remarks on dreams in Africa as to suggest a second area of influence, though the direction of that influence remains ambiguous. Van der Post may have borrowed directly from Jung's writings or from their discussions of Africa, but he may also have had personal familiarity in Africa with dream-related details that could have influenced Jung. To begin with, van der Post often mentions the idea that there is a dream dreaming us.[4] The notion appears in *Place* when François recalls that "Old Koba had told him all Bushmen believed that there was a dream dreaming them" (243). In *Memories, Dreams, Reflections*, Jung records how he awoke from a dream of a yogi and said, "Aha, so he is the one who is meditating me. He has a dream, and I am it" (323). The two novels also echo the concept of "big dreams," which Jung learned from his interviews with African dreamers on his Bugishu Psychological Expedition in 1925–1926. Being numinous and prophetic rather than merely personal, big dreams often convey information important to a group of people. For example, uLangalibalela has such a dream in which Umkulunkulu ("the first great spirit") appears to warn him that the terrorists are advancing (*Wind* 342); and Xhabbo's "great dream" of a singing woman bound to a tree, with crocodiles and hippos barring the way to her, is a precognitive image of Maria's captivity at the singing tree (*Place* 242–43).

A third apparent borrowing from Jung's expedition is Mopani's reply to the modern condemnation of "any relationship between the mind and spirit of civilized man and the mind of the natural world." He teaches François that

> there was the most delicate relationship between what went on in their
> own minds and the awareness of the animal world of Africa. He had found,

for instance, that when he and his father had gone out into the bush to kill, the behaviour of birds and animals was totally different from those occasions when they rode out without any intention of killing.

(*Wind* 277)

The point directly echoes Jung's recollection of hunting in Africa. Regarding one specific animal, the natives told him, "It is not bad, it is *our* lion." Additional evidence came when Jung realized "the fact that leopards go hunting with you provided you carry your shotgun and not your big caliber gun; when you carry your big gun no leopard will appear" (qtd. in Burleson 135–36).[5] In a similar locution, François speaks of "our lions" to Nonnie, meaning that they are "good lions . . . because they never give us any trouble" (*Wind* 242). It is quite possible that van der Post plucked these details about animals directly from his conversations with Jung about his African expedition, or perhaps they arrived independently at the same conclusion.

Various principles of psychotherapy, a fourth area of influence, appear in the novels and may have come from van der Post's reading of Jung, his conversations with his wife or with Jung, or some combination. Jungian analysts must themselves undergo analysis for the reason that Ouwa once impressed on François: "no one could take others further than he had taken himself" (*Place* 111). If that condition is fulfilled, then talking to an analyst provides benefit for the reason that van der Post articulates in *Jung and the Story of Our Time*: "Jung came to the conclusion that every human being had a story, or to put it in its most evolved form, a myth of [his or her] own" (118). Persons' psychological health improves when they share their stories with a professional. François and Nonnie experience some of the benefit of talk therapy when they finally begin to discuss the loss of their parents and friends:

> From then on for the first time too Nonnie and François found themselves talking openly about the figure, thereby confirming a law of whose existence Xhabbo's remark the night before had been as implicit as midnight is with noon of day. It is simply that until one acknowledges one's whole past, however painful and humiliating the process might be, and dignifies it with an honest frank and full admission of its nature into one's daylight self, one is not free for a future of one's own.
>
> (*Place* 235)

In other words, if the shadow (what we hide from others) is acknowledged, it becomes a source of strength. Another version of talk therapy appears a few pages later when Nonnie chides François for "being such an old Huguenot with such a fanatical conscience!" She adds, "As a good Catholic, I'll just have to be your Father-confessor [or 'Jungian analyst'] and pronounce absolution, total and complete from your crime" (239). The "crime" refers to François's confession of his gratuitous killing of a worm—the only creature he has ever killed unnecessarily. He also recalls

'Bamuthi's teaching that "the knowledge of the unspoken evil a man has done is a worm eating his heart away" (239). Earlier 'Bamuthi shares a similar adage with François—"He who has killed in secret will hear it announced to all the world by the grass of the veld" (*Wind* 78)—which resembles what Jung says in *Memories, Dreams, Reflections* about a murderess whose secret guilt was reflected in isolation from others and separation from animals. Jung writes, "Sometimes it seems as if even animals and plants 'know' it" (123). The shadow, which one conceals from the public, has external resonance, but the implications and consequences of secret guilt can be avoided by talking about it.

The problem of modern life

From the general range of Jungian echoes and analogies in the previous section, we turn to the central problem in van der Post's two novels, which Lloyd identifies as the dominance of rationality over the unconscious in Western civilization. As Jamal En-nehas accurately states, *Wind* and *Place* "belong to the collective unconscious [that] civilized man obdurately represses" (146). More specifically, it is modern persons' unconscious primitive side that must be acknowledged if individuation is to take place. The primitive, if cleansed of Jung's racist rhetoric, describes the archaic—what is far down in the psyche, far back in time, and characteristic of human origins. The archaic includes nonrational modes of thought such as instinct and intuition, which civilization ignores but Bushmen—"the oldest living people in the world" (*Place* 72) and "a living image of what we had rejected and betrayed of our own aboriginal spirit" (*Mantis* 104)—still embrace. As van der Post notes in *Jung and the Story of Our Time*, Jung was receptive to alternative ways of knowing because his mother had nurtured him in "the non-rational, at times, parapsychological phenomena of life so despised by the intellectual establishment of his day" (89).[6] The fundamental problem is "the singular lack of grief, the ominous incapacity of contemporary men for experiencing sorrow, that impoverishes the life of our time" (*Place* 300). The lack of feeling and, more generally, of the archaic with all its feminine connotations is the central problem of modernity: the anima is not properly mediating between the rational and the unconscious.

The best example is that the terrorists who take over Hunter's Drift do so because they lack individuation in general and suffer detachment from the anima, men's inner feminine, in particular. Jung would diagnose their problem as "fanatical one-sidedness," meaning a "loss of anima" (*CW* 9i, par. 147), a point that plays out in François's reflections. He knows that being "a partial, provisional version instead of a whole, committed version of [one]self" is the genesis of tyranny, for when "a part of the whole of man [reason, consciousness] masquerade[s] as his full self and suppress[es] the rest [for example, the anima]," brutality results. In other words, "All started within before it manifested itself without and tyranny began with partial concepts of ourselves [lack of individuation, wholeness] and our roles in life" (*Place* 111). As within, so without: from an unbalanced psyche proceed negative consequences; more specifically, terrorism is really a form of projection, as François tells Nonnie: "I think unnecessary killing is the only real killing there is, because we kill others then out of something we hate and don't understand [in ourselves]—at least that's what Mopani says" (*Place* 239). In short, terrorism projects the shadow and represses of the anima.

Lack of integration of unconscious content and the detrimental effects of repression receive further elaboration in van der Post's works. François suspects, for example, that growing up is a process "of being educated out of reality, above all the great invisible realities which matter so much more to a young person than the physical ones by which men set by far a greater store as they grow older" (*Wind* 131). If "reality" means attunement to the archaic and to the unconscious in general, "unreality" means suppression of all that it represents, as van der Post explains in *Venture to the Interior*. In that work, the loss of Vance in a river sweeping through a gorge is an allegory of what happens within individual persons. Repression opens up an inner gorge between the archaic and the civilized, and that gorge corresponds to divisions among peoples. The distance between the archaic and the civilized in one person begets distance between and among groups of persons, as van der Post explains:

> The distance between them and us was the distance of their unreality; just as the distance between us all to-day [sic] is created by our unreality. . . . For this unreality starts in our incomplete awareness of ourselves; it starts in the elevation of a part of ourselves [reason] at the expense of the whole. Then, out of this dark gorge which we have allowed to open up between the two halves of ourselves, out of this division between the Europe and the Africa in us, unreality rises up to overwhelm us.
>
> (*Venture* 225)

Civilization stifles the individuation process by repressing the archaic, something deep down and fundamental to our personal and societal well-being. One must bridge that inner gorge if society is to be healed, and it is van der Post's objective as author to show us how.[7]

Wind and *Place* dramatize the consequences of modern persons' failure to acknowledge the archaic, instinctual inheritance that constitutes psychic reality: that failure is the books' central problem and the driver of various actions. As van der Post puts it in *The Dark Eye in Africa*, there are "the two extremities of human nature—the natural, instinctive pagan element and the rational, conscious, forward-moving Christian awareness" (68).[8] Ouwa's overemphasis on reason illustrates the latter, for he is described as "a person essentially of an analytical and enquiring mind" without "the accepting and trusting spirit so necessary for the 'Bamuthi or [even the] Mopani approach to life" (*Wind* 137). Ouwa was formerly employed by the government as Director of Education for a vast territory in Africa. Not only does Ouwa practice Western rationality, but he also once represented a government that funds an educational system whose purpose is to extract "the life-giving riches" of "one's aboriginal self," as though the natives were children who have to be educated out of bad behavior (*Wind* 195–96). Because his personal objective, which was to help all races work toward harmony and unity to achieve "a common non-racial destiny" (*Wind* 54), was out of step with the government's expectations, he eventually resigned and moved to Hunter's Drift where the farm cooperative enacts a version of his vision for Africa at large.

The government is called "this formidable old gentleman" (*Wind* 53), which is a euphemism for the devil, and so it turns out to be. Ouwa gets sick for some reason that even South Africa's finest doctors cannot detect but that François and the other magic-minded characters believe to be rejection by the government. Ouwa is a man without a country: separated from the system he once served but unable fully to embrace the native Africa around him. The man took himself out of the government, but the government's extreme rationality cannot be taken out of the man. According to the narrator, "Lammie and Ouwa themselves had been caught unawares in some of this mechanism of rejection of the natural man in Africa." Their embrace of reason is "a form of overcompensation for their unawareness of some vital element in themselves" (*Wind* 194). Ouwa's rationality, now severed from its source, causes him to wither so that he experiences a slow death on the outer physical plane that both corresponds to and arises from the inner "unreality" of which van der Post speaks. In *Man and the Shadow*, published a year earlier, the author refers to the same "erosive process of rationalism which has deprived us of the language of the primitives" (10). Ouwa dies because he has been sucked into a psychic gorge as surely as Vance disappears in a literal one. As a result of this loss, François responds by attaching himself "more firmly than ever to the African influences of his surroundings" (*Wind* 196).

Western persons must strike a proper balance between extremes, and it is possible to chart the books' main characters with respect to a continuum between reason and the faculties the West considers archaic. At the far left extreme are the psychic pagans, uLangalibalela and Xhabbo, as well as recollections of Koba, the Bushman woman who helped transform François into a white Bushman (*Wind* 312). A step further to the right is 'Bamuthi, a black African, and Ousie-Johanna, a Christian, who both believe in witchcraft and magic. In roughly the center of the continuum, one finds François, a Christian of European extraction who also believes in the witch-doctor's abilities. Then there is the more rationally minded Mopani, another European Christian who reads the Bible and *Pilgrim's Progress* and with whom François does not share his visit to uLangalibalela for fear of criticism. Mopani, however, is open-minded enough to tell François: "Little Cousin, always remember in Africa that what we Europeans call superstition, is just the wrong explanation for the right truth. It is, in fact, an attempt to draw attention to mysterious facts and laws of nature which Europeans ignore because they cannot explain them with their brains" (*Wind* 228). From Ouwa, François receives no such latitude: the father is a straightforward rational European educator whose objective is to bring civilization to the Africans at Hunter's Drift and to establish a partnership with the Matabele. On the positive side, he does entrust his son to Ousie-Johanna and 'Bamuthi; and he schools François in the importance of an intuitive "leap into the dark"—feeling over reasoning—as an alternative to common sense (*Wind* 297). This limited openness puts him to the right of Mopani and the left of Sir James Archibald Sinclair Monckton, Nonnie's father, who continues to work for Great Britain, criticizes François for making a decision about a campsite on the basis of a native superstition, but later admires him for his rationality. Monckton, rather than Ouwa, is the true colonialist in the first novel because his estate will not be a family-like partnership. Believing that there is nothing to learn from Africa's denizens, he will simply be his native workers' employer. Furthest to the right is the government itself, the bureaucratic embodiment of European rationality.

The far right of the continuum reflects the statement in *The Dark Eye in Africa* that William Blake in *The Marriage of Heaven and Hell* criticizes the one-sided rationality of his time (121). It would have been better to note Blake's use of "Single vision & Newton's sleep" in a letter to Thomas Butts dated November 22, 1802 (Keynes 79). In Blake's view, Newtonian science's one-sided focus on the physical world distorts the human personality. Since single vision suggests a single eye, the Cyclops becomes an emblem in *Dark Eye* of the problem van der Post wishes to correct (120). The French mercenary Jean Armand's glass eye makes him cyclopean, and indeed his compatriot Mister Lauder criticizes him for knowing "only a logic of the mind and forget[ting] the logic of the heart," for emphasizing Descartes and ignoring Pascal (*Place* 103).[9] Their overheard fireside conversation duplicates and reinforces the problem that drives the larger narrative. The association of Cyclops and elephant, however, is imperfect and introduces an aporia. According to the narrator, "the elephant in the Bushman world . . . played the same role as one-eyed giants in François's Greek legends or wicked giants in his European fairy tales" (*Wind* 94). Uprooter of Great Trees is such a destroyer. But later 'Bamuthi contrasts the rhinoceros, which hurries in a straight line, destroying things in its way, with elephants, which "go slowly in and out, round and about, making their way through the bush as the wise among men go through life" (*Wind* 164). The juxtaposition provides a little allegory of ways of knowing: the rationality of Ouwa and Monckton on the right (rhino) versus the intuition of Xhabbo and the others on the left (elephant). As in Mopani's favorite maxim, "the longest way round was the shortest way there" (*Wind* 275), the rational rhumb line is not always the best course to steer.

Since rationality is linked to tragedy, van der Post establishes Hunter's Drift as an Eden-like place from which there will be a fall. The farm is a paradise "where animal, bird, flower, fruit and man had been so at one" (*Place* 66) but where its human overseers, Ouwa and Lammie, emphasize reason over feeling. Both Ouwa in his educational practices and Lammie in treating François as "another little person" do not provide sufficient emotional warmth (*Place* 299). Therefore, he "turns for more spontaneous manifestations of human feelings to the coloured and black people around him" (*Place* 2). That Ouwa falls to the old gentleman and Lammie to the terrorists signifies their original sin in van der Post's allegory. The imagery even incorporates the angel with the fiery sword who banishes Adam and Eve from the garden (*Place* 66). "Chaos and old night," a phrase from *Paradise Lost*, Book 1, characterizes the situation of the two teenagers who have escaped the massacre at Hunter's Drift (*Place* 80, 129). Whereas in Milton the fallen angels' shout "Frighted the Reign of *Chaos* and old Night" (line 543), in van der Post the phrase underscores the terror that François and Nonnie face in their exile.

Another myth adds to the notion of the lost archaic. Van der Post reads Prometheus's gift of fire to man as the dawning of consciousness, which corrupts us and causes us to spoil the earth ("Our Mother" 10–11). "The Promethean sin" refers to a focus on reason to the exclusion of nonrational ways of knowing (*Dark Eye* 68) and a separation "from our animal selves" (*Man* 19). Yet, in a corresponding myth, "the Bushman God had first discovered fire, to give it to the people of the early race": *discovered*, not *stolen* (*Place* 272). As Xhabbo and Nuin-Tara illustrate, fire/consciousness does not have to be a sin or mark a fall from wholeness, nor does its presence mean the absence of instinct and intuition. Much like Ouwa's death, the fall of Hunter's Drift is an outer loss that signals the inner consequence of harboring reason in the extreme. Unlike his parents, François survives because he cultivates alternative ways of knowing through the agency of the anima.

The anima as *mediatrix*

If neglect of the archaic causes the "one-sidedness" in Europeans and if the anima can be a "mediator" between consciousness and the unconscious, as van der Post suggests (*Man* 15), then the feminine is crucial to addressing the problem described in the previous section, and so it is in *Wind* and *Place*. Whereas Hunter's Drift stands for European reason, the characters' flight into the bush and across the desert signifies an encounter with nonrational, feminine qualities such as emotion, instinct, and intuition. As the two novels demonstrate, it is the anima, in its widely varied forms, that connects consciousness to the archaic/natural in the collective unconscious. In turn, the collective unconscious opens into the riches of the *unus mundus*. As a connector, then, the anima is the antidote to the malaise of the twentieth century, the bridge over the chasm dividing ancient and modern, and the access key to all that is.

In Jung's writings, the anima is not only a contrasexual principle but also a broad energetic field. If, as Hillman points out, the anima is all-inclusive, then it may contain the *unus mundus*, rather than the other way around. To begin with, Hillman notes the anima's relationship to *eros*, as in a man's connections to Helen and Eve, but overlooks the more general category of *feeling*, which has links to instinct and intuition. Further, if "the anima [is] the foundation of relationship" (*Anima* 37), then to live in touch with her means syzygy consciousness; but Hillman mentions only the male-female syzygy. If "anima [is] a unity" or "a uni-personality" (147, 151), then it must include and enable other syzygies such as flesh and spirit, man and beast, ancient and modern, European and African. As Hillman explains, the anima expands further still, for she is a "mediatrix [sic] to the eternally unknowable" (133); anima facilitates individuation by "mediat[ing] the ceaseless movement of interiority" (139). She is not just the guide between consciousness and the vast reaches of the unconscious but also "the archetype of psyche itself," which is "synonymous with psychic life and actually personifies the collective unconscious" (67, 73). Even more broadly, Jung calls her "the archetype of life" (51). Since Africa commingles geographical matter, the archaic, native cultures, "the pre-conscious life of nature" (141), and much more, it must be her continent. One suspects that she may even be a *mediatrix* to the spirit world, which imbricates but lies mostly beyond psyche. Such broad inclusivity, which far transcends our two Jungian systems, the Kore and the "stages of eroticism," suggests, according to Hillman, not that the anima is in us but that we are in her (81). Anima is a field of energy in which the parts of the *unus mundus* communicate with each other, including the microcosm of the individual psyche, the macrocosm of nature, and the spirit world—all that is.

Van der Post's treatment of the anima in *Wind* and *Place* is very clearly more than the contrasexual in men. To begin with, the African continent is unequivocally anima-related. As he writes in *Venture*, "On one side, under the heading 'AFRICA,' I would group unconscious, female, feminine, mother; and under 'EUROPE' on the other: conscious, male, masculine, father" (13). The connection between Africa and the feminine is nowhere clearer than in his rendition of African mythology. Mopani has told François that the Singing Tree, "the original tree of life . . . had originally been in the keeping of 'a white feminine presence' . . . a kind of white high priestess, or goddess." Like Mt. Sinai for Moses's people, the tree is the place "from which originally [Africans] had received their commandments and to which their prophets and seers, in the past, went in times of trouble for consultation and guidance" (*Wind* 284–85).[10] This information issues from the tree in song; and the terrorists capitalize on the belief that, when the tree sings again, it will be time for Africans to unite and push the white people back into the sea.

In van der Post's writings, the anima ranges from the contrasexual principle in men to a larger creative force. He defines the anima as "this delicate annunciation of woman in the spirit of man, this awareness of a re-creative feminine element in the masculine dominants of life and time which led the rough belted knights of Arthur on their quest" (*Dark Eye* 170). "Annunciation" and "re-creative feminine element" suggest the contrasexual principle in men but hint that the anima transcends its local habitation in the male psyche. A fuller articulation of the anima's greater dimension includes the image of "an elegant and most bewitching white lady" on an ancient rock painting. Van der Post's explication sounds akin to Hillman's description of the anima: "Also I find this white lady on a rock [to be] evidence of the profound mythological force which is active in the heart of all living matter, giving our little lives their direction, meaning and fullness in time" (*Dark Eye* 174). The woman on the rock figures forth both the feminine within the ancient artist and the creative impulse that human beings share with nature.

Wind and *Place* dramatize the feminine by illustrating the stages of eroticism. The maternal, in its biological and emotional senses, is particularly present. In the first book, Ousie-Johanna (like the memory of Koba) is a powerful maternal image, doing with food for the Joubert family what François does for Xhabbo with medicine. She also has a powerful maternal reaction when François brings home three bustard chicks that evoke her "under-employed maternal heart," and she makes sure that the local chickens adopt them (106). Maternal devotion is admired in another bird, the Francolin partridge, which "never allow[s] herself to be pushed off her eggs" (*Wind* 328). Lammie is the only human mother, but there is an implied connection to the maternal in Nonnie when the natives call her "a true 'little old impala lamb'" (*Wind* 226), as if she will receive the projection of François's maternal anima after his mother's death. She is too inexperienced in the bush to care for him, but nursing the wounded Hintza awakens "the mother latent in Nonnie" (*Wind* 369). After François, exhausted from running a long distance, returns to Mantis's Cave, the narrator describes her reaction in language that recalls van der Post's definition of the anima: "All that was latent and maternal in her flared into a quick flame that threatened to destroy her strained self-control. . . . It was her first clear *annunciation* of the role in which women are compelled at one and the same time to be both mistress and mother [Helen and Mary] to their men" (*Place* 124; emphasis added). Of course, Nonnie is certainly no Helen figure, as she notes when protesting treatment by her governess. She complains that Amelia carries on as if Nonnie were "a dancer about to do a striptease," which she is not about to do (*Wind* 246). A later comment adds a different sort of edge to her maternal role—"a kind of heroic Amazon, fighting off the world to give François the time to grow into the man who would deliver her from any need of playing the unfeminine role to herself" (*Place* 269–70). Teenage Nonnie wishes to take care of François so that he can take care of her adult self later on; she embraces the masculine so that she will have the luxury of greater femininity in the future. This trajectory deconstructs van der Post's recollection in *Jung and the Story of Our Time* that Toni Wolff's essay on psychological types refers to the Amazon as "the woman with a calling of her own, self-contained and independent of man" (173).[11]

Meanwhile, the novels' male-female syzygies illustrate the wifely role of Eve: Ouwa and Lammie "were profoundly attached to each other. Their relationship in fact was so complete that they were utterly content in each other's company," much as Xhabbo calls "Nuin-Tara . . . utterly my woman" (*Wind* 58, 361). When put through the crucible of exile and flight, the ideal Western relationship nascent in François and Nonnie takes on the intuitive closeness to nature of the Bushman couple in order to achieve *coniunctio*, "the union of opposites and the birth of new possibilities" (Sharp 42). Even the Bushman language plays a part in the young couple's transformation, for it "may lack logic and reason but more than compensates for them in feeling" (*Wind* 50). The teenagers become partners for life, as Nonnie announces just before the close of *Place*: it really does not matter what they do or where they go as long as she, François, and Hintza are "never separated for a split second again" (308). In the end, their relationship is not a clone of his parents' marriage or the Bushman couple's union but something new, which combines what is best in both.

Van der Post's critics, however, have puzzled over the apparent lack of sexuality—of *eros*, the Helen/mistress stage—between François and Nonnie. Martin Tucker downplays the lack of eroticism in stating: "Sexual love rarely occurs in his novels; the passion of friendship, of deep platonic affection, takes its place. He substitutes symbolic and emotional identity for sexual union" (213). Jones observes that "during twelve months in the bush and desert there is never a hint of a sexual current between these two epitomes of innocence, clearly though they are destined for each other" (306). Regarding the scene in which Nuin-Tara makes François lie down with Nonnie, Farrell seems more on point in stating, "François' emotional crisis as he lies next to Nonnie is not only a sexual awakening, then, but also part of his journey towards a Jungian actualization of self" (par. 6). He is already in love with her (*Wind* 304), declaring a bit later his feeling that they have always known each other, to which the lion "old Chaliapin gave one of his greatest roars" (*Wind* 332). Lying down with her evokes feelings of oneness with Nonnie, and he is "overwhelmed by the many feelings released in him by so simple and natural an event" (*Place* 36–37). Perhaps those who criticize the absence of sexual sparks underestimate the importance that van der Post places on decorum. For example, François describes the long ordeal to the press, "though obviously still without intimate personal matters and shades of thought and feeling too delicate for public discussion" (*Place* 293). Might these "intimate personal matters" include sexual arousal while they sleep next to each other at their hundreds of campsites? On the other hand, many factors are afoot to dampen their ardor. Teenagers who come from strict Calvinist and Catholic upbringings, they are grieving for their murdered parents, fleeing for their lives, walking all day, getting baked by the sun, and not eating or drinking properly. In addition, as the narrator notes regarding their closeness with the Bushman couple, "how at one they had all become" (*Place* 205). Van der Post well knows that now is the time for the survival of the group, not for eroticism. Sexual love will follow in later life.

It may also seem odd that *Wind* begins with twenty pages of narration on the coming of Hintza into François's life, but this feature of the novel is not difficult to understand in light of the importance van der Post places on instinct, one of the qualities to which the anima enables access. The first book begins with great attention to the dog because he is "the plenipotentiary of all that was natural and instinctive in life" (*Place* 69). More specifically, in *A Mantis Carol* van der Post identifies "the hunter in human imagination . . . as a *plenipotentiary* of that part of the human personality which is . . . in search of new and greater meaning" (18–19; emphasis added). Hunting is one channel into which instinct may be directed, and François has trained Hintza as a hunting dog to understand and respond to commands in the Bushman language. Unlike the mongrels at Hunter's Drift, Hintza sleeps indoors, becoming not so much a creature of pure instinct as a liminal figure halfway between wild animal and human being. The novels resemble children's stories in the sense that the ridgeback commingles instinct with human qualities, even sometimes the appearance of reason. Thus, he is a synthesis somewhat akin, strangely enough, to what Jung called his No. 2 personality (the part linked to the collective unconscious), which the human characters, Ouwa most of all, fail to emulate at their peril. As a masculine dog who radiates the feminine instinct that Xhabbo achieves on the human plane, Hintza is a human dog versus Xhabbo, a natural man. Finally, Hintza is the novels' greatest hero, for without him François would never have met

Xhabbo whose warning call motivates the dog to wake François up at the crucial moment. Without their four-legged friend, the youngsters would have died at Hunter's Drift along with their parents. Given his importance to the narrative and its themes, the coming of Hintza is as good a place to begin as any.

In Africa, the anima broadens from the contrasexual in the psyche of men to include nature and intuition. For example, Africans are in touch "with those overwhelming aspects of nature which are incomprehensible to reason and quite beyond conscious control and rational articulation" (*Dark Eye* 60). The statement relates to the novels' implication that ocean, bush, desert, and sleep all represent the unconscious mind. Jung associates the ocean with the collective unconscious; and if van der Post associates the bush and the desert with the ocean, then the setting figures forth the unconscious mind. *Wind* speaks of "that bush, full of as many voices as the five oceans, and so full of hidden forces" (160). Ordinarily, sleep is considered a medium in which consciousness and the personal unconscious commingle, but here "the deep sea of sleep" suggests that sleep is at one with the deep unconscious (*Place* 173). Simply put, Africa resembles the collective unconscious, which the anima personifies; as "this ancient treasure house of the lost original way of life" (*Dark Eye* 53), Africa echoes Jung's description of the collective unconscious as the "treasure-house of primordial images" (*CW* 7, par. 110).

Van der Post implies that getting in touch with the anima in Africa provides access, via emotion and imagination, to aspects of psyche that lie below and beyond the rational and the contrasexual. As *Wind*'s imagery suggests, it is the anima-related faculties that enable an emotional connection to the scene and a perception of the unity of man and beast in the bush/unconscious. Seeing "a great full moon," a traditional Romantic symbol of the imagination, François has a "warm feeling that the barriers between man and animal were downed by the moon and that they were all a single unit of life made one with the mystery of the bush full upon them" (*Wind* 169–70). The full moon, as a sphere, symbolizes the wholeness of the Self (Jung's archetype of wholeness) and relates to a similar image: "two large, round gold medallions on which the names of Xhabbo and Nuin-Tara were inscribed" (*Place* 297). At the end of the journey to the sea, François bestows these symbols of individuation on his Bushman friends. The medals, which unite Europe and Africa because they instruct any British citizen to aid the African bearers, contrast with the system of metal disks that Monckton formerly designed to identify every person of tax-paying age. The Matabele were supposed to wear them around their necks like an I.D., but the disks were instead "beaten into ornaments for women" (*Wind* 260), a distortion that affirms the feminine symbolism of their original shape over the masculine intent behind their design. As a similar image, the medals suggest that François and Nonnie have evolved beyond the limitations of Monckton's rational colonialism.

Moreover, the anima mediates between consciousness and the archetypes, which create a unity among all persons. That is exactly what happens when François observes Mister Lauder and Jean Armand as they discuss the war by firelight. Strangely, François realizes this anima-related unity because he too experiences the warrior and the hunter archetypes. To begin with, Ouwa has taught him that "all men tend to become the thing they oppose" (*Place* 112; cf. *Jung* 217); therefore, killing the two shadow figures would mark François as a shadow–possessed murderer. Instead, he chooses a more pacific alternative. In addition to their discussion of heart and head, Armand describes how he feels in battle "as if I hear the tramp of all the men who have ever fought for life since the beginning of time come marching up from the other side of the world [perhaps the unconscious] to stand at my side in battle." He is describing how battle connects him with the warrior archetype to produce "a calm that passes all understanding," an ironic echo of Philippians 4.7 (*Place* 107). François is able to see the humanity in his enemies because he has already had a similar experience when hooking little fingers with Xhabbo, which causes "a stream of strength and understanding" to flow into him, as if through the Bushman he connects to the hunter archetype (*Wind* 367). The hunter arises again after he leaves the officers' campsite: "A strange, yet definite kind of reassurance entered him through the soles of his feet from the track itself, as if all the countless feet of the forgotten men [hunters] who had trodden it over the years still lay there in the bush defined like a line in the palm of a black hand, had imprinted upon it the message for their successors" (*Place* 116). Later still, when he destroys the helicopter, "something else utterly beyond his powers of definition and expression [the warrior archetype], must have stirred deep down in François" (*Place* 204). This experience of sharing a connection to the archetypes with his would-be murderers is a sign of "their common humanity" (*Place* 99). Reason might have spurred François to murder Mister Lauder and Jean Armand, but the mutual experience of archetypal connection enables him to perceive something of himself in his enemies and vice versa. Because he does not kill gratuitously, the shadow withdraws its projection and becomes a source of further strength. Proof that the shadow becomes his friend appears at the end of *Place* when it is reported that Mister Lauder, now disillusioned with the war and back home in Scotland, anonymously supports François's account of the events at Hunter's Drift. It would be as wrong for François to kill the terrorists as to become one of them, and he achieves a middle way through the agency of the anima by fostering understanding and forgiveness rather than revenge.

Van der Post's larger point is not that one should abandon European reason in a total embrace of African feeling but that a Western person must achieve a proper synthesis, which the image pattern of the cross represents. In *Venture to the Interior*, van der Post notes that "a gulf bridged makes a cross; a split defeated is a cross" (242). In a similar phrase, Jung states that the anima provides "a bridge to the unconscious" (*CW* 13, par. 62). Xhabbo has a lot to do with how the point plays out in the second novel. He is named "dream" and is identified as "the unconscious man" (*Wind* 35); appropriately, a Bushman represents "our dreaming selves" (*Mantis* 20). In addition, if his "people [are] immediate with instinct" (*Place* 233), the Bushman is a fitting guide for François and Nonnie as they bridge the psychic gorge, as when Xhabbo draws "a large, symmetrical cross" on the floor of Mantis's womb-like cave. François reflects, "The cross, as he knew from Koba and Xhabbo, was not only a magic sign of healing for the Bushman but was also used a great deal in desert and bush, to show the place where two vital tracts met" (*Wind* 122), like the binaries that must be united. The cross is a fitting image to represent the unity of masculine and feminine, *Logos* and *eros,* consciousness and the unconscious.

As a result, the cave feels to François like "a naturally sacred place" (*Wind* 199). There is also "a cross painted in red by some long-forgotten Stone Age hand" on the cave's wall (*Wind* 351). He puts the painting of Saint Hubert next to it, later kneeling with Nonnie before this shrine to say a prayer for safety and deliverance now that François the hunter and his friends have become the hunted. The cross images unite the ancient Bushman pagan who drew the red cross, Xhabbo who marks the cave's floor, and the two young persons' Calvinist and Catholic strains of modern Christianity. Both Nonnie and François form the cross image—she makes the Catholic gesture, he a cross in the manner of Xhabbo's drawing (*Wind* 12, 66). In van der Post's hands, the cross image not only recalls the mark made on Old Testament doors at Passover (*Place* 127), the New Testament cross of Jesus's execution, and (as a quaternity image) the Jungian Self; it also signifies that in François and Nonnie all of these modes coalesce in a synthesis of Europe and Africa, which illustrates the anima as a principle of harmony and unity.

More specifically, the pagan cross, like the anima-as-*mediatrix*, signifies the meeting of conscious intention and assistance from the unconscious. As François explains, "That [red] cross was painted long, long before the crucifixion. . . . Bushmen have painted that sign of the cross to mark places where their asking in moments of despair, and what they call the answer and the asking-in-tapping meet" (*Place* 17). Tapping, which is similar to other gifts of the anima such as precognition and clairvoyance, puts Xhabbo in the same psychic league as uLangalibalela. In fact, the Bushman is "perhaps the greatest expert alive in this radar of meaning, built into every living being" (*Place* 17). It manifests as a literal thumping inside the chest but is more fundamentally a tapping or uniting of fields of energy within the *unus mundus*, especially the collective unconscious where information is not subject to the laws of time and space. Tapping is not available to rationalists like Ouwa and Monckton but only to those who are attuned to psyche's subjective feminine side, and it adds a moral dimension to the cross image. In van der Post's novels, then, the cross is a physical mark, stands for individuation, honors the moment of moral choice, and represents Christian salvation. Thus, it commingles all four traditional "senses" of interpretation—literal, allegorical, tropological, and anagogical.

François's world view is a similar synthesis of Europe and Africa, masculine and feminine. It is abundantly clear that both Mopani and 'Bamuthi are major reasons for François's hybrid approach to life. In fact, van der Post repeatedly mentions their dual influence. Both are wise old men, but "his chief instructors" bring different points of view to François's education (*Wind* 93). One is an African tribesman and a pagan who believes in magic. The other, a Christian of European extraction, reads the bush like "the writing in the Bible of nature" (*Wind* 133). Van der Post's statement in his summary of the first novel is that 'Bamuthi is to François in "a primitive sense" what Mopani is to François in "European pioneering terms" (*Place* 3). Indeed, "so well had François been trained in these things [moving stealthily through the bush] by Mopani Théron and 'Bamuthi" that he feels guided even in their absence (*Wind* 33). Because of "the lessons and examples of 'Bamuthi and Mopani," he finds "himself guided not so much by a rational self as by all the experience and love 'Bamuthi and Mopani had put into his upbringing" (*Place* 49). It is as though the older men have put him through an initiation at the men's house that Jung speaks of—a version perhaps of the shadow work that he maintains must precede successful work with the contrasexual. In short, they have provided a masculine training in ways of interacting with the feminine heart of Africa.

Following his two mentors, François develops a similarly hybrid spiritual position that reflects mediation by the anima. He is a Christian with a "Calvinist sediment" who, by nurturing "the pagan Matabele and Bushman aspects of his character," develops a "pagan-puritan conscience" (*Wind* 314, 132, and 220). Remarkably, he is a Calvinist who places his confidence in a witch-doctor. After he prays, "The Lord is my Shepherd as Koeggen-A is Xhabbo's shepherd," the narrator observes, "So complex a mixture had François become that he found nothing contradictory or even the least bit incongruous in joining the name of Christian overlord and pagan god in one and the same poetic prayer" (*Wind* 107). In other words, by fostering an anima-like inclusivity, "he was free of the mistrust of instinct and intuition wherein contemporary Europe tends to imprison human imagination, and . . . the pagan influences of his environment encouraged an unquestioning acceptance of this impulse which came to him" (*Wind* 124). The same theological mixture appears in another passage: "A faint feeling came to him that a tide of fate might have turned for him. But in the primitive fashion he did not allow himself to take it for granted, in case Providence found him presumptuous and reversed it again" (*Place* 116–17). Here the classical emphasis on fate (François is fond of Homer) mingles with Bushman practicality ("primitive fashion") and a Christian acknowledgement of God's will.

Citing "a new form of the Lord's prayer," Lloyd states that François's synthesis of Christian and pagan is not complete until the end of the tale (329). The comment refers to the following passage: "Our Father, which art in Heaven, Thy will be done. Our mother, which art in earth, thy love be fulfilled, and love and will made one" (*Place* 307). The new Lord's Prayer expresses the unity that results when the anima mediates between opposites such as heaven and earth, father and mother, will and love. However, it is uttered not by François but by Mopani who has himself come to the sort of realization that François manifests when he joins Nonnie in prayer at the shrine in Mantis's Cave. That is, François achieves something similar hundreds of pages earlier as illustrated by a saint and a pagan cross in an ancient cave—a synthesis of male and female, heaven and earth, Christian and pagan. It appears that François embraces a hybrid faith practically from the start of the tale and that Mopani's sermon, a continuation of his earlier "self-made Sermon of his own Mount" regarding the "dignity" of all life (*Place* 79), illustrates van der Post's heavy-handed didacticism.

Unity abounds

The anima not only is the contrasexual principle in men but also encompasses such faculties as *eros*, intuition, and imagination, which characterize the unconscious. As a place that honors, facilitates, and embodies these traits, Africa is anima country. Since the anima and the *unus mundus* are both connective fields, the final Jungian feature of the narration is the incorporation of details that reflect the unitary world. The novels are not about binary opposition because van der Post is not suggesting reason and emotion as mutually exclusive alternatives. Rather than overthrowing reason in favor of the unconscious mind, he prefers a balanced synthesis such as François's hybrid of Ouwa's rationality and Xhabbo's intuition. Opposites must unite, for individuation is not a zero-sum game. François tells Nonnie: "You can't just think about things in the bush, as Mopani has always told me. Thinking has its place, he says, but only when one is confronted with known facts and statistics. When you're in the unknown and the dark, as we are here, Mopani says, you surrender your thinking in trust to the feelings that come to you, out of the bush" (*Place* 183). He could as easily have said "out of the unconscious." Just as reason needs emotion, metropolitan man needs natural man as a complement, as for example the cerebral Jacob must reconcile with the hunter Esau (*Place* 302).[12] The ultimate goal is the sort of individuation that François achieves in realizing, "Yes, Lammie was at last in the blessed company at his side. They were only technically dead. Koba, Ousie-Johanna, 'Bamuthi, Lammie, Ouwa and many more, had almost acquired a living definition and dynamic clarity in death which they had not possessed in life and their voices would be with him always" (*Place* 300). If each of the deceased represents a part of François's psyche and these parts are now speaking to him, he has achieved what Mopani considers "a new journey within . . . [to] make what was first and oldest in us, new and immediate" and perhaps also "a true partnership with animals, birds, insects, plants, flowers and instinctive men" (302).

François has further inner work to do with Nonnie in the city, but what he has achieved so far on the personal level is the third stage of the hero's journey, synthesis and reintegration; and the young couple's long march to the sea and rescue by the British are a reverse image of the Great Trek of Europeans to the African interior, mentioned by van der Post in *The Dark Eye in Africa* (1980). The author signals that François achieves the synthesis that not only addresses twentieth-century malaise— Mopani (van der Post) calls it "the feeling of not belonging"—but also serves as a prerequisite for "the journey to the stars" (*Place* 301–302).[13] To the extent that François is really Laurens in teenage disguise, van der Post's implication that he is ready to be Earth's emissary to extraterrestrial civilizations is inflationary in the extreme.

Moreover, van der Post emphasizes "the reality of the singular" (*Wind* 276), the overarching unity of all things, in "the Bushman spirit," which rejects the idea that the large is greater than the small, for "long before the poet Blake, it had discovered infinity in the grains of sand of the desert" (*Wind* 269). The reference is to Blake's "Auguries of Innocence":

To see a World in a Grain of Sand
And a Heaven in a Wild Flower,
Hold Infinity in the palm of your hand
And Eternity in an hour.

(lines 1–4)

The lines suggest that the minutest physical detail contains the whole universe, that matter and spirit mingle, and that a moment contains all of time. Van der Post claims to have introduced Jung to a similar statement by Sir Thomas Browne, who writes, "We carry with us the wonders we seek without us: there is all Africa and her prodigies in us."[14] Van der Post describes Jung's reaction as follows: "He was deeply moved, wrote it down, and exclaimed, 'That was and is just it! But it needed the Africa without to drive home the point in my own self'" (*Jung* 50–51). For both men, the feminine heart of Africa makes the reality of the *unus mundus* perceptible to the conscious mind.

In the Africa of *Wind* and *Place*, signs of unity are everywhere, and all three parts of the *unus mundus* are present. 'Bamuthi associates wind with the first spirit, which uLangalibalela calls Umkulunkulu (*Place* 121; *Wind* 63). In the same paragraph that emphasizes "the reality of the singular," the narrator emphasizes the "profound inter-relationship existing with the life of the great world beyond" and warring man's effect on nature (*Wind* 276). The statement combines spirit, psyche, and matter in one tight bundle. Elsewhere, an Owl signals that spirits of those slain at Hunter's Drift have arrived in the spirit world (*Place* 14–15). On the physical plane, the nearby Hunter's Road joins people and places, providing an image of connectedness, just as the farm itself is a liminal place that brings together Europeans and Africans. In the African setting, coincidences frequently occur, and locations have psychoid resonance. In the spirit of the psychoid principle, naming campsites suggests that places retain an imprint of human experiences. Physical objects also have psychic resonance, which is why uLangalibalela needs something of Ouwa's in order to attempt a healing. On the cosmic scale, there are correspondences between celestial events and those on earth. François underscores this sense of unity when he tells Nonnie, "You know, Old Koba always used to say that there was nothing on earth that you cannot find in the sky; and nothing in the sky above that cannot be found below on earth" (*Wind* 325). There is also unity between animals and humans, as numerous examples attest. Animals are said to understand the Bushman language (Hintza certainly does), the birds change their tune in sympathy with human events like world war, the Conscience Bird (Isala) underscores human guilt, Old Chaliapin the lion roars at the moment François and Nonnie seem to become boyfriend and girlfriend, a Crow speaks through a retarded girl, and Old Back Lightning (another lion) works in tandem with the Bushmen and seems to shepherd the four travelers through the desert. The idea that all of life is a unity seems particularly true at sunset.

The bird known as the Honey Guide, however, is the novels' foremost illustration of the unity of nature, psyche, and spirit. It has "the most wonderful relationship ever evolved between bird and man," "a natural kinship," "a sense of common purpose and interdependence in all living and existing things." The bird even seems to be a living symbol of the *unus mundus*. First, it unites "four [physical] dimensions of reality" (plant, insect, bird, and human) and "carries fertilizing pollen from one growth to another, joining [with an implication of the psychological] the feminine in one growth to the masculine in another." Second, the bird's powers are even likened to the sacrament of transubstantiation in that it guides men to a physical food that transforms to infuse the spirit (*Place* 159–60).[15] Thus, by seeming to forge connections among the physical, the psychological, and the spiritual, the Honey Guide performs a function in the natural world that is akin to van der Post's role in bringing together continents, peoples, and ages of man in a single tale that enacts the journey to individuation through the recovery of the lost archaic.

Conclusion

Although *A Story like the Wind* and *A Far-Off Place* are not great art (they are the author's psychological fantasy rather than a visionary welling up of art from the collective unconscious), they illustrate how a tale may take shape around Jungian principles. A synergy of the anima and the *unus mundus* underscores connections among matter, psyche, and spirit in an African setting that is synonymous with the feminine. There, François and Nonnie undergo a version of the hero's three-part journey, which is both psychological and geographical, inner and outer. They must leave behind their European lifestyle, which has failed to protect them; embrace ancient African habits, including intuitive ways of knowing like tapping; and are finally reintegrated into Western civilization. In order to survive, the youngsters must tack toward the Bushman side; Nonnie especially must learn to think in a new way, and her new leather dress signifies that she has indeed "become a new person" (*Place* 231). But by the end of the second novel, they negotiate a balanced middle way between extremes of Western reason and native superstition. Rescued by agents of the British government, they will take with them some measure of their rich experience with the Bushmen when they study in a metropolitan setting but will then return to rural Africa and apply what they have learned in school. As this trajectory suggests, the proper orientation combines the best of Western rationality with complementary subjective faculties that are our archaic inheritance—a synthesis very much like what Jung achieved by recognizing and valuing his No. 2 personality. Jung identifies the difficulty of finding the right balance in the following statement: "Nature *must not* win the game, but she cannot lose. And whenever the conscious mind clings to hard and fast concepts and gets caught in its own rules and regulations—as is unavoidable and of the essence of civilized consciousness — nature pops up with her inescapable demands" (*CW* 13, par. 229). By avoiding the *enantiodromia* implicit in this statement and striking the right psychic balance, the two teenagers embody van der Post's solution to the malaise of modern civilization.

Notes

1 Van der Post believes that the natural and rational selves parted company at some point during the Renaissance, and he considers the Calvinist to be "the extreme form of this post-Renaissance" rationality (*Man* 11–12).

2 In *Man and the Shadow*, van der Post locates the origin of "colour prejudice" in the projection of the natural self and the shadow onto black Africans. He claims that the Nazis' similar "one-sidedness" resulted in the persecution of the Jews (13–14). A particular Jew, Jesus, is the greatest personification of the "despised and rejected self" (*Mantis* 134, 156).

3 Connections between *A Story like the Wind* and van der Post's life suggest that he is really writing about himself. His mother's name was Lammie, and he claimed to have had a Bushman nurse named Klara, the model for Koba. If so, then, like François, he may have learned some of the Bushman language as a boy, unless, as Jones believes, Klara was invented (82, 103). Van der Post did not go to a university; François vows never to do so and will go only after the close of *Place*. Both are Calvinists and could be considered "white bushmen" (see *A Walk with a White Bushman*). Van der Post served in World War II, as Ouwa and Mopani served in World War I. Like Ouwa the author was a proponent of education and an opponent of apartheid. Like Mopani he held the rank of colonel and later became a conservationist. Like Monckton he was knighted and served the British government (Monckton, regarding aid to Africa; van der Post, on the subject of African development). On a darker note, van der Post seduced a fourteen-year-old girl named Bonny Kohler-Baker whom he was chaperoning on board a ship bound for England. He later kept her as a mistress rather than properly delivering her to a London ballet school. She became pregnant and had a daughter, Cari, whom he never acknowledged as his own. As van der Post managed to keep the crime of statutory rape a secret until after his death, François develops a secret personality around his encounter with Xhabbo and Mantis's Cave. The names Nonnie and Luciana echo Bonny and Lucia, the name of van der Post's legitimate daughter by his first wife. (For the story of Bonny, see Jones 193ff.) He also concealed his mistress, Frances Baruch, from his second wife, Ingaret Giffard. In addition, van der Post borrowed various things from his experience of reading W. H. I. Bleek and L. C. Lloyd's *Specimens of Bushman Folklore*, which he calls "a sort of Stone Age Bible" (*Heart of the Hunter* xv). These include the names of Xhabbo and Nuin-Tara, the concept of tapping, and Mantis (van der Post makes Mantis the Bushman god, whereas Mantis appears to be mainly a trickster in Bleek and Lloyd; for Mantis see also *Heart*, ch. 12 and 14). Finally, *Wind* takes its title from Bleek's Xhabbo's statement that "a story is like the wind. It is wont to float along to another place" (qtd. in Jones 235). An adaptation of Xhabbo's statement serves as the epigraph to each novel.

4 Similar statements appear in *The Heart of the Hunter* (148, 152), *Jung and the Story of Our Time* (13), *The Lost World of the Kalahari* (269), and *A Mantis Carol* (23).

5 See Jung's *Visions: Notes of the Seminar Given in 1930–1934 by C. G. Jung* 1.470–71.

6 Van der Post as a young boy had significant dreams and "was nicknamed 'Joseph the Dreamer'" (*Jung* 9). Unlike Jung's mother, however, his grandfather warned him not to speak out about his ability. Van der Post is undoubtedly thinking of his younger self when he has François explain to Nonnie the name of a bird called "Little-Joseph-feather-in-cap": "'Little Joseph' because it has a coat of many colours, and besides the Bushmen say he is a great dreamer, as the Bible says Joseph was" (*Wind* 304).

7 After slightly misquoting Gerard Manley Hopkins's "No Worst, There Is None"—"O the mind, mind has mountains; cliffs of fall / Frightful, sheer, no-man-fathomed" (lines 9–10)—van der Post states, "Here you have from the artist an intimation that within man there is a great objective landscape, with mountains, valleys, chasms, rivers and jungles, and this is what makes parallels so real, and which makes poetic imagery apply, because we have this great world within which is related to the world without" (*Man* 6).

8 The opposition is a bit like van der Post's recollection that Jung spoke of a "country mind" and a "town mind" (*Walk* 37–38), corresponding, one supposes, to Africa and Europe. Psychic ability seems to be an aspect of the country mind. When asked if Bushmen "*have*

some psychic power unknown to us," van der Post replied, "No, I think we all have it in us, but they take intuition much more seriously than we do" (152).

9 A similar statement appears in *The Heart of the Hunter*. For example, "We have abolished superstition of the heart only to install a superstition of the intellect in its place" (137).

10 Jones's point that the two novels are "a classic quest tale" (306) is well taken because van der Post mentions Rider Haggard in both. "Dressed in this fashion ['khaki slacks, safari jacket and bush hat,' François] might have stepped straight out of the Africa of the great Rider Haggard" (*Wind* 249). Similarly, "the episode of the 'Singing Tree' . . . had puzzled the house [of Commons] to such an extent that the Leader of the Opposition had dismissed it as pure Rider Haggard" (*Place* 291). Of course, the white goddess may be directly borrowed from Haggard's *She*.

11 Wolff identifies the following feminine types: mother, Hataera (friend, companion), Amazon, and "medial woman" (5ff.). These resemble the stages of eroticism, which van der Post mentions: "Jung personified the evolution of the feminine in four self-evident ascending feminine models, of Eve, Helen, Maria, and Sophia" (*Jung* 241). Jung understood Maria to represent religious feeling and Eve to represent biological motherhood; however, since the four personifications are *stages*, this chapter considers Maria as mother and Eve as wife. Thus, a man relates first to his mother (Maria), then to a girlfriend/mistress/whore (Helen), then to a wife (Eve), and finally to wisdom (Sophia). Van der Post's claim that "the feminine soul in man is the go-between and guide to reconciliation of man and his shadow" (*Jung* 224) distorts Jung's sense that shadow work, which a male does with other males, precedes and enables progress with the anima. For the "apprentice-piece" (shadow) and the "master-piece" (anima), see *CW* 9i, par. 61.

12 Jacob and Esau are also mentioned in *Mantis* (99, 103, 126, and 155) and *Heart* (86). Michael Vannoy Adams (ch. 9) discusses van der Post's understanding of the differences between modern man and natural man but does not mention the Jacob-Esau opposition.

13 The point also appears in *Dark Eye*: "Not until we have travelled and known those great continents within as we have travelled and known them without, shall we be ready for our next great physical adventure which I truly believe will be to the stars" (217).

14 The quotation is from Browne's *Religio Medici* 474.

15 Van der Post's *The Heart of the Hunter* (dedicated to Jung) includes a chapter entitled "Ratel and Honey-Diviner," which like Caliban and Ariel represent earth and sky, respectively. The two creatures' partnership therefore suggests the "reconciliation of opposites" (67). *Heart* continues the story of the author's search for the lost Bushmen, begun in *The Lost World of the Kalahari*. Since van der Post describes the outer journey in *Lost World* and turns inward in *Heart*, the two travel books illustrate his principle that a journey is both geographical and psychological.

5

"WE ARE ALL SAILORS"

C. G. Jung's *Memories, Dreams, Reflections* and Doris Lessing's *Briefing for a Descent into Hell*

When James Hillman states, "We have no myths of the *nekyia* [descent into the underworld or the collective unconscious]. . . . Dante's underworld was our culture's last, and it was imagined even before the Renaissance had properly begun" (*Dream* 64), one may be forgiven for raising an eyebrow. Edward F. Edinger considers *Moby-Dick* an American *nekyia*, and what is *Heart of Darkness* if not a modern story of descent into the unconscious? One must also acknowledge *The Red Book* as a *nekyia*, for as R. F. C. Hull says of the time period it records, "Jung was a walking asylum in himself, as well as its head physician" and "went through everything an insane person goes through" (qtd. in van der Berk 74). A summary of his inner experiences appears in "Confrontation with the Unconscious," chapter 6 in *Memories, Dreams, Reflections*, and chapter 10 describes his near-death experience (NDE). Although there is no record of which Jungian texts Doris Lessing read, her novel *Briefing for a Descent into Hell* includes enough parallels to suggest that she had Jung's visions and NDE in mind when crafting the novel (the English translation of *MDR* was published in 1961, Lessing's novel in 1971). The purpose of this chapter, then, is to suggest that *Memories, Dreams, Reflections* provided Lessing with a successful *nekyia*, a hero's journey into the mind, by which to measure the experiences of the protagonist, Professor Charles Watkins. Ultimately, his encounter with the unconscious, though compensatory, is unlike Jung's *nekyia* in not effecting change in his conscious life; therefore, rather than achieving a lasting wholeness in which the unconscious informs waking life through imaginal ways of knowing, Watkins rejects the fruits of the unconscious by reaffirming rationality and the limits of conscious awareness.

Lessing and her novel have various parallels to authors and works considered in previous chapters. The vision includes a Haggard-like adventure story in which Watkins meets an exotic, dark-haired Yugoslavian Partisan named Konstantina Ribar; Watkins "remembers" a short happy life with her before she is killed protecting him from a female deer.[1] Like Olive Schreiner, one of Lessing's literary "elder sisters" (*Under My Skin* 202), the author grew up in Africa (Southern Rhodesia) and moved to London, carrying with her the manuscript of her first novel, *The Grass Is Singing*, much as Schreiner had brought *The Story of an African Farm* with her to London—each woman destined to become a feminist icon. There are other similarities: Laurens van der Post moved from Africa to London, neither he nor Lessing ever moved back or earned a university degree (Laurens finished high school; Doris dropped out of school at the age of fourteen), but both were self-educated professional writers. They were familiar with Jungian psychology (van der Post more deeply and publically, Lessing more critically), and he would certainly have resented her remark about his falling under the spell of papa Jung (Robb, par. 10, 29) because he considered himself Jung's peer and equal—an obvious inflation. Despite Lessing's qualified view of Jung's work, *Briefing* is remarkably Jungian, probably more than she realized, in its depiction of Watkins as being subject to the same problem that van der Post's Ouwa experiences, the debilitating effects of modern civilization's one-sided rationalism on the male psyche. Van der Post and Lessing also share an interest in the mind's transpersonal dimension, but she adds to his sense of overarching unity (the *unus mundus*) the importance of achieving harmony and love.[2]

Lessing and Jung

The previous criticism on *Briefing* has examined three main strands of influence: Sufism, R. D. Laing, and Jung. Lessing's debt to Sufism, which has been previously documented, need not concern us here.[3] Laing's *The Politics of Experience*, however, is more directly relevant. As Carole Klein points out, he and Lessing were both interested in the expansion of consciousness and in the possibility that madness can provide psychological healing (195, 204). Lessing denies the latter position in *Walking in the Shade*, saying that she never believed "that to go mad is to receive the ultimate in revelation" (276). She also denies that Laing's book influenced her at all. In a letter to Roberta Rubenstein, she writes: "I have not taken Laing as my starting point. I had not read the piece in question by him, or the book *The Politics of Experience*." She also claims that she found the name Watkins in the phone book (Rubenstein, *Vision* 196–97). Various critics consider Lessing's claims to be a mystification. For example, Marion Vlastos states that "it is hard to believe that Charles and the sculptor Jesse [Watkins], whose [schizophrenic] experience Laing records, have the same last name out of pure coincidence" (253).[4] Despite the enigma of Lessing's conscious intention, the two characters' visions both depict the broad outline of human evolution. Laing sums up Jesse's experience "as going further 'in,' as going back through one's personal life, in and back and through and beyond into the experience of all mankind, of the primal man, of Adam and perhaps even further into the beings of animals, vegetables and minerals" (87). It is exactly so with Charles. The two characters, however, return to normalcy in different ways. Whereas electric shock jolts Charles back to reality but deprives him of any memory of the unconscious realm, Jesse is able to describe his inner journey into Laing's tape recorder. For Jesse, then, the journey is a "natural *healing* process" of moving "from ego to self." "Can we not see," Laing adds, "that *this voyage is not what we need to be cured of, but that it is itself a natural way of healing our own appalling state of alienation called normality?*" (88, 93, and 116).

Since Jung is considered Lessing's psychological "mentor" (Rubenstein, *Vision* 9), various Jungian concepts are relevant to *Briefing*.[5] For example, Lorelei Cederstrom states that Watkins, who aligns with masculine *Logos*, has an archetypal vision of the Self that underscores the importance of feminine *eros* (13, 135, and 138). Strangely, Cederstrom does not specifically mention the anima in her chapter on the novel and seems unaware that the anima, which personifies the unconscious, is a psychopomp. All studies, however, concur that Watkins's unconscious compensates for his conscious life. A statement regarding compensation in Jung's chapter "Anima and Animus" is relevant here: "The repression of feminine traits and inclinations naturally causes these contrasexual demands to accumulate in the unconscious"; then "[t]he anima, being of feminine gender, is exclusively a figure that compensates the masculine consciousness"; as a result, "the man has, floating before him, in clear outlines, the alluring form of a Circe or a Calypso" (*CW* 7, par. 297, 328, and 338). The Homeric references are particularly apt because Lessing casts Watkins not only as a modern Everyman, as critics have observed, but also as a modern Odysseus who explores what the title page calls "Inner-space fiction . . . For there is never anywhere to go but in." Inner space is the realm of the anima.

Klein states that "Doris Lessing would briefly examine the ideas of Carl Jung" (110), but how much Jungian psychology did Lessing actually know? Her first exposure to Jung was probably in discussions that she and her second husband, Gottfried Lessing, had among friends. Someone in this group told her that Jung was one "of the main influences of our time," but she herself wondered if Freud and Jung were passing phenomena (*Under My Skin* 336). Her several years of twice- or thrice-weekly sessions with a Jungian therapist, Mrs. Toni Sussman, in London were a more significant influence. Sussman's approach was eclectic, but Lessing "didn't care about ideologies—Freud, Jung, and so forth"; "hated the labels"; and disliked Sussman's creedal interpretations because she, Doris, "had always been at home in these [psychological] realms" (*Walking in the Shade* 147, 39–40). Perhaps her most critical statement about Jung comes in a letter to Rubenstein:

> I think Jung's views are good as far as they go, but he took them from Eastern philosophers who go much further. Ibn El Arabi and El Ghazzali, in the [M]iddle [A]ges, had more developed ideas about the "unconscious," collective or otherwise, than Jung, among others. He was a limited man. But useful as far as he went. Both Jung and Freud were useful as far as they went.
>
> (qtd. in Rubenstein, *Vision* 230–31)[6]

The statement is not entirely fair-minded because Lessing agrees with Jung on numerous points and illustrates many Jungian concepts in her fiction. Most fundamentally, she embraces the idea that the mind is "above and beyond material conditions" (Howe 420). As Cederstrom notes, Lessing believes in the personal and collective aspects of the unconscious; in the archetypes, particularly shadow, anima/animus, and the Self;[7] in the confrontation with those archetypes as part of the individuation process; and in the idea that change within individual persons can spark societal change (4, 9–10, 12–13, and 135). Lessing understands too that the unconscious compensates so that what is repressed manifests in unexpected and unacceptable ways (Klein 244), much as Jung believes that "when an inner situation is not made conscious, it happens outside as fate" (*CW* 9ii, par. 126). In addition, Lessing shares Jung's essentialism, specifically stating that "men and women are biologically programmed to want different things" (*Walking* 371). Dreams were especially important to her, especially "'Jungian dreams'—wonderful, those layers of ancient common experience" (*Walking* 40). In fact, she frequently relied on dreams to solve problems in her writing. So when she states that "I liked Jung, as all artists do" (*Walking* 39), she may be thinking of Jung's acknowledgement that "[t]he modern artist, after all, seeks to create art out of the unconscious" (*MDR* 195). Lessing makes a similar statement in the preface to *Shikasta*: "Yes, I do believe that it is possible, and not only for novelists, to 'plug in' to an overmind, or Ur-mind, or unconscious, or what you will, and that this accounts for a great many improbabilities and 'coincidences'" (n.p.).

Although Lessing considered Jung "a limited man," she absorbed many Jungian principles and employed them in her work. Critics and probably even Lessing herself, however, have not noticed the full extent of *Briefing*'s use of Jungian concepts and imagery. There is, of course, commentary about mandala and quaternity images, but many examples of these images have gone unnoticed. More significantly, no one mentions active imagination, *abaissement du niveau mental* (a lowering of the mental level), Jung's work on *dementia praecox* (schizophrenia), the link between schizophrenia and "big dreams,"[8] psychic functioning (psi), the primitive/archaic, UFOs, quantum physics, or the *unus mundus*. All of this Jungian material informs *Briefing*, and Lessing even selects as her protagonist a character whose initials, C. W., are the usual abbreviation for *The Collected Works of C. G. Jung*, though this is more likely a synchronicity for readers than an intentional move on her part. The web of Jungian connections implies that *Briefing* is not strictly a visionary upwelling of the psyche's "hinterlands" like Henry Rider Haggard's *She* (*CW* 15, par. 137, 141–42) or a reflection of the author's personal unconscious but rather a book whose composition incorporates the *Zeitgeist*.[9] Watkins's *experience* is visionary, but Lessing assembled the novel from cultural fragments such as psychology, ufology, and evolution. The most significant omission from the scholarship, however, is the author's apparent borrowing of details from *Memories, Dreams, Reflections* regarding Jung's descent into madness and NDE.

Jung's *Memories, Dreams, Reflections*

In his autobiography Jung provides two examples of a successful *nekyia* or descent into the psychic underworld—his dreams and visions, which started less than a year before World War I, and a brush with death later in life. The many images common to *Memories, Dreams, Reflections* and *Briefing* suggest that Lessing used Jung's work the way she may have used Jesse Watkins's account in Laing's *Politics*. If so, the autobiography provided a model for a successful encounter with the unconscious.

The white bird. Following his break with Freud, Jung finds himself in "a state of disorientation" and in late 1912 dreams of a white bird (a dove or seagull) that transforms into an eight-year-old blonde girl and then back into a bird, whereupon it says to him, "Only in the first hours of the night can I transform myself into a human being, while the male dove is busy with the twelve dead" (172). The passage introduces various images/motifs that can be found in Lessing's novel: a white bird, the anima, the land of the dead (the unconscious), and the number twelve. Rubenstein's comment on the child is instructive, though she is unaware of the image's autobiographical significance and is not writing about *Briefing*: "According to Jung, the appearance of the child archetype in individual psychic development is an anticipation of the synthesis of conscious and unconscious elements within the personality, as well as a symbol of healing, of wholeness, of opposites mediated" (*Vision* 223). In that spirit of wholeness, Jung considers the symbolism of the number twelve ("the twelve apostles, the twelve months of the year, the signs of the zodiac, etc."), the key point being that it represents the wholeness of a completed cycle. In addition, his reference to Hermes Trismegistos, who "was said to have left behind him a table upon which the basic tenets of alchemical wisdom were engraved in Greek," may refer to the twelve alchemical stages (*MDR* 172). Notably, Hermes/Mercury is the god who delivers the briefing in Lessing's novel.

World War. After seeing corpses and a city, Jung mentions several of his late works, including *Flying Saucers: A Modern Myth of Things Seen in the Skies* (Lessing 172, 175; cf. Jung, *CW* 10). In 1913 he has a recurring precognitive vision of much of Europe engulfed by a sea of blood, a warning that world war was imminent. The city, the corpses, and UFOs have parallels in *Briefing* to the corpses of apes and rat-dogs that litter the city square, which Watkins tries to keep clear as a landing site for the crystal UFO that has taken up his friends from their sailing vessel. The battle between the apes and the rat-dogs appears to be his retrospective on World War II.[10]

The archetypes. Finally, in late 1913 Jung lets go—"Then I let myself drop" (179)—and experiences the unfiltered power of the archetypal realm. He writes, "I plunged down into dark depths," much as Watkins and Miles Bovey parachute into blackness over Yugoslavia in the former's false memory.[11] Jung sees a corpse, more blood, "a glowing red crystal," and "an unknown brown-skinned man, a savage" who represents "the primitive shadow" (179–81). He next encounters Elijah and Salome, "Logos and Eros" (181–82), the same duality that characterizes Watkins's academic work and his visions, respectively. Jung now knows "that there is something in me which can say things that I do not know and do not intend, things which may even be directed against me" (183), much like the unconscious forces that cause stuttering in Watkins and Larson. Jung notes that the anima/soul plays a key role in the psychic life of men; that by writing down his visions he is really writing letters to her; that she can be positive or destructive; and that she is "the mouthpiece of the unconscious" (187), allowing unconscious information to reach conscious awareness. In other words, the anima provides "a bridge to the unconscious" (*CW* 13, par. 62). Significantly, the police find Watkins near the Waterloo Bridge, a symbol not only of transition but also of the anima's role in transporting unconscious content to conscious awareness.

Staying sane. Jung frankly acknowledges that his visions constitute "the same psychic material which is the stuff of psychosis and is found in the insane," a "matrix of a mythopoeic imagination which has vanished from our rational age" (188), yet he remains sane by several means. Along with writing down his visions, he paints mandalas in his Black Book and later transfers them into what became *The Red Book*. His family and profession also help to ground him in the concrete world. Without these forces as a "counterpoise" (189) to his inner experiences, he would be psychologically at sea, which is where Watkins literally finds himself as the novel opens. Jung realizes, furthermore, that his visions carry an "ethical responsibility" not to revert to his earlier persona (193). Instead, he chooses to withdraw from his academic position in order to pursue further exploration of the unconscious. Watkins, of course, resumes his academic work.

At last, toward the end of World War I, the darkness begins to lift, and Jung's mandalas begin to reveal their meaning. They represent the wholeness and harmony of the Self, the path to individuation. Each one, he now realizes, is a cryptogram or microcosm of his psychic state on a given day. For example, a dream set in Liverpool includes both mandala and quaternity images, which resonate powerfully with *Briefing*. "The various quarters of the city were arranged radially around the square. In the center was a round pool, and in the middle of it a small island" (198). He is describing a mandala within a mandala within an image of quaternity within another image of quaternity. Similarly, in the center of the ancient city that Watkins discovers is a square with a circle within it, and within the circle, apparently, are signs of the zodiac (another twelve)—"geometrical patterns, that suggested flowers and gardens and their correspondence with the movements of the sky" (54). Here again are *Logos* (the square) and *eros* (the circle), now brought into balance with each other in a both/and way that is so eerily similar to images in *Memories, Dreams, Reflections* as to suggest that Lessing's debt to Jung is greater than anyone has previously realized.

Near-death experience. Jung, like Laing and Lessing, is aware that a traumatic incident of one type or another can trigger an inner journey. For Jesse, it is a dog bite; for Charles, a robbery; and for Jung, a broken foot and a heart attack. He nearly dies but instead of entering a tunnel of light, as in the classic NDE, he finds himself one thousand miles out in space, staring down at India and surrounding areas, much as Charles finds himself out in space, looking back at Earth. Jung is summoned back to his physical body by his physician, Dr. H., who dies shortly thereafter. Watkins's doctors' names (X., Y., and Z.) are also abbreviated, not to conceal identity as in Jung's case but to imply the insufficient rationality of the medical profession. The doctors are mathematical symbols of stark materialism masquerading as health-care providers.

The hero's journey. Jung's dreams/visions and his NDE constitute a successful *nekyia* because, in each case, he does not resume his former persona but weaves the visionary material into his conscious life—he returns able to integrate the bounty of the unconscious. A successful descent requires proper integration as in Jung's experiences, which are a psychological version of the departure, descent, and return, which Joseph Campbell considers the hero's journey.[12] Of course, the account of Jung's madness in *Memories, Dreams, Reflections* is a synthesis of the experiences that are recorded in *The Red Book*, whose comments on the descent into hell flesh out the anatomy of Jung's hero's journey. The beginning of his descent is marked by an either/or imbalance:

> the spirit of this time does not leave a man and forces him to see only the surface, to deny the spirit of the depths and to take himself for the spirit of the times. The spirit of this time is ungodly, the spirit of the depths is ungodly, balance is godly. Because I was caught up in the spirit of this time [was unbalanced in favor of ratiocination], precisely what happened to me on this night had to happen to me, namely that the spirit of the depths erupted with force, and swept away the spirit of the time with a powerful wave.
>
> (*Red* 238)

It is clear that Western scientific rationalism is at fault, for Jung states, "Keep it far from me, science that clever knower, that bad prison master who binds the soul and imprisons it in a lightless cell" (*Red* 238). In William Blake's terms, the goal is to transcend the "single vision" of Western scientific rationalism (Newton and Locke) and to embrace visionary ways of knowing.[13]

In the middle stage of the journey, Jung and Watkins encounter the unconscious mind's compensatory impulse toward psychic balance. First, they both experience an *abaissement du niveau mental*, a lowering of the mental level that restricts the conscious personality. The lowering occurs when "the individual parts of the personality make themselves independent and thus escape from the control of the conscious mind, as in the case of anaesthetic areas or [like Watkins] systematic amnesias" (*CW* 9i, par. 213–14). Significantly, the lowering "can be the result of physical and mental fatigue, bodily illness, violent emotions, and shock [like the robbery]." Watkins's sleep—with sleep being in Jung's words a "more or less complete oblivion of the ego"—is also considered an *abaissement* (*CW* 3, par. 523). Lessing seems to understand the value of sleep/dream in the self-healing process when she writes about her own breakdown: "I needed to sleep and dream myself whole. I was full of division" (*Under* 297). Although one's symptoms would lead a doctor to diagnose mental illness, Jung writes that "there is a divine [compensatory] madness [afoot] which is nothing other than the overpowering of the spirit of this time through the spirit of the depths" (*Red* 238). The acknowledgement of the shadow is a second key element of the descent: "He who does not want evil will have no chance to save his soul from Hell. So long as he remains in the light of the upper world, he will become a shadow of himself. But his soul will languish in the dungeons of the daimons. This will act as a counterbalance that will forever constrain him" (*Red* 289).

The result of confronting the shadow is a balanced psyche in which shadow lends its strength to consciousness and opposites become more complementary. That is, the goal of individuation is to achieve synthesis by collapsing the unconscious/ conscious binary. As Jung states, "Depths and surface should mix so that new life can develop" (*MDR* 239). With regard to this idea, some of Lessing's critics are on the right track. Cederstrom notes that "the goal of individuation is to harmonize the known self with its darker unknown face, to make peace between the conscious personality and the powers of the unconscious" (8–9). Whittaker emphasizes that Lessing's concern in *Briefing* is to depict "a holistic approach to living that takes account of both the external, everyday life, and the internal psychic life of a character" (83). Exactly right. Or as Sanford L. Drob states in his commentary on *The Red Book*, there must be a "dialectic" between visionary experience of the unconscious and conscious attention to reason (31).

For Jung, there has been a departure (a dropping into the unconscious), a confrontation with the unconscious in dream/vision, and a return that finds him changed in fundamental ways. Now he resigns his academic position, transforms his visions into psychological theory, allows ideas to well up within him, approaches his clients more from the Self than from the ego, paints mandalas, and works with stone. In other words, he successfully brings his experience of the deep psyche into physical manifestation and himself into a more holistic orientation with everyday life. He achieves, as a result, the "true" sanity that Laing describes, which "entails in one way or another the dissolution of the normal ego, that false self competently adjusted to our alienated social reality; the emergence of the 'inner' archetypal mediators of divine power, and through this death a rebirth, and the eventual reestablishment of *a new kind of ego-functioning*, the ego now being the servant of the divine, no longer its betrayer" (Laing 101; emphasis added). *Memories, Dreams, Reflections*, then, appears significant to Lessing not only as a source of images that appear in *Briefing* but also for the pattern of successful *nekyia* that Jung's experiences establish. His concern with accessing and confronting unconscious material has its counterpoint in Lessing's depiction in *Briefing* of Watkins's lack of individuation. The next section explores how Watkins fails to measure up to the wholeness Jung achieves.

The anima and Africa

Charles Watkins's problem. In a passage overlooked by critics, Watkins and Doctor Y. have the following exchange:

> DOCTOR Y.   I'd like you to try something else, Professor. I'd like you to sit down and let yourself relax and try writing down anything that comes to you.
>
> PATIENT.   What sort of thing?

DOCTOR Y.	Anything. Anything that might give us a lead in.
PATIENT.	Ariadne's thread.
DOCTOR Y.	Exactly so. But let's hope there is no Minotaur.
PATIENT.	But perhaps he would turn out to be an old friend too?

(200)

Their dialogue is easy allegory: Doctor Y. wants Watkins to use writing (active imagination) to draw memories up from the unconscious. Here the desired path leads *into* the depths, for that is where his forgotten memories now reside. The anima, as Ariadne, provides the thread, the necessary linkage, which like a telephone wire allows the unconscious to talk to the conscious mind. Doctor Y. is pleasantly apprehensive about what might come up because Watkins may encounter not just any monster but the Minotaur, a creature whose hybrid form suggests the tension between the human/civilized and the bestial/atavistic as well as the possibility that the unconscious may be a place of horrors rather than of healing. Whereas Doctor Y. shows his insensitivity to psyche by offhandedly minimizing the shadow/Minotaur's threat, Watkins wisely realizes that it can be "an old friend too," a source of wholeness and strength if it is properly integrated. However, having already realized a fellow-feeling with the shadowy rat-dogs and the atavistic apes,[14] he writes what could be a stand-alone short story about the parachute drop into Yugoslavia and his love of Konstantina. In other words, shadow work *seems* to provide a foundation for anima work—in Jung's terms, the "apprentice-piece" precedes the "master-piece" (*CW* 9i, par. 61).

Still, this brief exchange between doctor and patient conveys the sense that Watkins's most basic problem is lack of psychic integration or individuation. Other details reinforce the main character's lack of self-knowledge. As Watkins watches the Crystal depart with his eleven friends, he notes: "And inside were eleven men, my friends, whom I knew better than I knew myself. Since we do know our friends better than we know ourselves" (22). To know even good friends better than oneself, or to think so at any rate, suggests that Watkins, like King Lear, "hath ever but slenderly known himself" (*Lr.* 1.1.296–97). Even worse, Watkins identified in earlier life with his persona, mimicking Jeremy Thorne's dress, manner, and haircut, becoming, as the latter puts it, "a monstrous caricature of myself" and neglecting inner work (185). Jung accurately critiques the wrong path that Watkins has taken: "Every calling or profession, for example, has its own characteristic persona. . . . Only, the danger is that they become identical with their personas—the professor with his text-book, the tenor with his voice. Then the damage is done; henceforth he lives exclusively against the background of his own biography" (*CW* 9i, par. 221). The trouble, then, is that "[t]he man with the persona is blind to the existence of inner realities" (*CW* 7, par. 319). Even from a young age, Watkins has been incapable of expressing gratitude, as when years before Thorne gave him his place on a yachting trip. Now that Watkins is at the top of the classics profession, he is egocentric in the extreme as evinced by his infidelity to Felicity (he has absented himself from Felicity well before he cannot remember her), his apparent lack of regard for the students he teaches,[15] his insensitivity toward his mistress and their son, and his indifference toward Baines and Larson. Doing too much work and getting too little sleep cause him to begin stammering during his lectures, and perhaps Mary Ann Singleton is right that stammering is "a physical reaction to a deep, unconscious sense that what he teaches is meaningless" (148).[16] Although it is nearly a quarter of a century after the end of World War II, it is also possible that he still suffers from post-traumatic stress disorder, for as Bovey writes to Doctor Y., Charles's wartime experience involved "hard routine work, maximum physical discomfort, maximum boredom, and pretty steady doses of danger and death" (224).

Whatever causes may underlie his madness, the great man of words is reduced to incoherent blabbering in the Central Intake Hospital: "Last week. Last *when?* That was no weak, that was my wife." *Week, weak,* and *wife* are all four-letter words beginning with *w,* and perhaps he has been weak in matters involving his wife, but his mind seems to operate only on the order of homonymic and orthographic similarity. A bit more coherently, he also says, "The eye that would measure the pace of sand horses, as I watch the rolling gallop of sea horses would be an eye indeed. Aye Aye. I. I could catch a horse, perhaps and ride it, but for me a sea horse" (10). He is talking about waves, and the passage anticipates the later egocentrism of "I, I, I, I, I . . . struck lunatic, made moonmad" (103). As with the "wife" comment, there may also be a kind of sense below the lunacy of his utterance. Because he is psychically at sea, isolated from others and himself, his words mean the following: *I must now say aye (yes) to the contents of the sea (the unconscious) so that I can see (understand) myself more deeply.* Because his conscious resources have been exhausted, there is need for a *nekyia,* which Edinger calls an "innate, necessary psychic move-ment which must take place sooner or later when the conscious ego has exhausted the resources and energies of a given life attitude" (*Melville's* 27). Indeed, these passages indicate that he has already begun his descent.

Africa as a counterpoint. Briefing takes place in England in 1969, and Watkins's visions are set mainly in Brazil, yet Lessing uses Africa as a *leit-motif* to underscore several things—Watkins's bad verbal behavior, the unfulfilled human potential he shares with Larson, and disunity among humans in war—that oppose the briefing's central message (harmony/unity) and the imperative of individuation. Africa is a boundary of the Atlantic, and Watkins refers to the Guinea Current and the Diamond Coast. Bovey informs Doctor Y. that Watkins served in north Africa during World War II, and Africa is a staging ground in the Yugoslav operation. Africa comes up again in Thorne's letter to Doctor Y. along with, perhaps, Lessing's residual colonialism. Thorne writes that Watkins once spent an afternoon telling Thorne's wife that he (Watkins) might have married her (and Thorne, Felicity), if circumstances had been different "and that we all were much too personal about the whole thing." Incensed by the remark, Thorne harrumphs, "Yes, 'we are all much too personal about the whole thing.' He was talking about marriage after all. After all, we aren't Hottentots" (187). The report of Watkins's remarks strikes Thorne as boorish, for after all the two couples are not uncivilized primitives like those in Africa, and marriage *should* be something that is contemplated feelingly.

(Incidentally, the apes and references to the Brazilian savannah serve as reminders that, well before the Hottentots, *homo sapiens* evolved on the African savannah.)

Rosemary Baines's letter describes Frederick Larson's archeological work with a native African tribe in a way that upholds the briefing's message of natural unity. Putting family before work and not sleeping enough, Larson is Watkins's foil. A compensatory desire is to work in Africa again, but Larson turns down an offer to work at a site in the Sudan. He now experiences a version of Watkins's ailment—a heightening of perception like "a condition of extra wakefulness" (160), followed by stammering during his lectures on Homer, contrary inner voices, and doctor-prescribed sedatives. Baines sums up his situation in the phrase "male menopause and manic depression" (162). Apparently, his condition results from a lifestyle that violates what he witnessed over ten years before while visiting "a tribe whose life is based on the movements of a river. The river floods every year, and a large plain disappears under water" (163), much as Watkins's conscious awareness is flooded by the unconscious. Because these archaic people live in a state of unity and harmony with the earth and the cosmos, Larson considers them admirable. Baines writes:

> Yet, Frederick said, if you judge a society by harmony, responsibility towards its members, and lack of aggression towards neighbours, it was a society on a high level indeed . . . a society more integrated with nature than any he could remember, and for Africa that is saying a great deal . . . it was very highly ritualized around the seasons, the winds, the sun, the moon, the Earth.
>
> (164)

The suggestion is that the native people have achieved a high level of individuation because they maintain close ties to nature and each other, live in sync with the rhythms of earth and sky, and have done sufficient inner work to live in peace. Seasonal ritual suggests the holism of the natives' existence as a counterpoint to Watkins's persona-driven profession and empty life. Larson's "chief thought was that our society was [inferior because it was] dominated by things, artefacts [sic], possessions, machines, objects, and that we judged previous societies by artefacts—things" (164). As a result of choosing the lesser good over the greater, he has recently experienced a crisis of conscience—"Profound Doubts about what was going on in Archaeology, Doubts about its bases, premises, methods, and above all, its unconscious biases" (168)—exactly parallel to Watkins's denunciation, prior to the opening of the novel, of all previous scholarship in the classics field.

Through the Watkins-Larson parallel, Lessing indicts the academic profession for its lack of balance and for its loss of touch with what the native Africans represent. Europeans do not need to sell their homes and live off the land alongside a river, but they must achieve a balance of intellection and harmony with nature, lest they end up stammering in public because something essential has been allowed to languish in the unconscious and is straining to communicate with the conscious mind. As Jung writes, "Nature *must not* win the game, but she *cannot* lose" (*CW*, 13, par. 229). Like the shadow, our link to nature must be acknowledged, or our conscious lives will wither.

Analogies to legendary sailors

Along with mentioning Africa, Lessing includes another detail that provides a way to critique Watkins's progress: namely, frequent references to famous mariners from ancient stories to whom he does not measure up. These include Jonah, Jason, and Sinbad. Watkins's chant—"Sin bad. Sin bad. Bad sin" (15)—indicates that he has harmed his psyche and his family. But by far the most frequent and significant allusion is to Odysseus, which provides another link to Jung. As Sonu Shamdasani points out, *The Red Book* likens Jung's visionary experience to Odysseus's *nekyia* (100). In the novel, a late reference identifies Watkins with the Odysseus who fought the Trojans, casting Watkins's imagined time with the Yugoslav Partisans in Homeric terms: "Their heroism had the simplicity of other days, a clean straightforwardness, like the heroes outside Troy" (207). Many of the allusions, however, link Watkins with Odysseus's physical struggle to reach home. "[T]he Scyllas and the Charibs," the fact that his companions "tied [him] to a mast," and women who later sing on shore—all suggest forces that lurk within the unconscious as well as the half-measures a man may take in resisting the seductive anima (11, 18). The "one-eyed giant" and "men with one eye in the middle of their foreheads" signify the "single vision" of the doctors' scientific materialism and Watkins's own excessive ratiocination (20, 49). Still, he is no cyclops but rather thinks that his name might be Odysseus or "Crafty" (27–28), an appropriate epithet for a star classicist who cheats on his wife.

References to the anima figures Odysseus encounters further illuminate Watkins's tenuous situation. In the vision, Watkins builds a raft in order to leave the ship and later contemplates "build[ing himself] a raft from driftwood" (71), Odysseus's means of leaving Calypso on Ogygia. The vision also includes a reference to "poor Odysseus pining there in the arms of the enchantress [Calypso] and wishing only to go home" (108). She represents oblivion, the temptation to forget home by staying abroad in the arms of a goddess, as for Watkins the temptation is to embrace amnesia and the visionary unconscious, the fake memory of Konstantina, or life with Violet, never to return to his family. A parallel oblivion is the long, drug-induced sleep, which makes him a kind of lotus eater. In the briefing section, we read: "'Father,' says Jupiter's efficient and bossy daughter. 'Why don't you send down Mercury to do something about that poor voyager, stranded there on his drugged island?'" (111). At no point is Odysseus drugged, even by Circe on Aiaia; but Watkins is, his body becoming a kind of "drugged island" that strands him in the unconscious. Other Odyssean details in *Briefing* relate to Odysseus's encounters with anima figures on the human plane. The women in Homer's poem correspond to characters in the novel: Penelope/Felicity, the wife who waits; Circe/Constance, the temptation to infidelity; and Nausikaa/Violet, the opportunity to start life over with a younger woman.

Homer's tale unfolds with strong connections to the sea, which is Jung's "favourite symbol for the unconscious" (*CW* 9i, par. 298).[17] In the vision, Watkins thinks, "here I am, voyager, Odysseus bound for home at last, the seeker in home waters, spiteful Neptune outwitted and Jupiter's daughter my friend and guide" (104). Here is a similar comment: "Odysseus the brave wanderer was hated by some force to do with the sea, the ocean in its drugged condition, its moonmadness, always tagging along after the moon. It was the ocean Odysseus displeased, could not remain in harmony with, the ocean, our moon's creature and slave" (108–09). These statements suggest that Watkins is out of sync with the oceanic collective unconscious; and their light implication, that Neptune is to shadow as Athena is to anima, points to his problem of individuation: one must befriend, not outwit, the shadow. Contrary to the implication of the banter about Ariadne and the Minotaur, Watkins has lurched ahead in relationships with women without having first done proper shadow work with other men, which is ironic because fighting Nazis and bonding with comrades provided many opportunities to do the first stage of the individuation process. Perhaps these wartime experiences were negated because Watkins on two occasions lost all his companions to enemy fire, much as Odysseus on his way home to Ithaca loses all his crewmen.

The longest and most confusing references to *The Odyssey* appear in Watkins's initial love letter to Felicity, in which he declares his interest in her. Here is the statement with suggested glosses in brackets:

> I love you [Felicity]. Yes, that is it, I know—you would never keep me a pig in your pen [as Circe does to Odysseus's men]—no, I'm sure. She [Circe] had bright yellow hair and blue eyes too, she must have had—but it is the soul [like yours, Felicity] that counts. Not like that dark one [Helen], black hair and white teeth and red lips—those are the colours for pig-keepers. And in wartime [the Trojan war] too—The light and the dark of it. But the yellow-hair [Circe] locked *him* [Odysseus] in her pen and fed him husks [no, she did not; a strange gaffe for a classics professor unless it refers to the prodigal son in a foreign land, to whom the next phrase alludes]. Later a fatted calf? [Affirming Felicity/anima parallels the prodigal son's return to the father.] But I don't dare [risk my manhood]—Yes [that is the problem with me]. Would you [Felicity, treat a man like that?]—I've never dared [to speak thus to a woman, as I am now speaking to you], I've been alone for fear of that [enslavement to emotion or the feminine]. *She* died [his anima was repressed], and so could never lock me in her sty.
> (181)

In the love letter, Watkins, then a vulnerable young academic, rewrites the Circe story to reflect the ambivalence of his emotions: he is attracted to Felicity but simultaneously scared of the way in which strong emotion scrambles his academic brain. In addition, he blends it together with a biblical homecoming, hoping that Felicity will welcome him as the father embraces his wayward son yet still fearing that she will reduce him to a husk-eater in an emotional sty. He fears that opening himself to the feminine by way of a love relationship could usher in degradation, subservience, loss of identity, and even loss of humanity. Just as surely, he loses his I.D., his identity, and all the fruits of his nearly photographic memory in the robbery and later identifies in the vision with the subhuman apes and rat-dogs. Moreover, through mention of oblivion—forgetting home and the imperative to return there—the love letter makes *The Odyssey* analogous to the situation described in the briefing. Specifically, the fear is that those who will descend into hell (be born on Earth) will forget their "brainprints" (125) and the message of unity and harmony that they are being sent to deliver, becoming so wrapped up in earthly vicissitudes that they neglect their purpose.[18] Watkins's letter expresses a similar fear of forgetting himself, which makes falling in love (confronting woman and the anima) a parallel descent into hell.

The important thing is to remember, as Watkins apparently does early in the novel, that "[w]e are all sailors" (13). Like Odysseus and the other mariners, every living person is a voyager from a transcendent realm. Human life involves departure from that realm, a sojourn on Earth, and a return. As Katherine Fishburn notes, "Charles is voicing the universal patterns of mythic voyages" (26). Not only are all of us sailors in that respect (heroes on a journey), some more successfully than others, for "[n]ot everyone has known these depths" of the oceanic unconscious (34). But all sailors are also in each of us—we are they, and they are we—because of the fundamental "Unity of Life" that Mercury describes (120). We are evidently all *soldiers* as well, for Watkins's "memory" of Yugoslavia draws on another man's experiences.[19] The message of universal unity may be overwhelming, but one must simply take the journey a step at a time and remember the destination. For Odysseus the important task is to return to family, to kin, which is why Watkins's nurse is named Alice Kincaid—Alice, because his journey is down a rabbit hole; Kincaid, because *kin* can *aid* someone in his unsound state of mind. Ultimately, he does return to Felicity and their two sons, but forgetting his visions makes him unlike Odysseus, who brings home with him the psychological benefits of his wanderings. Watkins, therefore, could be considered an illustration of T. S. Eliot's sense in "*Ulysses*, Order, and Myth" that the "mythical method" juxtaposes a classical hero and a modern character in order to underscore the latter's shortcomings (178).

Two further matters probably lie beyond Lessing's understanding of *The Odyssey*. First, as Joseph Russo points out in "A Jungian Analysis of Homer's Odysseus," Hermes/Mercury (who provides the briefing in the novel) is the father of Autolykos, who is the father of Laertes, who is the father of Odysseus (247). It makes sense that the trickster god would be the great grandfather of the crafty Odysseus, and the fact that he not only receives moly from Hermes but also is the god's blood relative strengthens the novel's Watkins-Odysseus-Hermes nexus. Second, in *The Collected Works* Jung significantly misreads Odysseus's *nekyia* in book 11 of *The Odyssey*, referring to "the Descent into the Cave, the Nekyia" and adding in a footnote, "Cf. the passage in Odysseus' journey to Hades, where he meets his mother" (*CW* 5, par. 634, n. 26). Although Odysseus visits his dead mother and other shades, he does *not* descend into Hades. His descent is figurative.[20] He simply journeys to a meadow of asphodel, sacrifices two sheep, and waits for their blood to draw the dead up out of Hades in reverse chronological order of their deaths. The detail recalls *Briefing*'s anti-clockwise currents in the southern hemisphere: he looks further into the past as the visitation continues. Despite all the Odyssean parallels that Lessing builds into the novel, Odysseus's and Watkins's experiences of *nekyia* diverge significantly. Alfred Tennyson sums up the proper incorporation of the past when his Ulysses states, "I am a part of all that I have met" (line 18). Homer's Odysseus can say the same; Lessing's Watkins cannot.

Wholeness, unity, and the quantum

Lessing reinforces Mercury's message of unity/harmony in a variety of ways, some of which have gone unnoticed in the previous criticism. All underscore the wholeness that Watkins fails to achieve. To begin with, the number twelve—a probable echo of *Memories, Dreams, Reflections*—appears with surprising frequency. Including Watkins, there are twelve people on the ship (19); the raft he makes of balsa wood is twelve by twelve (24); the white bird's wingspan "was ten or twelve feet" (80); when he gets taken up in the Crystal, twelve days have passed in the real world (87); Watkins wonders, "what of Jupiter [the planet] with his—is it now twelve?—subsidiaries [moons]?" (108); and in Yugoslavia, "the band [of Partisans] remained in numbers between twelve and thirty" (209). These half dozen references to the number twelve parallel and reinforce Mercury's message of unity and harmony, primarily because of their association with the months of the year and its division into seasons. For Jung, "The seasons refer to the quartering of the circle which corresponds to the cycle of a year" (*CW* 12, par. 283). The statement includes his two favorite images of wholeness, the quaternity and the mandala.

These images are subtly built into the beginning of Watkins's vision. His drifting in the Atlantic is framed by a geographical quaternity: the Caribbean and Florida (northwest), Europe (northeast), Africa (southeast), and Brazil (southwest). Moreover, each hemisphere is itself a mandala or clock image. At first he drifts clockwise in the northern hemisphere (*Logos*, time's forward march), then anti-clockwise in the southern (*eros*, a journey backward in time).[21] One may recall Jung's notation in *Psychology and Alchemy* (*CW* 12, par. 309) of the world clock as a mandala. There are many other round or spherical objects in *Briefing*: a compass (10), flowers in one of the poems (19), the crystal disk,[22] "this little bubble of Earth" (48), the sun and moon, the solar system (55), Earth's biosphere seen from space (97, 99), an alarm clock (129), Baines's mention that her "letter is like a snake swallowing its tail" (146), various references to webs, and the parachutes that lower Watkins and Bovey into Yugoslavia (202). Among these, flying saucer, snake, globe, and clock are mandala symbols in Jung's works. In particular, he identifies flying saucers as "manifestations of totality whose simple round form portrays the archetype of the self" as opposed to the ego (*CW* 10, par 622; 12, par. 126). Mandalas are thus symbols of transformation (such as the one Watkins undergoes when the Crystal finally takes him), for "Mandalas are birth-places, vessels of birth in the most literal sense" (*CW* 9i, par. 234).

The mandala image that has received the most attention is the one Watkins discovers in the ruined city: "The square was perhaps seventy or a hundred yards across, and in it was an inner circle, about fifty yards across. . . . I had to prepare this circle lying in its square, by clearing away all the loose dirt and pulling out the grass" (53). A square (quaternity image) contains a circle (mandala), which in turn contains zodiacal markings (another mandala). Writing about Lessing's *The Four-Gated City*, Rubenstein suggests that the square represents consciousness since, for Jung, "fourness" signifies "rational wholeness and completion," while the circle corresponds to the unconscious mind (*Vision* 107). In the same way, "the Sun, man's father and creator" (*Briefing* 56) represents the masculine, while the moon, in addition to signifying lunacy (being "moonstruck" or, for Rubenstein, embracing the irrational [*Vision* 182]), represents the feminine.

Strangely, no one has noticed the most obvious image of mandala-in-quaternity—the doctors' names. Doctors X. and Y. suggest the X and Y axes and thus a two-dimensional (limited) approach to treating mental disorder and a general indictment of scientific materialism. Since the axes form four quadrants that constitute a quaternity image, the doctors' names also suggest the wholeness that they seek to bring about in Watkins and the holism in medicine that they currently lack. There is also a Doctor Z., whose only letter to Doctor Y. appears roughly two-thirds of the way through the novel (171). It is Z. who initially prescribed Librium (liberation from the unconscious) for Watkins's stammering. If a Z axis is added to X and Y, one has the three axes of a sphere, another image of wholeness.

Watkins's journey from the ocean to dry land and from there via the Crystal to the briefing enables him to experience the evolution of life on Earth, that is, the fundamental unity of all species. The novel presents more, however, than "an allegory of the evolution of the human condition" (Whittaker 79). Watkins's vision is a tour of the historical dimension of the collective unconscious. Rubenstein accurately states that he experiences "through the exploration of the microcosm of his own consciousness the experience of the human race" or a journey "through the collective unconscious" (*Vision* 178, 184). As he says early on, "I've learned to breathe water" and identifies with fish and microscopic life in the sea (32). The porpoise, for Douglas Bolling, signals the transition of life from ocean to land because it lives in the sea but breathes air (559). The Brazilian forest resembles Eden, being a "paradise for birds and for monkeys" where there is a comfortable fellow-feeling between Watkins and a large cat (*Briefing* 40). He experiences the Fall (joining the meat-eating women in their bloody ritual) and witnesses humanity's bestial origins in the apes and rat-dogs whose conflict suggests "the insanity of modern warfare" (Bolling 559). In short, Watkins experiences the ideal of natural unity along with the fall away from it through violence and pollution.

Many of Lessing's poems in the novel comment on the stages of evolution, but one in particular seems to sum up the position of modern humans. As Watkins rides on the back of the white bird within sight of the Portuguese coast, his poem refers to our liminal position: "Not ape, nor God, to swing from tree to tree, / Or bid the sea be still from fear of me, / Divided, dwarfed, a botched thing in between" (81). That these lines are perfect blank verse, like most of the other poetry in the novel, may suggest Watkins's effort to impose order on the chaos of the unconscious and return to sanity. More importantly, the lines suggest that we are neither "ape, nor God" but "a botched thing in between," much as Hamlet considers man "like an angel" yet still "the paragon of animals" (*Ham.* 2.2.307–08). As Watkins will discover, we have not only an animal body that grounds us in nature but also a spiritual body that has access to a realm of archetypes or Forms. Similarly, the unity that the briefing depicts is not only for humans; it applies equally to matter, psyche, and spirit—Jung's *unus mundus*.

Thus, evolution is an image of wholeness and connectedness in the novel, and Lessing underscores the unity among human beings in numerous passages. After Watkins has been taken up into the Crystal, the ideal that all persons participate in the One Mind is stated:

> In that dimension minds lay side by side, fishes in a school, cells in honeycomb, flames in fire, and together we made a whole in such a way that it was not possible to say, Here Charles begins, here John or Miles or Felicity or Constance ends. And so with us all . . . comprehension, only possible at all because of my fusion with the people who were friends, companions, lovers and associates, a wholeness.
>
> (91)

> It was the mind of humanity that I saw, but this was not at all to be separated from the animal mind which married and fused with it everywhere . . . all sympathetic knowledge must be . . . like a web whose strand is linked and vibrates with every other.
>
> (92)

> On every level: even myself and my friends whom the Crystal had absorbed into a whole . . . in the great singing dance, everything linked and moved together. My mind was the facet of a mind, like cells in a honeycomb . . . together we [Watkins and his friends] were a whole, connecting in this wholeness with the myriad differing wholes that each of these people had formed in their lives.
>
> (96)[23]

We are connected to each other and to nature, and Unity extends all the way down to the microscopic realm: "these microbes are a whole, they form a unity, they have a single mind, a single being, and never can they say I, I, without making the celestial waters roll with laughter or weep with pity" (103). But when people forget natural unity, they revert to egocentrism: "I (who am not I, but part of a whole composed of other human beings as they are of me) [am] hovering as if between the wings of a great white bird . . . [and when people forget] their true understanding [that all life is a unity] . . . most have said I, I, I, I, I, I, I and cannot, save for a few, say We . . . the sweet sanity of We" (103).[24] The truth, however, is that everyone is linked because everyone is God (136).

[DOCTOR Y.]	So you are God, too, are you?
[WATKINS]	You as well.
[DOCTOR Y.]	I don't aim so high, I assure you.
[WATKINS]	Stupid. You don't have a choice.

(136)

Given this universal participation in the divine, all events and all peoples make up a unity. Watkins notes, therefore, that "all events are equally important, whether war, a game, the weather, the craft of plant-growing, a fashion show, a police hunt" (157). Likewise, the Partisans in Yugoslavia enact a kind of unity, though being at war qualifies the point: "This group of young soldiers contained Serbs, Croats, Montenegrins, Catholics and Moslems. Nowhere but in these mountains, among these soldiers, these comrades, could it be possible for two people to meet, take each other's hands, call each other by name . . . take the Red Star as their bond, and forget the rest" (208). Unlike the Yugoslav fantasy, the college memory of the commingling honeysuckle and camellia becomes a point of debate with himself as he writes—whether the honeysuckle spray swings to reach the camellia or whether the wind blows it in that direction. He concludes this second exercise in active imagination by delivering the message of the briefing to Doctor Y.: "The surfer and the wave. The plant swinging in the wind. And it's just the same with—well, everything, and that's what I have to say, Doctor. Why can't you see that?" (243).[25] Even though electroshock therapy blocks or erases his memory of the vision, the message has gotten through and may do some good.

Images of upward progress throughout the novel also augment the sense of potential that Watkins fails to achieve when his memory of the unconscious is lost. The porpoise helps him make a transition from sea to land; he climbs upward out of the forest of the ancestral unconscious (Singleton calls this "a metaphor for man's ascent to consciousness" [150]); the white bird elevates him into the air;[26] and the Crystal lifts him into itself via a vortex so that, in a rarefied version of himself, he sees the Earth from outer space (as did Jung during his NDE) and experiences the archetypes or Forms of earthly things. First, the Crystal lifts Watkins into the astral dimension. Inside the Crystal

time had shifted gear and vibrated differently. . . . The dragging pain of gravity had gone: this dimension was as free and delicious as skating or flight lying between the wings of a guardian bird. Yet I had a body. But it was a different substance, lighter, finer, tenuous, though I recognized its likeness to my usual shape of matter . . . my new body . . . the new dimension, or level, of vibration . . . my own body was now a shape in light.

(88)

In the background is Saint Paul's distinction between the physical body and the spiritual body in 1 Cor. 15.45; part of the verse appears in the illustration to Blake's "To Tirzah," which Lessing probably knew: "It is raised a spiritual body," which is what seems to have happened to Watkins. Now he sees the city's inner blueprint or pattern and the Forms of things on the physical plane, realizing that "there were no such things as judges, but only Judge, not soldiers, but Soldier, not artists, but Artist . . . and not clerks but Clerk, and Gardener, and Teacher" (95–96). This material obviously refers to Platonic Forms, which Jung equates with the archetypes, stating that "'Archetype' is an explanatory paraphrase of the Platonic εἶδος" (*CW* 9i, par. 5) and describing archetypes in a way that resonates with Lessing's "brainprints"—"An archetype means a *typos* [imprint]" (*CW* 18, par. 80; Jung's insertion). His statement that archetypes are form without content also resonates with the crystal nature of the UFO. An archetype's form, he says,

> might perhaps be compared to the axial system of a crystal, which, as it were, preforms the crystalline structure in the mother liquid, although it has no material existence of its own. . . . The archetype in itself is empty and purely formal, nothing but a *facultas praeformandi*, a possibility of representation which is given *a priori*. . . . With regard to the definiteness of the form, our comparison with the crystal is illuminating inasmuch as the axial system determines only the stereometric structure but not the concrete form of the individual crystal. This may be either large or small, and it may vary endlessly by reason of the different size of its planes or by the growing together of two crystals.
>
> (*CW* 9i, par. 155)

Lessing probably did not know the passage, but it still lends credence to the view that the Crystal transports Watkins into an ethereal realm where things exist only as Form whose potential becomes content in the material world, much as an archetype becomes a literary image.

By including in Watkins's vision not only three locales within the physical world (sea, land, and air) but also in *Briefing* three realms of experience (the physical world, the collective unconscious, and the astral plane of Platonic Forms or Jungian archetypes—the entire *unus mundus*),[27] Lessing suggests that the proper orientation to human life is a both/and openness to multiple dimensions of experience, which is Jung's basic message in *Memories, Dreams, Reflections*. If all things are a unity, which is the view of the new science, then it follows that there would be traces of quantum physics in the novel as when Watkins, in a paragraph about the moon, muses, "So each one of us, walking or sitting or sleeping, is at least two scales of time wrapped together like the yolk and white of an egg" (57). Here are the temporal and the timeless: the soul transcends physical matter, but for a time the two are held together, like the yolk and the egg white, much as archetypes have concrete reflections. These dyads resemble physicist David Bohm's distinction between the implicate and explicate orders (the enfolded order and the unfolded order, what is invisible within and what is visible without). That Lessing is talking about unity is even clearer when she writes that "the enclosing web of light (inner or outer as one chose to view it), was not at all a question of individual entities, as those entities saw themselves, but a question of Wholes. . . . All over the globe ran these pulses or lines, linking groups of individuals" (94).

Lessing also includes two further ideas that the new science has embraced. The first is that matter is conscious, as when Watkins says, "I looked at this crumb of matter [the moon] and knew it had thoughts, if that is the word for it, thoughts, feelings, a knowledge of its existence, just as I had, a man lying on a rock in the dark" (57–58). If human beings are made out of the same matter as celestial bodies, and if we are conscious, should they not be as well? The second, the concept of fractals (each piece contains a pattern of the whole in which it participates), is relevant to the epigraphs by Mahmoud Shabistari and Rachel Carson. The Shabistari poem directly locates the large within the small—"a hundred seas" in a raindrop, a thousand harvests in a single grain. The poem also states: "The world within a grain of millet's heart. The universe in the mosquito's wing." Whittaker (78) rightly associates the lines with Blake's "Auguries of Innocence," which begins,

> To see a World in a Grain of Sand
> And a Heaven in a Wild Flower
> Hold Infinity in the palm of your hand
> And Eternity in an hour.
>
> (lines 1–4)

In such tiny spaces, says Shabistari, "two worlds commingled may be seen." Such statements actually frame the novel because the Afterword quotes Blake's first Memorable Fancy in *The Marriage of Heaven and Hell*: "How do you know but every Bird that cuts the airy way, / Is an immense world of delight, closed by your senses five?" (250).

The novel's second epigraph, from Carson's *The Edge of the Sea*, deals with the "miniscule world of the sand grains" in a way that anticipates the microscopic world that Watkins encounters in the ocean. Coming right after Shabistari's poem, the Carson passage implies that even a microscopic organism contains the whole universe of which it is a part. Later in the novel the image of "grains of sand" continues the echo of "Auguries" and connects with the concept of fractals, each grain resonating or oscillating with the whole:

> Within patches that seemed stationary, motionless, minute particles moved, but in set patterns, so that looking down at one fragment of this crust of matter, smaller than the tiniest of grains of sand or dust of pollen, it seemed

that even the curve made by a journey of a group of such items from one continent to another was a flicker of an oscillation in a great web of patterning oscillations and quiverings.

(93)

Watkins addresses the kind of seeing that Blake has in mind during his final conversation with Violet Stoke the night before his electroshock therapy. His basic point is another possibility supported by quantum physics, that psi is real because the unconscious talks to us:

> "There are lots of things in our ordinary life that are—shadows. Like coincidences [synchronicities], or dreaming, the kinds of thing that are an angle to ordinary life. . . . The important thing is this—to remember that some things reach out to us from that level of living, to here. Anxiety is one. The sense of urgency. Oh, they make an illness of it, they charm it away with their magic drugs. But it isn't for nothing. It isn't unconnected. *They* say, 'an anxiety state', as they say, paranoia, but all these things, they have a meaning, they are reflections from that other part of ourselves, and that part of ourselves knows things we don't know."

(245–46)

He is referring to the same enhanced perception that Baines writes about in her letter (she calls it a feeling of being on a higher wavelength [153]). Therefore, Watkins feels the imperative to tell others who are asleep about communication from within: "I have to tell people. . . . They are not awake" (247). Lessing herself is likely speaking here, for as Klein points out, the author believes "that actions were guided by forces more powerful than consciousness" and "lamented that Western civilization rejects these kinds of psychic and extrasensory faculties" (105, 44). As Lessing expresses in an interview, "other cultures have accepted the unconscious as a helpful force, and I think we should learn to see it that way too" (Raskin 68).[28] Although Watkins's memory of the briefing is limited, he remembers at least the possibility that human beings are more than conscious awareness, and he wants to be a Mercury-like messenger to those who slumber. Sadly, electric shock therapy takes even that glimmer of memory from his conscious awareness, a loss that turns his hero's journey tragic by obviating the positive return. The content of the vision, with its suggestions of the potential for wholeness and its reminders of the fundamental unity of all things, is lost to conscious awareness. As Lessing comments in *Walking in the Shade*, "Professor Watkins in *A Briefing for a Descent into Hell*, who loses his memory for a while, has the opportunity to know himself better, but refuses it" (268).

Conclusion

Following the electric shock therapy, Watkins informs his department chair that he will be able to deliver a series of lectures on *The Iliad*. Lecturing on *The Odyssey* would suggest that, like Odysseus in Ithaca, he remembers his *nekyia*. His subject, the everyday world of grinding toil and conflict, is appropriate because the Odyssean numinous is no longer available to him. In other words, Watkins does not live up to the standard of successful individuation that *Memories, Dreams, Reflections* sets out—a conscious life informed by memory of visionary experience. Returning to the status quo, he lacks the enlargement of personality that comes from within (*CW* 9i, par. 215) and does not achieve the "sacrifice of . . . egoistic aspirations and desires," a central theme of *The Red Book* (Drob 36). He is simply back where he began and is welcomed into the routine rationality of his former life, which caused his breakdown in the first place. All of the novel's hints with regard to a hero's journey of the mind and all its reminders of unity and harmony ultimately come to naught.

Briefing and Lessing's novella "The Temptation of Jack Orkney" are frequently considered companion pieces, but the endings differ significantly. Following the death of his father, Orkney begins having numinous dreams. Taking sleeping pills corresponds to Watkins's electric shock therapy, but Orkney's *nekyia* produces an alternation of personality in the third part of the hero's journey. His dream memory is not wiped clean. Instead, as the story concludes, the narrator states:

> Now, in spite of everything, although he knew that fear would lie in wait there, his sleep had become another country, lying just behind his daytime one. Into that country he went nightly, with an alert, even if ironical interest—the irony was due to his habits of obedience to his past—for a gift had been made to him. Behind the face of the sceptical [sic] world was another, which no conscious decision of his could stop him exploring.
>
> (308)

Just as Jung honors his visions and dreams by adjusting his everyday life, Orkney decides that he and his wife will move to Nigeria so that he can take a job that has been offered to him. "Spending two years in Africa would change them both, and they did not want to admit that they had become reluctant to change," says the narrator (307). Whereas Watkins simply returns to his former life, the Orkneys' temporary sacrifice of their comfortable life in England will lead to personal growth, perhaps through exposure to the positive connection to nature in Larson's experience of the river people in Africa. For the Orkneys, a change that Jung would approve of is on the horizon.

Notes

1 Lessing may have been aware that in June 1968 Ivan Ribar died. A Yugoslav politician, Ribar lost his wife and two sons during World War II. Both sons fought in the war ("Ivan Ribar").

2 In the novel, love figures importantly in various ways. One way not mentioned in the previous criticism is the allusion to the lyric "Western Wind." Watkins's interior monologue includes "blow blow blow my love to me" and "blow my love to me" (12, 30). An

anonymous Middle English poet writes, "Westron wind, when will thou blow?" The speaker longs for spring and wishes that his love were in his arms and that he were in his bed again. Ernest Hemingway, as Lessing surely knew, alludes more fully to the same poem in *A Farewell to Arms* (197; ch. 28).

3 Nancy Shields Hardin emphasizes that for Lessing the physical world and the imaginal world are in a complementary (both/and) rather than a binary (either/or) relationship (571). Phyllis Sternberg Perrakis discusses connections between the Jungian and Sufist background of Lessing's work.

4 The following critics are of the same opinion: Joan Didion (193), Carole Klein (205), Roberta Rubenstein (*Vision* 88–89), Paul Schlueter (123), Michael Thorpe (31–32), and Virginia Tiger (88). Both Laing and Jung define "schizophrenia" etymologically. Laing states that it is a compound of "Schiz" (broken) and "Phrenos" (soul or heart) (90). Jung, following Bleuler, calls schizophrenia a "split mind" (*CW* 3, par. 497). To be schizophrenic means to be broken or divided in heart, mind, and soul.

5 The only monograph dealing exclusively with Lessing and Jung is Lorelei Cederstrom's *Fine-Tuning the Feminine Psyche*. Jungian commentary can also be found in Douglas Bolling; Perrakis; Roberta Rubenstein, *The Novelistic Vision*; Mary Ann Singleton; and Ruth Whittaker.

6 The inserted capital letters are Rubenstein's addition. A similar statement appears in Lessing's introduction to Idries Shah's *Learning How To Learn*: "But the 'discoveries' of Freud and Jung are to be found in Al Ghazzali and Ibu El Arabi, who died in the twelfth century, and in other great thinkers of the time. (Jung acknowledged his debt to the East. Is it not remarkable that his disciples are not curious about what else there might be?)" (n.p.).

7 Cederstrom erroneously considers the persona to be an archetype (10). Jung writes, "The persona is . . . a functional *complex* that comes into existence for reasons of adaptation or personal convenience" (*CW* 6, par. 801; emphasis added).

8 See *CW* 3, par. 528: "the schizophrenic state of mind, so far as it yields archaic material, has all the characteristics of a 'big dream'—in other words, that it is an important event, exhibiting the same 'numinous' quality which in primitive cultures is attributed to a magic ritual." In par. 549 Jung adds that big dreams are archetypal in the sense that their images are like those in mythology.

9 I am in accord here with Rubenstein's "Notes for Proteus: Doris Lessing Reads the *Zeitgeist*." Rubenstein argues that *Briefing* and several other novels by Lessing are "instructive fables about life on this earth during our own era of relentless aggression and destruction" (14).

10 Witnessing the carnage, Watkins reaches what *Heart of Darkness* calls "the very bottom of there" (Conrad 33), experiencing a *nigredo* or moment of despair: "Now I believed that everything was ended, and there was no hope anywhere for man or for the animals of the Earth" (85). *Nigredo* literally means blackness, which may have some connection to Nurse Black at the end of the novel. In addition, Nurse Black's name suggests black-and-white, either/or thinking rather than the inclusive both/and that Lessing favors. For example, it is Nurse Black who attempts to shut down Watkins's important conversation with Violet Stoke about alternative ways of knowing.

11 The Yugoslavian episode, which includes falling in love with Konstantina, is apparently an imaginal embellishment of Bovey's wartime experience.

12 Hillman's description of Jungian psychology as "thoroughly oppositional" (*Dream* 75) is somewhat reductive, for although oppositions such as anima/animus and conscious/ unconscious are accurate descriptors, the goal of individuation is a both/and synthesis of the unconscious and conscious awareness.

13 I discuss Blake's four types of vision in *The One Mind* (195–204). In brief, single vision involves scientific perception; twofold vision, intellectual/moral reflection; threefold vision, Jung's visionary mode; and fourfold vision, access to the spirit world via psychic functioning. The four types of vision appear in Blake's letter to Thomas Butts dated November 22, 1802 (Keynes 79).

14 The apes and rat-dogs are one of Lessing's echoes of Jonathan Swift's *Gulliver's Travels*. Thorpe states that the rat-dogs are "Yahoo-like creatures" (31), and Vlastos calls the setting they inhabit "a Swiftian land" (255). Comments about these creatures are actually descriptions of England and of world war, much as what Gulliver encounters reflects the England that he has left.

15 In the Yugoslav fantasy, Watkins writes: "I believe that a man who fought with those young people [the Partisans] who now has to stand up on a platform in a big hall to lecture, or teach, must often, a quarter of a century later, look down on the upturned faces of students who are rioting and sullen and critical and undisciplined and who in every country of the world reject what their society offers them . . . this man, a professor perhaps, with responsibility, a place in society, looks at those faces and thinks how young people exactly like them, 'children' to their elders, fought the most vicious and terrifying army in history, Hitler's, fought short of weapons, short of warm clothes, often without food, always outnumbered—fought and won, and created a new nation" (208; ellipsis in the original).

16 Lessing's awareness of the role of sleep deprivation in madness is clear when she writes, "I deliberately drove myself crazy by not eating and not sleeping out of curiosity" (*Walking* 267). Jung states, "*Disturbances of sleep* are quite usual in dementia praecox [sic] and manifest themselves in a variety of ways" (*CW* 3, par. 181). His basic point is that the unconscious breaks through into consciousness. Lessing exaggerates this effect by having Watkins's consciousness switch completely off.

17 In *Briefing*, the Atlantic represents the unconscious, but so do the forests in Brazil and Yugoslavia, the forest being Lessing's image for the unconscious in *Walking in the Shade* (40).

18 In the background is William Wordsworth's "Ode: Intimations of Immortality," lines 67–68: "Shades of the prison-house begin to close / Upon the growing Boy." Rosemary Baines's letter specifically refers to "those 'prison shades'" (152). The Wordsworthian connection has been previously noted by Whittaker (81) and Schlueter (120).

19 When Lessing comments in *Walking in the Shade* on "the extraordinary slipperiness of memory" (67), she is getting at the way two people's memory of the same event can differ markedly. She also thinks of memory as "a tiny part of what is in our brains" and not "the full, real record" below conscious awareness (104). *Briefing* offers a different take on memory. Watkins "remembers" another person's experiences as his own and may also concoct parts of the story. Cederstrom maintains that the Yugoslavia story "indicates that Watkins can relate archetypal patterns to modern life" and that the account "represents his only moments of wholeness before the electric shock treatments" (148–49). Perrakis (citing Annis Pratt, *Archetypal* [81] who draws on Northrop Frye's work on Shakespeare) mentions "the green world . . . an archetypal realm of oneness with nature" (108), which describes some aspects of the Yugoslavia of Watkins's false memory. For Margaret Moan Rowe, Watkins journeys "in inner space where any number of narratives are appropriated by the voyager" (64). Rubenstein reads the episode as an experience of collectivity, wholeness, harmony, and union in which Konstantina is an idealized version of Constance (*Vision* 192). And Susan Watkins considers the paradox that the memory is genuine, though not his own (60). Here are three further possibilities: that Watkins is re-visioning his wartime experience and coming to terms with residual PTSD; that falling in love with an attractive guerilla fighter is every dispirited academic man's compensatory fantasy; and that Watkins is encountering the anima in the person of Konstantina in much the same way that Lessing's character Jack Orkney encounters the anima in a dream. A woman may embody different aspects of the anima. Orkney's vision of a "female figure in white" is "a composite of his mother, his wife and his daughters" ("The Temptation of Jack Orkney" 290). Similarly, Konstantina is a young woman who shifts easily among medic, warrior, and civilian as well as between mature object of male desire and little girl.

20 Jung uses a lighter touch in *Psychology and Alchemy*, considering *nekyia* the title of *The Odyssey*'s Book 11 and defining it as "the sacrifice to the dead for conjuring up the departed from Hades." The term "is therefore an apt designation for the 'journey to

Hades,' the descent into the land of the dead." Jung cites, as examples of *nekyia*, *The Divine Comedy*, *Faust*, and Christ's descent into hell in the Apocrypha (*CW* 12, par. 61, n. 2). Excerpts from the passage are one of the epigraphs in Edinger's study of *Moby-Dick*.

21 Rubenstein states that anti-clockwise movement suggests movement backward in time (*Vision* 180). *Logos* and *eros* are my own suggestion.

22 Bolling quotes Marie-Louise von Franz as stating that "the Self . . . appears as a crystal" and involves "the union of extreme opposites—of matter and spirit" (557). Vlastos points out that a "crystalline gleam" in Lessing's *The Four-Gated City* is associated with extrasensory perception. The critic calls it "the divine order that contains the balance of the universe" (252, 255).

23 Some of the images—particularly "flames in fire" and "the great singing dance"—are reminiscent of William Butler Yeats's "Byzantium," which mentions how "flames begotten of flame" are "Dying into a dance" (lines 27 and 30). Of course, Byzantium depicts the afterlife, not a realm of Forms.

24 There is a strong connection here to the ending of Lessing's novella "Hunger." "*We*, says Jabavu over and over again, *We*. And it is as if in his empty hands are the warm hands of brothers" (331).

25 Watkins also delivers the message earlier when he says, "It's knowing. Harmony. God's law." Doctor Y. replies, "Now, now, shhhhhh, don't get so excited, there's a good chap" (133).

26 Jung states, "For a symbol is the intimation of a meaning beyond the level of our present power of comprehension" (*CW* 15, par. 118). The white bird is such a symbol because it is multivalent. Marchino calls it "the white bird of truth" (259); Cederstrom, a "Jungian symbol of transcendence" (143); and Singleton, "Hermes the divine messenger" (155). Jung himself equates birds with "thoughts and the flight of thought" (*CW* 12, par. 305). Thoughts *take flight*. The point is that the white bird is an exception to Lessing's allegorical method throughout much of *Briefing*. Perhaps Lessing gives us a white bird because a white rabbit would be merely allegorical.

27 Similarly, Vlastos states that Watkins discovers three levels of consciousness: "human, god disguised as human, and pure god" (256).

28 Lessing probably knew and would have affirmed Blake's statement in *Marriage*: "If the doors of perception were cleansed every thing would appear to man as it is, infinite" (Plate 14).

6

"NOT A BAD MAN BUT NOT GOOD EITHER"

The Anima and Individuation in J. M. Coetzee's *Disgrace*

J. M. Coetzee's *Disgrace* presents another disaffected academic, but there are important differences between Charles Watkins and David Lurie. Both are widely published, but whereas Watkins is a star scholar at Cambridge University, Lurie's three books mean very little because the former modern languages professor has been downgraded to a mere adjunct in communications following the transition of Cape Town University College to Cape Technical University. Whereas Watkins disrespects classical scholarship, Lurie cares only for scholarship. He hates the introductory level communications courses he teaches and is fed up with his Romantic poetry students' boredom and shallow intellect. The two characters' psychological problems also diverge, for Watkins's overemphasis on reason is unlike Lurie's anima possession and compulsion for sexual gratification. In their personal lives, Watkins is a family man who is still married to his wife Felicity; Lurie is twice divorced from Evelina and Rosalind. Although both men have involvements with female students, Watkins waits until the semester is over; having sex with a current student is fatal to Lurie's career. Overall, Watkins's story appears to be comic (he returns to his family and his job) but is actually tragic (he forgets his experience of the unconscious); Lurie's journey appears tragic (he is ruined in worldly terms) but is comic because he is the beneficiary of inner work.

Although *Disgrace* (2000) is the most recently published work discussed in *Anima and Africa*, nearly three hundred articles about it already appear on the MLA Bibliography. Psychological criticism, however, remains underrepresented. Even though the novel is shot through with depth psychology, there is strangely no Jungian analysis among the previous studies, though some critics touch on issues relevant to the approach below.[1] The present chapter addresses this lacuna by arguing that a dysfunctional relationship with the anima lies at the heart of Lurie's problems so that the question "does he have it in him to be the woman?" (160)—somewhat reminiscent of Olive Schreiner's section on "Gregory's Womanhood"—becomes the relevant question. Does Lurie make progress with his inner feminine? The affirmative answer proposed here does not negate the narrator's sense that Lurie is "[n]ot a bad man but not good either" (195); however, shadow work, a miniature version of the *nekyia* that Watkins experiences, and various images of transformation underscore the fact that Lurie does do some inner work. Chapter 6 also considers Coetzee's allusion to the Faust legend: one of Lurie's three monographs deals with the origin of Arrigo Boito's opera *Mefistofele*, and that origin is obviously one of Jung's favorite books, Johan Wolfgang von Goethe's *Faust*. Because Coetzee treats the Faust story as a source of images and motifs the way Doris Lessing apparently uses *Memories, Dreams, Reflections*, the Boito-Goethe nexus serves as both a thematic touchstone and a template for understanding and evaluating Lurie's journey with the anima.

David Lurie's anima problem

In stating that "a highly esteemed professor in his seventies abandons his family and runs off with a young red-headed actress" (*CW* 9i, par. 62), Jung imagines a situation that resonates with David Lurie's. As a man ages, the object of his projected anima becomes younger so that "an adult man [prefers] the figure of a younger woman" (*CW* 9i, par. 357). Melanie Isaacs, a twenty-year-old brunette theater major with a "[c]unning little weasel body" (189) and hips "as slim as a twelve-year-old's" (19), definitely qualifies. Lurie, age 52, true to his name, proceeds to *lure* her into a *lurid* affair.[2] She also illustrates Jung's sense that the anima is multi-faceted. "Mistress? Daughter?" Lurie wonders (27), and his student becomes his mistress-daughter when he has sex with her in his daughter Lucy's former room in his home. Both young women are probably on his mind when he thinks: "as a father grows older he turns more and more—it cannot be helped—toward his daughter. She becomes his second salvation, the bride of his youth reborn. No wonder, in fairy-stories, queens try to hound their daughters to their death!" (86–87).

Anima projection seems to be the major psychological process that drives and goads Lurie into relationships with females. The narrator tells us: "His childhood was spent in a family of women. As mothers, aunts, sisters fell away, they were replaced in due course by mistresses, wives, a daughter. The company of women made of him a lover of women and, to an extent, a womanizer" (7). In other words, his focus is on external surface rather than inner depth: not having made friends with the anima, he dwells in a state of non-individuation. More fundamentally, he is an example of "men who do not readily make friends, whose attitude toward friendship between men is corroded with skepticism" (102). Reinforcing his projection is the fact that he has not done shadow work, which Jung considers the "apprentice-piece" (*CW* 9i, par. 61), and chooses compartmentalization over wholeness: "He is all for double lives, triple lives, lives lived in compartments" (6). There is little wonder, then, that he is unprepared for the "master-piece" with the anima when Melanie appears in his classroom.

As their affair unfolds, Lurie's psychological problems echo in his lesson on Wordsworth's *The Prelude* in his Romantic poetry course. In "Lines Composed a Few Miles above Tintern Abbey" Wordsworth emphasizes the "eye, and ear,— both what they half create / And what perceive" (lines 106–07), which suggests a dialectical or two-way interplay between the mind and nature: the eye not only takes in sensory information but also colors the object under observation. That reciprocal process is not present in what Lurie quotes to his students, a passage whose theme is disappointment.

> we also first beheld
> Unveiled the summit of Mont Blanc, and grieved
> To have a soulless image on the eye
> That had usurped upon a living thought
> That never more could be.
>
> (21; *Prel.* 6.524–28)

Upon finally seeing the summit he has previously imagined, Wordsworth is disappointed because the setting does not match his "living thought" (the projection, the expected image). Instead, the "soulless image" impinges on the eye and is not colored by it, which creates a jarring contrast between expectation and reality. In other words, Wordsworth describes a kind of perceptual corrective process similar to what Lurie experiences with Melanie. The summit unveiled (her naked body, unresisting but void of passion) is a "soulless image" (disappointment) because she does not and cannot live up to his "living thought" (fantasy, projection) of Woman (the anima archetype). As Lurie explains to his class, "[t]he great archetypes of the mind, pure ideas, find themselves usurped by mere sense-images" (22). An analogy to male-female relationship brings the passage into focus for his students: what Wordsworth is describing is like the way reality intrudes into one's fantasy about another person; one sees her with "cold clarity" rather than "in [the] archetypal, goddesslike form" (22). The Mont Blanc episode, then, foreshadows the disappointment ("grieved") to which an affair based on anima projection leads.

The professor's comments about the perfective tense augment his reading of the passage, signal the negative end of projection, and introduce one of the novel's important motifs. He states: "*usurp upon* means to intrude or encroach upon. *Usurp*, to take over entirely, is the perfective of *usurp upon*; usurping completes the act of usurping upon" (21). The "soulless image" does the usurping in the passage, and "had" indicates a completed process so that the "living thought . . . never more could be." Wordsworth describes a process (usurping upon) that occurred in the more distant past but is now finished (his preconception of the mountain has been definitively destroyed). *Had usurped upon* conveys the experience of loss in the moment on Mont Blanc, but Lurie's grammatical explication signals a shift from being in the middle of something to a transition out of it into a state of being completely *usurped*. Similar locutions appear later in the novel. For example, he notes: "the distinction between *drink* and *drink up*, *burned* and *burnt*. The perfective, signifying an action carried through to its conclusion" (71). Another pair is "[d]rive, driven" (194), and a final example is Petrus's broken English, "it is finish[ed]" (201). Drink, drive, and finish signal a process; drink up, burnt, and finished parallel the finality in Wordsworth's loss of a "living thought," Lurie's loss of Melanie, and his transition from urban academia to rural unemployment. In his case, a perceptual process that exposes vain projections leads him to a different state of being in which a previous life is closed to him. If a life that has enabled psychological dysfunction to fester now yields to sober reality in which he must confront his shortcomings, then personal transformation—the individuation process—is an important motif in *Disgrace*.

At the heart of Lurie's psychological dysfunction is his infantile sexuality—he believes that one should satisfy one's lust. "Unacted desires," he tells Lucy, "can turn as ugly in the old as in the young" (70). It appears that he embraces the spirit of Blake's maxim: "Sooner murder an infant in its cradle than nurse unacted desires" (69; *The Marriage of Heaven and Hell*, plate 10). Desire drives him, for example, to commit an offense against Melanie, a woman more than thirty years younger who is under his tutelage. Such behavior is Luciferian, as Lurie seems to acknowledge when discussing a passage from Byron's "Lara" with his Romantic poetry class. Regarding the fiend, he states: "Good or bad, he just does it. He doesn't act on principle but on impulse, and the source of his impulses is dark to him" (33).[3] Inner darkness signals the shadow, which lurks unintegrated in the unconscious, and the idea that a man is free to do good or ill according to his desires is an apt description of Lurie's own lack of sexual ethics prior to the university's disciplinary action against him. That action may be considered a sort of repression: because he has acted on lust rather than properly integrating desire into his conscious life, external forces now make him answer for his deeds and encourage him to seek counseling, which he considers repressive rather than genuinely therapeutic. As he retreats to the Eastern Cape, he is not unlike the male dog there whose owners had beaten him whenever he got excited, which clouded the dog's desire for sex with fear. As a result, "the poor dog had begun to hate its own nature" (90). Lurie too has been punished for acting on his desire and now experiences desire-in-revulsion when he couples with "dumpy" Bev Shaw at her animal clinic (72). If he were to give up sex entirely in an act of total repression, he would be like the persons he describes: "to me animal-welfare people are a bit like Christians of a certain kind. Everyone is so cheerful and well-intentioned that after a while you itch to go off and do some raping and pillaging" (73). Lustful behavior and repression are in a relationship much like *enantiodromia*. Repression of desire leads to sin, which leads back to repression, unless desire is properly integrated into consciousness; otherwise, it remains an opponent and saboteur.

The owner-beaten dog suggests that Lurie encounters things in the country that illustrate his own psychological dysfunction, and this mirroring extends to the political situation in post-apartheid South Africa. Lurie suspects that Petrus's collusion with the thugs has its roots in something "*anthropological*" (118), that there is a deficiency inherent to black psychology that causes them to conspire against whites. Later he understands more accurately that a "history of wrong" was "speaking through them [blacks]" (156), much as, in the film Lurie shows Melanie, the stroboscopic effect is that "the instant of the present and the past of that instant, evanescent, [are] caught in the same space" (15).[4] Colonial oppression is specifically emblematized at Petrus's party when Lurie sees a middle-aged black man who wears a fist-sized medal around his neck, one of many "[s]ymbols [of empire] struck by the boxful in a foundry in Coventry or Birmingham" (135). *History of wrong* echoes more directly in Lurie's later statement that the university's inquiry "is the history" of his case (165), which implies that he has wronged Melanie as Westerners have wronged South Africa's natives. Now that apartheid is "gone with the wind" (133), much as slavery is a thing of the past in the southern United States, blacks strive to make inroads against whites. In the spirit of *enantiodromia*, they have gone from being oppressed to taking action against their former superiors through theft and rape. Blacks were denied opportunities because of their racial purity; now they dilute the racial purity of the white race through acts of sexual violence—they *do* rape, in the vernacular of the novel. Much as the university takes corrective action against Lurie for his mistreatment of Melanie, the thugs attempt to compensate for the ills of apartheid by targeting Lucy and her farm. Lurie feels the violation of his daughter more deeply than his own lost car or physical scars (the thugs pour methylated spirits on him and set him on fire), for now father and daughter are co-recipients of wrong, like Melanie who was not quite raped but suffered harm nonetheless.

Repression of sexual desire versus a swing to inappropriate sexual behavior is *enantiodromia* plain and simple. As such, Lurie's behavior also constitutes anima possession. Although appealing to women has been "the backbone of his life," his *raison d'être*, his attractiveness has faded; now he has sex with colleagues' wives, tourists, and prostitutes (7). In other words, he sleeps with women who are transient or emotionally unavailable so that he experiences the feminine only as a superficial pastime but remains a stranger to the feminine within his own psyche. However, because the unconscious manifests, Lurie's efforts to deny the anima backfire in the form of inappropriate behavior. Going to prostitutes is the main example of anima possession. Jung's position is that one who goes to a prostitute may victimize her but is "no less a victim of impulses from the unconscious" (*CW* 6, par. 805).[5] As a result, anima possession undermines the life of an outwardly upright public figure. Stalking is the best example. Like a "predator" (10), Lurie hires a private detective to find Soraya's real identity and later calls her on the phone in a violation of the code of anonymity between prostitute and customer. He also stalks Melanie, going to her rehearsal, "sitting in the dark spying on a girl," a behavior that he thinks of as "*letching*" (24). Near the end of the novel he stealthily attends the public performance of her play, *Sunset at the Globe Salon*, but is motivated to leave when her boyfriend Ryan hits him in the head with spitballs.[6] Stalking drives Lurie's self-identification as a Lucifer/Satan figure whose impulses lead to catastrophe. If he were to choose a totem, it would appropriately be the snake (2), and he seduces Melanie with "serpent's words" (16). After Mr. Isaacs likens the university to "a nest of vipers," Lurie acknowledges that he is such a "viper" (38). Later he realizes that the purpose of Soraya and his other sex partners is "to suck the complex proteins out of his blood like snake-venom, leaving him clear-headed and dry"

(185).[7] And his second ex-wife Rosalind, in calling him "[a] great deceiver and a great self-deceiver" (188), likens him to the devil. "So . . . how are the mighty fallen," comments Mr. Isaacs on Lurie/Lucifer (167).

At the root of Lurie's anima/sex addiction is archetypal possession. He realizes that "he is in the grip of something" (18) and that "nothing will stop him" (25) when he date rapes Melanie. "Suffice it to say that Eros entered," he tells the committee of inquiry.[8] "After that I was not the same. . . . I was not myself. I was no longer a fifty-year-old divorcé at a loose end. I became a servant of Eros" (52). He repeats the explanation to Lucy: "*I was a servant of Eros. . . . It was a god who acted through me.*" And then: "What vanity! Yet not a lie, not entirely. In the whole wretched business there was something generous that was doing its best to flower" (89). To the committee and to his daughter, his explanation must sound as hollow as Petrus's sophistical defense of Pollux's crime later in the novel.[9] As regards his employment, he does himself no favors because he lacks the humble contrition that the committee's members need to save his job. However, the inquiry sparks genuine self-reflection and a sense of depth psychology. He has been possessed by the anima archetype and must serve her because she is unintegrated. But insofar as he is beginning to make the unconscious conscious, his unfortunate statement to the press about his affair with Melanie—"I was enriched by the experience" (56)—is not entirely inaccurate. The man whose anima is becoming more integrated ("doing its best to flower") is soon to help Lucy bring flowers to the farmers' market, and such humble work makes a positive difference in his life. In an epiphany, he thinks about the word "enriched": "A stupid word to let slip, under the circumstances, yet now, at this moment, he would stand by it. By Melanie, by the girl in Touws River; by Rosalind, Bev Shaw, Soraya: by each of them he was enriched, and by the others too, even the least of them, even the failures" (192). Now his heart opens "[l]ike a flower blooming in his breast," and the narrator supposes that such moments are "[h]ypnogogic," that is, from the unconscious (192).

Signs of individuation

Regarding the anima, "[t]he question is, does he have it in him to be the woman?" (160). Laura Wright states that, no, he cannot *be* the woman but that he "may possibly" come to love "ordinary" Bev Shaw and that he develops empathy for rape victims who are analogous to animals that are slaughtered or euthanized (95, 97). But if the question is whether he makes any progress with anima integration, the answer is yes, though many layers of psychological problems abide. Lurie is in a better psychological place at the end of the novel than he is while visiting Soraya, having an affair with Melanie, or being questioned by the committee of inquiry, though he remains fettered to psychological dysfunction (for example, he picks up a street walker during his brief return to Cape Town). A principal agent of change is the rural environment, which mirrors his psychological state in various ways. In other words, he sees his personal unconscious allegorized in details of his new life, much as Charles Watkins experiences an allegory of the collective unconscious and the human condition in his vision. The first step is to acknowledge that there is a problem, and Coetzee's use of imagery implies the plausibility of that self-realization.

Among the first creatures Lurie sees is a bulldog bitch named Katy, which Lucy is boarding, though the dog has been abandoned by her owners. The dog's situation is essentially that of Lurie's anima upon his arrival at the farm—abandoned by his rational self yet sheltered and nurtured by his daughter. Shortly thereafter, he and Lucy see a sign that says, "Trespassers will be Prosecuted" (69). He has trespassed on forbidden territory with Melanie and has been prosecuted in a way by the committee of inquiry, convicted of personal misconduct and professional malfeasance, and punished by the university. Lurie's work on Wordsworth is relevant in this connection. His critical study, *Wordsworth and the Burden of the Past*, is about history, but the title resonates meaningfully with his own situation. He too is carrying a burden of the past, and Wordsworth's *The Prelude* includes an episode that links inappropriate sexuality at an earlier moment to present punishment. In Book 12, the poet mentions "spots of time," which have a "renovating virtue" by which "our minds / Are nourished and invisibly repaired" (lines 208, 210, 214–15). These are ordinary events that have extraordinary psychological impact. The passage mentions two such spots—the sight of a murderer who "had been hung in iron chains" (line 236) and a wind-blown girl for whom the young Wordsworth develops sexual feelings. He considers his father's death to be a "chastisement" for lust (line 311); when he bows low, God corrects his desires. Here is a paradigm for redemption: infraction, punishment, repentance, and improvement. Wordsworth is who he is because of his childhood experiences, but some of the burden of guilt has been lifted. Similarly, Lurie trespassed, was prosecuted, received punishment, and is now at work on repentance, which culminates in his apology to Mr. Isaacs and a literal bowing down before Mrs. Isaacs and Melanie's sister ("he gets to his knees and touches his forehead to the floor" [173]). For the moment, however, Lurie resembles what grows in the Shaws' backyard—"an apple tree dropping wormridden fruit" (73). The apple is Coetzee's heavy-handed symbol of the Fall, which Lurie, who is trying throughout the book to write an opera about Byron in Italy, would have identified with loss of virginity, as in Don Juan's case, or sexual misdeeds more generally, as with Byron and his Italian mistress, Contessa Teresa Guiccioli, who is roughly Melanie's age. Even worse, the apple is corrupted by phallic worms—"*I am the worm in the apple*, he should have said" (37)—that turn a source of potential nourishment into something useless for anything except compost. The Shaws' wormy apples are worse than the bulldog bitch, for they are abandoned or cast off like the dog but also corrupted at the core, much like the disgraced David Lurie. The injured dog and the ruined fruit are thus appropriate images of the dysfunctional anima, on which he must do inner work.

The next image that reflects Lurie's situation is one of Bev's injured animals—an old goat ("a fullgrown buck") with a mangled scrotum. "One half of his scrotum, yellow and purple, is swollen like a balloon" (82). Later it is referred to as "the old billy-goat with the ravaged testicles" (126). Also, "[h]e remembers Bev Shaw nuzzling the old billy-goat with the ravaged testicles, stroking him, comforting him, entering into his life" (126). On the one hand, Lurie himself is an old goat who has been figuratively injured in the scrotum by job loss and disgrace, and Bev strokes and comforts him when they fornicate on the floor of the clinic. On the other, by helping out there, Lurie is now "[p]laying right-hand man to a woman who specializes in sterilization and euthanasia" (91). Even before the affair with Melanie, he sees castration as a desirable option.

> Might one approach a doctor and ask for it? A simple enough operation, surely: they do it to animals every day, and animals survive well enough, if one ignores a certain residue of sadness. Severing, tying off: with local anaesthetic and a steady hand and a modicum of phlegm one might even do it oneself, out of a textbook. A man on a chair snipping away at himself: an ugly sight, but no more ugly, from a certain point of view, than the same man exercising himself on the body of a woman.
>
> (9)

Appearing directly after he has sex with Dawn, his department's secretary, the passage indicates Lurie's awareness that his sex drive must be controlled. Since he believes that he, as "a grown man," is "beyond the reach of counselling" (49), he wonders whether his problem could be solved by removal of the testicles. In other words, the professor thinks that sex drive is merely animalistic, that his misbehavior is driven by a physical mechanism, and that surgery on his body might be a feasible solution. What he does with his body, however, is an outer sign of an inner and psychological problem that no excision of parts will solve. Castration would finalize the repression of his sex drive, but it would not address the neglected anima—the bulldog bitch—that languishes within. Since one can wither the body and reduce sexual libido yet not engage fruitfully with the anima, there is no simple solution for Lurie. Later, as he and Lucy discuss the rape, the "Cycads sign" (159) that they drive by is a reminder that sexuality abides, for part of the cycads plant looks like an enormous upright phallus. Later still, at the performance of Melanie's play, "Ryan, the boyfriend with the ear-ring and the goatee" (193), is a young old goat who represents the part of Lurie that has still gone largely unaddressed, the shadow whom he must not flee but befriend in order to make progress with the anima.

In short, Lurie finds himself in an allegory, especially in the country, where details highlight his wounded, dysfunctional psychological state. To a significant extent, he is to the farm as Charles Watkins is to his inner vision; but whereas Watkins's inner vision is relevant mainly to humanity in general, Lurie's experiences in the Eastern Cape are relevant both to himself and to the country's post-apartheid growing pains. Petrus and the thugs, for example, are not only the object of Lurie's shadow projection but also an illustration of a power shift occurring in 1990s South Africa (the novel is set in 1997). The slowness of that political progress has a personal parallel—Lurie's intransigence before the committee of inquiry, which signals reluctance to change and grow. A bit later, "[h]is mind has become a refuge for old thoughts, idle, indigent, with nowhere else to go" (72). In addition, he agrees to work at Bev's clinic "only as long as I don't have to become a better person. I am not prepared to be reformed. I want to go on being myself" (77). Nonetheless, if seeing reflections of his psychic life in the external world is a first step in the direction of individuation, then he is "enriched" by more than the affair with Melanie. For example, there is a strong indication of anima work in his statement to Lucy: "Every woman I have been close to has taught me something about myself. To that extent they have made me a better person" (70). Coetzee presents an image of inner work when Lurie visits the Isaacs family's home upon his return to Cape Town. In his mind's eye, he sees himself laid out on an operating table as a surgeon extracts his organs one by one (171). The image, which conveys Lurie's profound discomfort in conversation with Mr. Isaacs, resembles the agony J. Alfred Prufrock feels when being stared at as if he were "sprawling on a pin" and "wriggling on the wall" (Eliot, lines 57–58). Lurie's apology for the trouble he has caused the Isaacs family suggests that he has at least become more circumspect. If he also becomes a slightly better, more individuated person, then the key issue involves the steps in his psychological process.

Lurie's individuation process

The shadow. As with Charles Watkins, a robbery is the catalyst for psychological progress. Lurie's confrontation with the dark African Other—with Petrus and the thugs serving as the object of shadow projection—signals that he is bringing up to consciousness the shadow that has contributed to his misdeeds in the city. These men personify not only his personal shadow but also South Africa's collective shadow so that the robbery, "another incident in the great campaign of redistribution" (176), compensates for years of personal and political repression. The confrontation is so violent because the shadow has been so long repressed in both senses. In particular, Pollux, a retarded boy who assists the adult thugs, represents apartheid's mind-numbing effect on the country's natives. Eventually, after spotting Pollux at a party, Lurie confronts Petrus who defends the boy, using arguments that parallel Lurie's self-justifications with regard to his offense against Melanie. Perhaps the parallel helps him understand that acting on selfish desires is untenable when doing so harms others. Indeed, like Satan, the beguiler beguiled, Lurie is a sexual thief who has now suffered a parallel robbery. It is a "punishment fitted to the crime" (210), which is the definition of *contrapasso*, the term for the punishments suffered in *The Inferno*. What he does to Mr. Isaacs's daughter is done more destructively to his own; and his act of passion, of sexual heat, against a young woman is punished by his being literally set on fire.

The robbery leads to further work with the shadow as the novel continues. Because the harm perpetrated against Lucy and her farm is something Lurie cannot abide, he takes matters into his own hands by hitting the peeping Pollux in a fit of "elemental rage" (206). Here is the kind of masculine awakening, a connection to primordial masculine strength, that Francis Macomber experiences during his final hunt. Although Lurie's anger is out of control, the shadow is now working *with* him rather than fueling sexual high jinks. Justice rather than projection drives the attack. Yet acknowledgement of the shadow also makes him subject to negative inflation. Ashamed of his action against Pollux, he condemns himself absolutely (208). He realizes earlier that he is a "troublemaker" who has caused Melanie "at least as much trouble as" she caused him (147) and that if "squat little tub" Bev "is poor, he is bankrupt" (149–50).[10] He even considers himself a "*harijan*," one who is inferior and untouchable (146).

Abaissement du niveau mental.   For Lurie, there is no days-long immersion in the collective unconscious such as Watkins experiences, but engagement with the shadow lowers and deepens his conscious awareness in the spirit of "*abaissement du niveau mental*, i.e., a weakness in the hierarchical order of the ego" (*CW* 16, par. 361). Jung's term resonates with Lurie's reaction to the media's coverage of the scandal: "Confessions, apologies: why this thirst for abasement?" (56). Now, with his body and rationality weakened by injuries, the unconscious—the anima—speaks to him. "He has a [dream] vision: Lucy has spoken to him; her words—'Come to me, save me!'—still echo in his ears" (103). Because the rape renders her incapable of work, he takes over much of the daily chores on the farm, and she also needs her father's help and understanding in order to heal psychologically. These things are only the surface truth, however. His anima, personified as Lucy, is crying out to him for acceptance and self-healing. The erotic anima, which he has projected on beautiful women, is not active here. Instead, the vision of Lucy is a call to compassion that transcends *eros*. What he has lost is asking to be found. What he has repressed and neglected is asking to be integrated into the Self.

Nigredo.   Shortly after the vision, Lurie has a second dimension of experience with the unconscious: *nigredo*, despair.

> He sees it quite clearly, and it fills him with (the word will not go away) despair. The blood of life is leaving his body and despair is taking its place, despair that is like a gas, odourless, tasteless, without nourishment. You breathe it in, your limbs relax, you cease to care, even at the moment when the steel touches your throat.
>
> (107–08)

The mention of starvation, gas, and knife suggests that suicide is a present possibility; and the placement of the passage—roughly the center of the book, chapter 13 of 24, pages 107–08 of 220—suggests the centrality of despair in Lurie's psychological journey. It is as if the first half of the novel is a descent leading to this moment of despair, followed by some degree of recovery in the second half. Having now reached what Joseph Conrad calls "the very bottom of there" (33), Lurie begins to lift out of *nigredo* by being busy in constructive work on the farm, much as Marlow emphasizes the saving benefits of work in *Heart of Darkness*. Work helps both characters to retain a sure footing in the concrete world, yet the unconscious is not done with the disgraced professor.

Nekyia. A bit later, the shock of the robbery and Lurie's burns result in a further *abaissement* that is reminiscent of Jung's precognitive image of World War I. Coetzee writes, "One night, half sleepwalking, half demented, he strips his own bed, even turns the mattress over, looking for stains" (121). First, he is in between waking and sleeping—the unconscious is manifesting in the physical world through the action of stripping the bed, an image that relates to what he has done *in bed* with Melanie. The stain for which he searches suggests perhaps the blood of a virgin (which Melanie is not) but definitely the stain of original sin, in which he is a guilty participant. If the stain is indeed blood from sex, then other images of blood and penetration are relevant. Lucy, a lesbian, describes sex as a knifing: "Pushing the knife in; exiting afterwards, leaving the body behind covered in blood" (158). Further on, "[t]he man who raped her, the leader of the gang, was like that. Like a blade cutting the wind" (170–71). The imagery of stabbing informs Lurie's reflection on his nightmare: "*Covered in blood.* What does she [Lucy] mean? Was he right after all when he dreamt of a bed of blood, a bath of blood?" (159). The reflection signals a growing awareness on his part that he may have harmed Melanie. What he has done with Melanie is a violation that, while not quite rape, is not completely different in spirit from what the thugs do to Lucy.[11]

Images of transformation. Lurie's injuries relate to several important images of transformation. First, when one of the thugs pours methylated spirits on Lurie's head and lights him on fire, he sustains serious damage to his scalp, one of his ears, and one eye. After he is bandaged up at the hospital, he pronounces himself "'[s]hipshape,' . . . but thinks: Like a mummy" (106). His bandaged head is not unlike his wishes for the farmhouse, which he would prefer that he and Lucy turn "into a fortress" (113). In appearance, both his head and her house are mummy-like, closed off, static; but in reality his bandages are more like a chrysalis, in which transformation is taking place. Two lines from *Faust* encapsulate the idea nicely: "The chrysalis, the caterpillar clinging, / Presage the butterfly's resplendent gleam" (lines 6729–30). The image, however, should not be overstated: Lurie does not emerge from his bandages a completely new man, like a caterpillar that becomes a butterfly. He is still "[n]ot a bad man but not good either" (195), but details point to inner progress. "He has recovered the sight of his eye completely," the narrator tells us (141). Although his physical eyesight is no better than it was before, it is now an eye through which painful experience enables him to see himself and the world more accurately.

The disposal of dogs provides a second image of transformation. People who bring dogs they cannot care for to Bev's clinic know that the animals will be disposed of without any apparent consequences. "What is being asked for is, in fact, *Lösung* (German always to hand with an appropriately blank abstraction): sublimation, as alcohol is sublimed from water, leaving no residue, no aftertaste" (142). The dogs' owners do not ask Bev to euthanize their dogs, but what they do say is *Lösung* (solution), which signifies the same.[12] Their objective is a clean disposal with no consequences or responsibilities, as in a transformation via sublimation. They drop the dogs off for killing that is up to others. Lurie's wounds, however, suggest that his own process of psychological transformation is not so clean. Just as he is one of the agents of the dogs' death (assisting in the killings, taking the corpses to be incinerated), he must be the agent of his own change, which does leave a residue or aftertaste.

For Charles Watkins and David Lurie, a robbery is the third catalyst for deeper psychological awareness; whereas Watkins loses his mind, Lurie is literally set on fire, which is part of a strand of references to fire that relates to increased self-awareness. To begin with, Lurie associates fire with his passion for Melanie: "In Melanie's case . . . something unexpected happened. I think of it as a fire. She struck up a fire in me" (166). Then his explanation to Mr. Isaacs lurches toward the archetypal: "Yet in the olden days people worshipped fire. They thought twice before letting a flame die, a flame-god. It was that kind of flame your daughter kindled in me. Not hot enough to burn me up, but real: real fire" (166). The statement echoes the lame idea, expressed earlier to Lucy, that he was possessed by a god, but he is now saying that he really was not. Melanie's effect on him is more like Percy Bysshe Shelley's analogy for the imagination in "A Defence of Poetry": the wind gives a dying coal a momentary increase in intensity (1143), just as Lurie's affair with Melanie is "[a] last leap of the flame of sense before it goes out" (27). Its heat is sufficient in Lurie's case to destroy a career but not to consume a mind.

During Lurie's first visit to Lucy's farm, two statements imply that he is beginning to consider his own fire/passion from a more mature perspective. He makes a comment to Bev Shaw about "foreknowledge," which means genetic memory or instinct. "This is Africa, after all. There have been goats here since the beginning of time. They don't have to be told what steel is for, and fire. They know how death comes to a goat. They are born prepared" (83–84). The goat image reinforces his own goatishness and implies that he is now acknowledging the instinctual within him, for there has been an old goat within man since the beginning of human experience. A later conversation with Lucy also suggests that Lurie is slowly coming to terms with his passions. "Vengeance is like a fire," he tells her. "The more it devours, the hungrier it gets" (112). He is lecturing her on the way the thugs' action against her is a step toward greater harm. The nature of vengeance applies equally to sexual passion; once lit, both irascibility and concupiscence have the potential to outweigh reason and common sense. Fearing for her safety if she does not report the rape, he is now counseling his daughter on how to deal with a sexual offense, much as he suspects that Mr. Isaacs has pushed Melanie into filing a complaint. The parallelism cannot be lost on someone of his intellectual acumen. Lucy replies: "Stop it, David! I don't want to hear this talk of plagues and fires. I am not just trying to save my skin. If that is what you think, you miss the point entirely" (112). The statement bespeaks a well-being that is more than surface deep; she needs to do more than put out the thugs' fiery lust for vengeance against white people. She is trying to deal with what is deeper than her own skin. Read psychologically, the statement says: *Stop trying to get me to worry about external safety when my inner life has been laid waste.* Lucy needs depth psychology, not firefighting.

Fire, stolen from the gods and given to man, represents both the dawning of consciousness in humans and the beginning of deeper insight in Lurie's individual psyche.[13] That suspicion, however, is somewhat muted in the following statement, to Mr. Isaacs: "But there was something . . . lyrical. I lack the lyrical. I manage love too well. Even when I burn I don't sing, if you understand me. For which I am sorry. I am sorry for what I took your daughter through. . . . I apologize for the grief I have caused you and Mrs. Isaacs. I ask for your pardon" (171). Sex is ordinarily for Lurie a mechanical act, a business transaction, something to be managed, and lust rather than love. As the quotation suggests, he has been a man with little music in his soul, yet Melanie apparently touches him deeply by awakening part of him that he never experienced before. If he is now capable of intellectual empathy and humility, seeing the affair from the Isaacs family's point of view and apologizing for his actions, then he truly has been "enriched by the experience" (56). Toward the end of the novel the music of his soul slowly but surely filters into his opera. Although he writes lyrics to be accompanied by a toy banjo rather than an orchestra, the fact that he is writing at all registers inner work and signals progress with a previously unacknowledged part of his psyche: the anima is on the move.[14]

From eros *to* agape.   The fire of *eros* does not yield to full-blown sacrificial love but does move closer to *agape*. Lurie is no saint, and he is never completely without lust; however, his anima is leading him from using Melanie because she is beautiful to having greater empathy despite the presence of unattractiveness in self and other. Jana María Giles accurately asserts that he does "develop sympathetic imagination for others when physical and emotional trauma makes him other to himself" (23). A clear sign of progress is that Eros no longer seems to be driving him: "If he is being led, then what god is doing the leading?" (Coetzee 192). The diminution of *eros* is quite clear when, halfway through the novel, he realizes that his days as a sexual adventurer are now behind him. Becoming "a country recluse" constitutes "[t]he end of roving" (120), just as returning to Cape Town signals "[t]he end of roaming" (175). Both are allusions to Byron's "So We'll Go No More a Roving," in which the poet realizes that sexual desire has outlived his physical capacity. As a result, Lurie has in store the likes of Bev Shaw: "After the sweet young flesh of Melanie Isaacs, this is what I have come to. This is what I will have to get used to, this and even less than this" (150). He is not now that womanizer who in old days could move any woman he fancied.

Like Byron, Lurie faces this painful transition by creating art, turning to a character in his opera about Byron in Italy. When he imagines the married Teresa as the Melanie-esque young woman she was when the poet wooed her, no music comes. That situation directly parallels the Lurie-Melanie dyad: "a passionate young woman and a once passionate but now less than passionate older man" (180). Then he sees Teresa as follows: "a woman past her prime, without prospects, living out her days in a dull provincial town, exchanging visits with women-friends, massaging her father's legs when they give him pain, sleeping alone. Can he [Lurie] find it in his heart to love this plain, ordinary woman?" (182). The answer is yes. In his mind's eye, when she flaunts her unworthy breasts to the sun and sings and strums despite others' smirks, the music comes to him. In that respect, "Teresa may be the last one left who can save him" (209) because, when Lurie finally comes to terms with how age affects his romantic prospects, active imagination facilitates a response.[15] Song is associated with "the need to fill out with sound the overlarge and rather empty human soul" (4), and the anima is finally singing back to him, not in the erotic siren-call that he projects onto Ms. Isaacs ("Melanie—melody; a meretricious rhyme" [18]) but in the tones of a mature, age-appropriate woman.

Thus, Lurie goes from erotic addiction to the beautiful to a frank acknowledgement of his fading attractiveness and an ability to appreciate less attractive women like Bev, not for how they look but for who they are. Along the way, his maternal anima grows in the capacity for empathy. Instead of preying on Melanie, he now watches over Lucy. Of course, "[t]his is not what he came for—to be struck in the back of beyond, warding off demons, nursing his daughter, attending to a dying enterprise" (121). As the quotation suggests, he is not a Gregory Rose-like figure of the maternal anima. Although he does not receive the soul-soothing he sought from his daughter, nursing her does diminish his egocentrism and foster empathy. Now his own wounds and the resulting nightmares help him understand "what women undergo at the hands of men" (111) and perhaps what a particular woman, Melanie, has undergone because of his own misbehavior. He realizes too that Lucy's shame parallels his own disgrace, for the story of the attack is spreading "[l]ike a stain" (115) similar to the bed stains in his dream, much as his own story has spread throughout the university and into the press.

Lurie's empathy also develops as a result of his encounters with dogs while he is in the Eastern Cape. To the extent that he "seems to have adopted as his own" the bulldog bitch named Katy (92), he begins to care about the undesirable. Thinking of her as "the abandoned one" provides an easy allegory (68). Not only have his university and his colleagues abandoned him, but he has also neglected his own anima. Now both he and Katy find themselves "sulking" (62) on Lucy's farm; but by caring about the abandoned dog, he begins to care about a long-lost part of himself.[16] In short, the animal helps him do inner work, and so it is with dogs later in the novel. Whereas Katy feels the disgrace of abandonment, he supposes that the dogs at the clinic "feel the disgrace of dying" (143). This time, however, there is no parallel to his own inner life; instead of egocentrism there is empathy: "He has learned by now, from [Bev], to concentrate all his attention on the animal they are killing, giving it what he no longer has difficulty in calling by its proper name: love" (219), which Shelley calls "the great secret of morals" (1135).

Just as "*it has fallen to [him] to guide*" Lucy, he now becomes "a dog psychopomp" (156). Lurie's work at the clinic sets the stage for inner work, and caring for the condemned dogs helps him foster selfless love. Since lower than this a proud academic is not likely to fall, he has now, in the words of Shakespeare, "sounded the very bass string of humility" (*1 Henry IV* 2.4.5–6); but his work with dogs resembles the anima's role in the psyche. He helps dogs transition into death as the anima guides the conscious mind into the unconscious. The implication is not necessarily that Lurie is becoming less than human but simply that he is doing inner work with his anima.

Lurie's empathy for dogs falls short of affirming the *unus mundus* but does involve a shift in his attitude toward the soul, which is the anima's original meaning. In a conversation about "a higher life" with her father, Lucy states: "This is the only life there is. Which we share with animals. That's the example that people like Bev try to set. That's the example I try to follow." Lurie responds: "We are of a different order of creation from the animals. Not higher, necessarily, just different" (74). Lucy's atheism results in her perception that sharing life with animals has moral implications. The difference between humans and animals, for Lurie, probably rests upon academic values like civilization, language, reason, education, and scholarly achievement. "Not higher, necessarily" is probably a rhetorical flourish that signals his belief in the opposite, but a strand of references to the soul illuminates his growing empathy and suggests that his disgrace is a portal to personal growth. Regarding dogs' souls, he first cites the Church Fathers in stating, "Their souls are tied to their bodies and die with them" (78). Sheep also appear to be inferior: they are "destined since birth for the butcher's knife" and "exist to be used, every last ounce of them . . . except perhaps the gall bladder, which no one will eat. Descartes should have thought of that. The soul suspended in the dark, bitter gall, hiding" (123–24). As the parts of the sheep are used, the soul takes refuge in what remains, presumably to be snuffed out—to die with the body—when the last organ is destroyed. Two pages later Lurie still does not "believe that animals have properly individual lives" (126).

He views the human soul in a more positive light. After the thugs attack the farm, the wounded Lurie thinks, "In a while the organism will repair itself, and I, the ghost within it, will be my old self again" (107). Here is evidence of thinking that humans are both higher than and different from dogs, that we are ghosts in biological machines, and that these ghosts are made of spiritual stuff that ensures the continuity of individual consciousness at the moment of death. In the novel's second half, however, he changes his mind about dogs. When he looks at the bags containing dogs' corpses, he considers "each [to have] . . . a body and a soul inside" (161). In the end, he believes that "the [euthanized dog's] soul is yanked out of the body; briefly it hangs about in the air, twisting and contorting; then it is sucked away and is gone" in direct contrast to his earlier view that an animal's soul dies with its body. The narrator adds, "It will be beyond him, this room that is not a room but a hole where one leaks out of existence" (219). That is, a canine soul's process of transition from physical existence to life in the spirit world is beyond his present power of comprehension. It is enough, however, that he now attributes spiritual continuity to the canine soul. The shift signals not only greater empathy but also inner work with his own anima: once he becomes more conscious of his inner feminine, it is easier for him to see the anima's etymology and most fundamental characteristic—soul—in creatures who are vulnerable. Moreover, in the reverie about women during Melanie's play, he realizes, in an allusion to Langland's *Piers Plowman*, a connection between himself and all the women he has loved: "*A fair field full of folk*: hundreds of lives all tangled with his" (192). This realization too falls short of the *unus mundus*, but it does signal a "going out of our own nature, and an identification of ourselves with the beautiful which exists in thought, action, or person, not our own," which is key to Shelley's definition of love (1135).

Although Lurie's anima may be on the move, his progress also stops short of *coniunctio*, "the union of opposites and the birth of new possibilities" (Sharp 42). At the end of the novel, he remains friends with Bev, but he has no wife or girlfriend. Also, he and Lucy are semi-estranged because she rejects his advice to have an abortion and plans to carry and keep a rapist's baby. Yet *Disgrace* is not without hints of *coniunctio*. At the beginning of Chapter 11, Lurie finds Lucy "watching the wild geese on the dam" (88). Geese mate for life, and in the background lurks Charlotte Brontë's statement in *Jane Eyre* that "birds were faithful to their mates; birds were emblems of love" (283; ch. 28). There is perhaps something in Lucy that inclines toward union, versus the bickering she and her father do as though they were a married couple (134). If so, this desire explains her decision to allow Petrus to tell whatever story he wants—that she is his third wife, for example—so that she and her farm will come under his protection. Lurie considers the deal a capitulation and an error, as unnatural as "[t]he marriage of Cronus and Harmony" or, one might add, the union of him and Melanie (190). But a Lucy-Petrus partnership is an incorporation of a sort, a coming together of disparate parts, a bit like Gonzalo's mention in *The Tempest* that Claribel found a husband at Tunis (5.1. 211). In both cases, a white woman's union with her dark African Other has positive implications. For Lucy, the arrangement may not be the *hieros gamos* (holy marriage) that Jung speaks of, but she will no longer be merely a part of "*We Westerners*" because she considers Pollux "*[m]y people*" (202, 201). More precisely, she now inhabits a liminal space where difference remains but vulnerability declines and where her baby will be "a child of this earth" (216), a native black child who will grow to be "[a] peasant, a *paysan*, a man of the country" (117) like Petrus, whose name, derived from *petram* (Latin: rock), implies that he is part of the living landscape.[17] Although Lurie detests her decision, his acceptance of it suggests that he at least tolerates the shadow within him and has made sufficient peace with the anima that he can allow his daughter to chart her own course. On a larger scale, Coetzee implies via Lucy that making progress toward racial harmony requires the intercession of the feminine.

One further strand suggests a similar coming to terms with things as they are and must be. Whereas Lurie has sex with Dawn early in the novel, shortly after he arrives on the farm he is up at five o'clock to cut flowers and witnesses the "dawn" at seven (70). Halfway through the novel, he is "busy from dawn to dusk" (120). The play on the word "dawn" suggests that he moves from sexual risk-taking as an antidote to professional boredom and personal unhappiness to a stronger connection with the natural world, a connection that is synergistic with inner work. Then, during the return visit to Cape Town, Lurie attends Melanie's play, *Sunset at the Globe Salon*.

The shift from Dawn to dawn and now to sunset parallels and reinforces his acknowledgement of his own aging and loss of attractiveness (the sun is going down on David Lurie versus the young, smart-mouthed beautician played by Melanie). Similarly, the image of the globe, which for Jung signifies the Self, reflects the progress he has made and points to the possibility of greater wholeness. At the play, for example, he watches the young woman not with a lecherous eye but with paternal pride until Ryan's spitballs force him to leave. Later still, his individuation is explicitly qualified: "He lacks the virtues of the old: equanimity, kindliness, patience" (217). But perhaps his restlessness will drive him not into the arms of God, as in George Herbert's "The Pulley," but toward further inner work. In the end, he achieves at least a simulacrum of those qualities he seems to lack.

Moving into town to await the birth of Lucy's baby, he continues his psychopomp work at the clinic, becoming friends with a dog named *Driepoot* that he helps euthanize. "Bearing him in his arms like a lamb, he re-enters the surgery. 'I thought you would save him for another week,' says Bev Shaw. 'Are you giving him up?' 'Yes, I am giving him up'" (220). Giving *him* up but not *giving* up: thus ends *Disgrace*. This is a somber way to end a sad novel, but "giving him up" is more positive than it may at first seem.[18] The phrase signals that Lurie will no longer rail at the world for thwarting his wishes and that he will now simply let happen what may. The psychological implication is openness to further individuation: he is more likely to recognize what lies within now that he no longer resists what lies without; being reconciled to external circumstances brings him into greater sync with his inner life. The whole novel has been but a prelude in the Wordsworthian sense. Lurie is not giving up on the psyche, and he has arrived at a state that will enable inner work to begin in earnest if he so desires.

The *Faust* allusion in *Disgrace*

Since *Disgrace* is by and about persons with advanced training in literature, the novel's literary allusions are frequent and widely varied, ranging from Greek mythology to Alice Walker, with emphasis on Wordsworth and Byron. Commenting properly on all of these allusions fills the pages of many articles, but one insufficiently explored source is particularly relevant to this chapter's approach. Among Lurie's monographs is a text that would be sure to catch Jung's attention: *Boito and the Faust Legend: The Genesis of Mefistofele*.[19] Arrigo Boito's *Mefistofele* and Johann Wolfgang von Goethe's *Faust*, on which it is based, are consistent with the view that Lurie's difficulties are conducive to individuation and that, although his worldly prospects look bleak, his inner life is on the rise. Coetzee is a careful craftsman, and he would not have invented Lurie's book title if the Faust legend were not relevant to an interpretation of Lurie's journey. This section pursues that line of reasoning with regard to *Mefistofele* and *Disgrace* in the larger context provided by Jung's extensive comments on *Faust*.

Summary of the opera. Boito's opera, a highly abridged version of Goethe's *Faust*, begins with a prologue in what seems to be outer space where Mefistofele thinks that man is an easy target. When the chorus objects by asserting Faust's incorruptibility, the fiend and the chorus make a wager: if Faust falls, Mefistofele wins a victory over God. Then, in a moment of foreshadowing, the soaring of boys' spirits from Limbo to Heaven implies that Faust's time of temptation will end with his salvation and a loss for the devil. In the meantime, Mary is invoked for help "'gainst passions' raging" (5). Act 1 takes place in Frankfort on Easter Sunday. As couples are dancing, Mefistofele appears as a grey friar. Wagner, Faust's associate, fears phantoms, but Faust can actually see that the "friar" leaves flaming footprints. Faust states that he has his passions in check and makes the "sign of Solomon" in self-defense (9). Now appearing as a knight, the devil offers to be Faust's "slave" or "servant" (10) but states that this arrangement will be reversed in hell. Mefistofele identifies himself as a spirit of negation and as an agent of chaos. The contract they agree upon stipulates that Faust will be damned if he should wish for a blissful moment to endure. Act 2 opens in a garden. Mefistofele and the rejuvenated Faust, now going by the name of Henry, encounter Martha and Margaret (Gretchen). Attracted to Gretchen's youth and beauty, Faust seduces her, and they plan an assignation at her home. He gives her a sleeping potion for her mother so that they can fornicate uninterrupted; however, three drops of the potion prove fatal. In the next scene it is revealed at a witches' Sabbath in the high mountains that Mefistofele is their king. They present him with a glass globe in which he sees the earth that he despises. In a vision, Faust sees Gretchen shackled and awaiting her execution. In Act 3, it becomes clear that she has not only poisoned her mother but also drowned her baby. Mefistofele opens the door to her prison cell, but when she sees the devil she shrinks away from Faust who hopes to rescue her. Man and fiend leave just before the executioner enters. Act 4, which takes place at night on the classical Sabbath on the shores of the Peneus in the Vale of Tempe, is primarily about Faust's attraction to Helen. She and Pantalis sing a hymn to the moon, and Faust (dressed as a fifteenth-century knight) is in awe of the scene's natural beauty. After Helen tells the story of Troy's destruction, he acknowledges her ideal female beauty, and they pledge their love to each other. In the epilogue, Faust is a very old man in his laboratory, nearing death and feeling disappointment. Hoping to ensure his damnation, Mefistofele wants him to fly through the air so that he will continue to focus on earthly matters, but he declines. When Mefistofele calls up a vision of sirens, Faust is not distracted because he has just had a glimpse of heaven and knows that it is the only place where he can experience tranquility. "Oh, stay thee, thou art blissful!" is Faust's call to God for salvation (28). Although the devil tries to intercept Faust's soul in transit, it soars upward to salvation in heaven.

Lurie and Boito's Faust. How does this outline of the opera's events relate to David Lurie? Although Mefistofele is a force of negation, ruin, death, and chaos, he is part of God's overall comic plan: "I am only a portion of that great force / That always and forever thinketh ill but well doeth" (10).[20] These lines foreshadow Faust's salvation after his realization that true bliss comes only from God. The trajectory of his growth, however, differs markedly from Lurie's. Faust's realization comes at the eleventh hour after a long period of dalliance with the devil; Lurie's initial fall leads to some measure of humility and a long process of abasement and slow individuation. Unlike Faust, he is not ushered into heaven at the end of the novel; instead he has been opened to the unconscious and may achieve further growth as a result. Despite these differences, however, Faust's enlargement comes—as it does for Lurie—through various encounters with passion and the feminine. First, Coetzee's fire imagery harkens back to Boito's association of Mefistofele with fire and passion: the devil's "tracks are flame" (8), there is wild fire at the witches' Sabbath (15), and fire corresponds to "the sweet fruits that vice doth offer" (4). Second, Faust experiences the feminine on two main levels—an actual young woman (Gretchen) and the archetype (Helen). The fact that he projects his anima onto Gretchen, ruins her life, and finds her in chains reflects his lack of individuation. Helen represents a "love far more sublime" (24), and he longs to immerse himself in the smell and sound of her "sweet idiom" (25). But since she too is merely an object of projection, he realizes at the end of the opera that neither experience of the feminine is satisfactory.

> All mortal mysteries I have proved—
> The Ideal [Helen], the Real [Gretchen];
> The love of simple maidenhood,
> And of the higher goddess—
> Yet the Real was sorrow, and but a dream the Ideal.
>
> (26)

This dual experience of the feminine also sums up a major part of Lurie's experience, which coalesces around Melanie who is simultaneously a young woman like Gretchen and a catalyst for archetypal possession.

If Lurie's *Boito and the Faust Legend: The Genesis of Mefistofele* concerns the *character* Mefistofele, then perhaps the title implies some interest in the origin and workings of the shadow. More likely, however, the monograph plumbs the origins of the opera in a more general way that includes Mefistofele but does not focus exclusively on him. If this assumption is correct, then Lurie's book probably deals with the work to which Boito is heavily indebted, Goethe's *Faust* (the opera consists of vignettes chosen from the drama, and Goethe quotations serve as epigraphs for the various acts). Two questions thus arise: How does *Disgrace* echo *Faust* in a way that is significant for a reading of Lurie and the anima? And how do Jung's insights on the drama enhance a reading of the novel? The answers will not add to the Jungian study of *Faust*, to which Edward F. Edinger's *Goethe's* Faust: *Notes for a Jungian Commentary* contributes a great deal, but considering Lurie in light of the ur-text will shed some light on Coetzee's allusive method.

Lurie and Goethe's Faust. Patricia Casey Sutcliffe establishes a number of important parallels between the two characters.[21] Both are disillusioned, aging professors who use women to keep their passion alive but eventually experience revelations, learn the value of selfless love, and connect to the eternal feminine. Lurie experiences the eternal feminine in an enjoyable moment that he would prolong forever, the kind for which Faust would surrender his soul: "There is a moment of utter stillness which he would wish prolonged for ever [sic]" (218). Sutcliffe also suggests that sacrificing *Driepoot* reverses Faust's attempt to save Gretchen and that Lurie is Mephistophelean in his capacity for deception and self-deception, as Rosalind points out (Coetzee 188). More can be said about the two scholars, however. Although they have much in common, Lurie is unlike Faust in journeying away from sensual delights and toward the things that promote psychological health and well-being. Lurie may not fully register the inner value of his experiences, but *Disgrace* is nonetheless a tale of individuation, as previously uncharted parallels between the novel and the drama bear out.

In *Faust* the repression of the natural man emerges as an academic person's fundamental problem in an exchange between Mephistopheles and a character identified as Student. The young man speaks negatively about the university's "maze of brick and wall" as well as its lack of green space, adding that in such a constricted setting he "cannot think or see or hear" (lines 1881–87). In other words, academic life requires the repression of the part of us that longs for a connection to nature—the same basic ill that Laurens van der Post diagnoses in modern man. It is also a privileging of mind and spirit over libido and the senses, the basic split in the Western psyche during the Christian era. A bit later (lines 2023–36), Mephistopheles urges the student to impress women with his title, lure them into his study, and seduce them. Goethe is describing the basic situation of David Lurie, a man whose professional role institutionalizes repression of the libido but who indulges in illicit sensuality with one of his own students. The split between body and spirit is the *psychomachia* that the following lines nicely express: "Two souls, alas, are dwelling in my breast, / And either would be severed from its brother"; one involves "earthly lust," while the other impels Faust to the "realms of lofty forebears" (lines 1112–17). The contrast is more starkly and beautifully stated in Christopher Marlowe's mighty line: "Hell strives with grace for conquest in my breast" (scene 17, line 70). As a result of this *psychomachia*, Faust leaves academia, and Lurie is ejected from it. Faust says, "The web of thought is all in slashes, / All knowledge long turned dust and ashes." Now he turns to "the depths of sensual life / [so that] The blaze of passions [may] be abated!" (lines 1748–51). In a clear *enantiodromia*, Faust abandons scholarship and embraces sensuality, believing that the latter will relieve his lust, but it is as if he were saying that gasoline can put out a fire. As Lurie discovers, the opposite results because lust perpetuates itself. The senses, once fed, react to years of repression by demanding more and more gratification. Faust summarizes his situation (and Lurie's) by stating that he is at a weird liminal time of life, "too old to be content with play / To[o] young to be without desire."[22] He envies the young men who indulge their sensuality at Burgdorf's Tavern yet realizes that what the world offers is hollow and that he should abstain (lines 1546–47).

Knowing that the senses are where Faust is most vulnerable, Mephistopheles becomes an agent of anti-individuation by attempting to corrode the scholar's will through the very things that academic life has denied him: songs, pictures, smells, tastes, and touch (lines 1436–46). Basically, the devil prompts Faust to choose the lesser good over the greater by exchanging "reflection," "introspection," "intelligence and science" for "dissipation" and "shallow insignificance" (lines 1828–30, 1851, and 1860–61). The goal, in short, is to lure Faust into becoming even more anima-possessed than Lurie. Referring to Helen, Mephistopheles states, "That paragon of women, sirrah, / Shall soon confront you in the flesh" (lines 2601–02), which seems to portend something positive, as in the idea that Helen and Paris are "Ideals female and male, ideally mated" (line 6185). But in an aside, the true intention is immediately revealed: "No fear—with this behind your shirt / You'll soon see Helen of Troy in every skirt" (lines 2603–04). Every woman, no matter how unattractive, will soon become a distracting delight; Mephistopheles hopes that Faust will reel "from desire to fulfillment, / And in fulfillment languish for desire" (lines 3249–50). Instead, Faust falls for Gretchen who is condemned for accidentally poisoning her mother and for drowning the child who results from their union. If he finds Gretchen beautiful, he considers Helen in Part II "Beauty made flesh" (line 6483), the anima sprung to life. All other women pale in comparison with her, and on her he projects "[d]esire, love, worship, adoration, frenzy!" (line 6500). As he loses himself in her, she becomes his "sole desire" (line 7412). Ironically, she herself utters a maxim that Faust ignores to his peril: "An ancient truth, alas, is proved once more through me: / That beauty and good fortune are but fleetly joined" (lines 9939–40). In the aftermath of Lurie's experience with Melanie, he experiences the full force of this disconnection. The psychological moral is nicely summed up by the character Erichtho: "For he who has not learnt to rule / His inner self, is only too intent to rule / His neighbor's will to suit his own imperious mind" (lines 7015–17).

Yet *Faust* also mentions a better way to lead one's life that has clear parallels in *Disgrace*. In the witch's kitchen scene, Faust and Mephistopheles discuss ways to transform Faust into a younger man. When the devil notes that "nature's way to youth is apter" (line 2348) for this purpose than a magic potion, Faust demands to know what that way is. Ironically, Mephistopheles gives an honest answer.

MEPHISTOPHELES
Go out into the fields, today,
Fall to a-hoeing, digging,
Contain yourself, your mind and mood,
Within the narrowest of spheres,
Subsist on uncommingled food,
Live as a beast with beasts and spurn not chores unsung,
In person spread your crop-fields with manure;
That is the best resource, you may be sure,
Through eighty years to stay forever young!

FAUST:
I am not used to that, it goes against my marrow
To put my hand to hoe or harrow.
A narrow life would suit me not at all.

(lines 2353–64)

The rural life, simple diet, and manual labor that Faust rejects as a viable way of reaching his goal are an apt description of the life that Lurie embraces when he moves to Lucy's smallholding. Much later in the play, the Astrologer also provides good advice—so good that Mephistopheles must be glad that Faust is not present: one should *be* what one wants to attract, promote joy through temperance, earn what one desires through hard work, and maintain a positive attitude (lines 5053–56). Neither Faust nor Lurie ever takes these suggestions to heart, which is why Lurie, though he makes psychological progress, remains "not a bad man but not good either." Having absented himself from the city, he consciously resists the kind of psychological makeover that would result from embracing the Astrologer's advice. In Ralph Waldo Emerson's terms, he takes his "giant" (shadow) with him when he travels to Lucy's house (104).

Consequently, Lurie never fully overcomes his shortcomings, as the discovery that his own house has been robbed makes clear. *Faust* again provides a parallel, this time in Phorcyas's words:

> He who remains at home, preserving choice estate,
> At pains as much to caulk the tall apartments' walls
> As to secure the roof before the thrust of rain,
> Will surely prosper all the long days of his life;
> But he who frivolously crosses, on flighty soles,
> The hallowed straight-rule of his threshold, lawless of mind,
> He will, returning, find the old place, to be sure,
> But altogether changed, if not destroyed outright.
>
> (lines 8974–81)

He who leaves his house while he is in in a lawless state of mind will find, upon his return, that the house, having been subject to lawless behavior (robbery), has become an emblem of his own psyche, and so it is upon Lurie's return to Cape Town. Obviously such progress as he makes during his absence is not full-blown individuation, but what really matters is that he makes an effort. He tries, and in *Faust* effort counts. As the Lord observes, "Man ever errs the while he strives" (line 317); the best that man can achieve is what the Angels call "ceaseless toil." To such a person God grants redemption, especially if love adds intercession (lines 11,935–41). Of course, *Disgrace* is not eschatological, but Lurie (unlike Faust) does continue to toil despite his many errors and, as a result, does make some progress.

Jung and Faust.   Believing that "[t]he Christian psyche is fatally split between Christ and Satan, spirit and nature, heaven and hell" (Edinger 42), Jung understands *Faust* to enact this fundamental split within modern persons.[23] Jung actually took his identification with Faust, the character, a step further by carving "Shrine of Philemon—Repentance of Faust" into stone over the entrance to Bollingen tower. The inscription relates to a scene late in the play where Faust mistreats an elderly couple, Philemon and Baucis, because he wants their land. The inscription in stone indicates that Jung "took upon himself the guilt [for this action] that Faust evaded" (Edinger 84). Whereas Faust himself lives a dissolute life but ascends to heaven nonetheless, Jung consciously worked toward wholeness throughout his life in ways that repair the rift within the modern psyche. The themes of guilt and redemption that characterize Jung's approach to *Faust* also inform an approach to Lurie's journey: although he is guilty like Faust, as he acknowledges to the committee of inquiry, his ejection from the university marks the start of his search for greater self-understanding.

In particular, Lurie shares Faust's confrontation with the shadow and struggle with the Promethean attitude. Jung considers Mephistopheles and Wagner to represent competing alternatives for Faust: the Promethean drive for sex and power (the shadow) versus the life of the thinker (*CW* 6, par. 345).[24] In other words, Faust is presented with the judgment of Paris—the choice among power (Hera), love (Venus), and knowledge (Athena) (Edinger 97). Whereas Faust "seek[s] a renewal of libido, the life energy that makes existence exciting and meaningful" (Edinger 32), Lurie must come to terms with the waning of sexual libido and physical attractiveness. In his case, the drive is perhaps for sex *as* power over Soraya and Melanie, and the affair with Melanie leads to various confrontations with Ryan, who with his goatee stands in for Mephistopheles by providing a reminder of the shadow, the part of the psyche that Lurie would rather keep hidden. There is little doubt that Jung would affirm this association because he identifies Goethe's devil as "the man with the pointed beard" (*CW* 11, par. 88–89, 119, 136–37, and 211). But whereas Mephistopheles is an agent of power, Ryan merely presents a challenge to Lurie's authority as a professor and, later at the theater, a reminder of past misdeeds.

Jung further considers the Promethean attitude in Faust to mean equating the ego and the Self—believing, for example, that gratifying the ego via the libido is one's highest good. In Edinger's words, "Faust does not make a distinction between the ego and the Self and thus falls into a grandiose inflation which must lead inevitably to a fall" (31). Indeed, Jung calls Faust "the medieval Prometheus" and notes "that the Faustian attitude must be abandoned before the individual can become an integrated whole" (*CW* 6, par. 315, 188). Jung also states: "Faust's redemption began at his death. The divine, Promethean character he had preserved all his life fell away from him only at death, with his rebirth. Psychologically, this means that the Faustian attitude must be abandoned before the individual can become an integrated whole" (*CW* 6, par. 317). Whereas Faust indulges his Promethean attitude for many years, Lurie is jolted out of that mindset by being fired. As this chapter has charted, that event starts a slow process of deflation that culminates in his anti-Promethean affirmation at the end of the novel. It is not, as Linda Seidel holds, that "the final event in the story [giving up *Driepoot* is] a kind of spiritual suicide on the part of a man who feels unmanned" (par. 15). Surrendering the dog is not negative inflation but negative capability; what Lurie achieves is not a sense of grace but simply a peaceful acceptance of a situation that he cannot control.[25]

Jung considers *Faust* to be a drama about the union of the masculine and feminine principles (*CW* 14, par. 327). Indeed, the drama is the source of his stages of eroticism, which can be used to track Faust's and Lurie's respective journeys.[26] Just as both characters move away from a Promethean attitude, so they also move from the purely biological aspect of the feminine to something higher. The first stage is Eve who represents instinct and biological motherhood; her representative in *Faust* is Gretchen and, in *Disgrace*, Lucy's mother Evelina as well as Lucy herself who is pregnant at the close of the novel.[27] Helen, or sexual *eros*, is present in *Disgrace* as Lurie's attitude toward prostitutes and Melanie.[28] However, the fact that the character Helen, Lucy's lesbian partner, has left the farm suggests the waning of *eros'* importance for the aging academic. Mary, religious devotion or spiritual motherhood, corresponds perhaps to Teresa Guiccioli in Lurie's chamber opera, for he is devoted to her in a purely spiritual sense as he is to no flesh-and-blood woman. Finally, "Woman Eternal" in *Faust* (line 12,110)—wisdom that is personified as Sophia or Sapientia in Jung—corresponds to the women who provide Lurie with sound advice: Rosalind, Lucy, and Bev.[29] Coetzee is quite clear that Lucy fits this category, for as Lurie watches her working in her field, he sees her as "a young woman, *das ewig Weibliche*," the eternal feminine (218).[30] Nor is it any coincidence that as the novel ends Lurie is with Bev at the animal clinic, for she has helped bring about his positive change.

For Jung, individuation in *Faust* involves not only such progress as Lurie achieves among the stages of eroticism but also a *nekyia* or encounter with the unconscious. In this connection, Jung mentions the witches' Sabbath and the "chimerical vision of classical antiquity" (*CW* 15, par. 212), but even more fundamentally the descent to the mothers is considered a descent into the collective unconscious. In preparation, Mephistopheles gives Faust a key and tells him to touch it to a tripod in that nether realm. Jung writes:

> In the realm of the mothers he [Faust] finds the tripod, the Hermetic vessel in which the "royal marriage" is consummated. But he needs the phallic wand [the key Mephistopheles gives him] in order to bring off the greatest wonder of all—the creation of Paris and Helen. The insignificant-looking tool in Faust's hand is the dark creative power of the unconscious, which reveals itself to those who follow its dictates and is indeed capable of working miracles.
>
> (*CW* 5, par. 182)

A tripod plus a key is a quaternity, which for Jung is a highly positive image of the Self. For example, in *Memories, Dreams, Reflections*, he quotes Mephistopheles's instructions regarding the tripod and the key (lines 6287–88) to emphasize the point:

> Only gradually did I discover what the mandala really is: "Formation, Transformation, Eternal mind's eternal recreation." And that is the self, the wholeness of the personality, which if all goes well is harmonious, but which cannot tolerate self-deception. My mandalas were cryptograms concerning the state of the self which were presented to me anew each day.
>
> (195–96)

Jung adds: "Touching the tripod with the key and the *hieros gamos* [sic] prefigure the 'chymical' marriage of Faust to Helen, the sister anima. Their child Euphorion is the third renewal form of Mercurius" (*CW* 18, par. 1698). Jung further notes that Euphorion, the Boy Charioteer, and Homunculus all die by fire.[31] *Disgrace* echoes this nexus of images. First, the tripod of the mothers and Faust's key/wand become a crippled dog and a syringe. *Driepoot* (Dutch and Afrikaans: tripod or three-legged), the dog who likes Lurie's music, and the needle filled with sedative are a quaternity that produces death.[32] Second, the immolation of the three characters in Faust corresponds to the thugs' crime of setting Lurie on fire with methylated spirits. The dog's literal death and Lurie's physical injury have their counterpart in figurative deaths in his life: the termination of his professional career, the theft of his truck, and the robbery at his home.

Conclusion

Of course, *Faust* is a drama in two parts; it is really two complete plays stitched together. Edinger suggests that Part I is about Faust's experience of the personal unconscious, whereas Part II concerns his archetypal encounters within the collective unconscious.[33] In other words, the juxtaposition is between conscious experience and deeper meaning. For example, Part I presents Faust's despair, and Part II dramatizes that quality on the collective, transpersonal level. *Faust*'s two parts therefore resemble the two main settings in *Disgrace*, Cape Town and the Eastern Cape. Although part two in both works includes persons and places from part one, Goethe's basic contrast, as Jung understood it, is a distinction between personal experience for its own sake and personal experience as a representation of collective experience. In neither work, however, is this distinction ironclad. Events, whether they are personal or have a collective resonance, happen to Faust throughout the drama, much as Lurie's point of view is maintained throughout the novel. Lurie's sexual dalliances in the early chapters have political resonance (Soraya, for example, has dark skin); and the thugs' actions in the province, though representative of struggles in post-apartheid South Africa, have clear personal consequences.

One can take the parallels between *Faust* and *Disgrace* no further because the two main characters' paths ultimately diverge. As Jung affirmed, Faust's healing takes place in the afterlife, but Lurie's disgrace promotes a slow process of individuation in this life. Although he is "[n]ot a bad man but not good either"—a mixture of Faust and Mephistopheles—there are undeniable signs of progress, particularly with the anima. At the end of the novel he illustrates Edinger's statement about Faust: "The Care anima, if accepted, could bring recognition of his feelings of guilt and remorse and thus lead to healing of his dissociation and redemption in this life rather than in the life beyond" (83). Whereas Faust's healing takes place post-mortem, Lurie's final acceptance of things as they may not ideally be signifies genuine change. In the psychological sense, the ending of *Disgrace* heralds a more hopeful future than "giving him up" may at first imply.

Notes

1 This note mentions the studies of *Disgrace* that are most relevant to a Jungian psycho-logical approach. Sounding Platonic rather than Jungian, Chris N. van der Merwe and Pumla Gobodo-Madikizela state, "The way to healing, *Disgrace* suggests, lies in the return to the great archetypes of the mind, especially beauty, goodness and love" (98). Although Laura Wright identifies Lucy "[a]s the feminine principle that denies male determinism" (83), Jungian archetypes and individuation are not present in the previous criticism. Instead, Lurie's psychological development is frequently discussed in terms of his imagination and its capacity for empathy or sympathy, particularly in connection with Wordsworth and Byron. For this approach, see Margot Beard (imagination overcomes psychological isolation), Philip Dickinson (sympathetic imagination is contaminated by stupidity and other affective states), Jana María Giles (sympathetic imagination results in John Keats's negative capability), Nora Hämäläinen (sympathetic imagination leads to something akin to Christian grace), and Claire Heaney (Lurie may not achieve sympa-thetic imagination). Other studies of Coetzee's use of the Romantic poets include those by Melinda Harvey (Wordsworth), Kai Easton (Byron), and Pieter Vermeulen (Wordsworth). For commentary on whether Lurie achieves a state of grace, see Derek Attridge (how grace/disgrace functions in the novel), Erik Grayson (Lurie achieves peace but not necessarily grace), and Charles Sarvan (Lurie moves toward grace and achieves a "secular salvation" [n.p.]).

2 Alternatively, Harvey suggests that Coetzee names his protagonist after two recent practitioners of the campus novel, David Lodge and Alison Lurie (95).

3 Beard explicates Lurie's misreading of "Lara" as follows: "he narrowly identifies Lara with Lucifer, thereby reducing the complexity of the character" (n.p.).

4 Reflecting on what Lucy has become, Lurie supposes that "perhaps history had the larger share" in producing her (61).

5 For a summary of Jung's insights on prostitution, see "The Anima and Prostitution" in my book *A Jungian Study of Shakespeare: The Visionary Mode* (124ff.).

6 The play, "a comedy of the new South Africa" (23), is set in Hillbrow, Johannesburg, where, as Attridge points out, racial mixing freely took place (n.p.).

7 The statement resonates with Mephistopheles's reference to "my cousin, the Snake" (Goethe, line 2048).

8 Harvey points out that the committee satirizes South Africa's Truth and Reconciliation Commission (105). In addition, Lurie's experience with colleagues on the committee makes the destruction of his career a faint parallel to the fall of Troy. Like the city, Lurie is sacked; but unlike what happens to Faust, his departure is no great loss to Cape Technical University or to its communications department.

9 In mythology, Leda gives birth to Helen and Pollux as a result of a rape by Zeus who takes the form of a swan. Seidel considers the rape of Leda by Zeus to be analogous to the rape of Africa by Europe (par. 18). Pollux and Castor, his mortal half brother, set Helen free after her kidnapping by Theseus and Pirithous. Goethe's Helena mentions Castor and Pollux at lines 8501 (childhood) and 8852 (rescue). Since Coetzee's Pollux is a child who *does* rape, the novel ironically inverts the classical character. Laurence Wright suggests that Castor and Pollux are in a yin/yang relationship and that Lurie ironically stands in for the more spiritual and intellectual Castor (162). Paul J. C. M. Franssen deals with the classical background of Coetzee's Pollux.

10 The statement echoes the end of Chapter 3: "But if she [Melanie] has got away with much, he has got away with more; if she is behaving badly, he has behaved worse" (28).

11 Beard is helpful regarding the contrast between Melanie (dark) and Lucy (light) but suggests that the two women come together in the opera, which is to be accompanied by Lucy's toy banjo. Since Wordsworth is to Lucy as Byron is to Teresa, "daughter and mistress, Wordsworth and Byron, symbolically fuse" (Beard n.p.). Sarvan points out that Melanie grew up in the region where Lucy now farms (n.p.). Harvey notes that "Mélani: the dark one" (Coetzee 18) links Melanie to the Middle Eastern Soraya and to Africa as the heart

of darkness (104). Van der Merwe and Gobodo-Madikizela note that Melanie "plays the role of a 'coloured' character" in her theater production (79). Laura Wright considers Melanie to be "biracial" (89–90).

12 Sutcliffe points out that the word *Lösung* resonates "with Hitler's *Endlösung* ('final solution'), [which] means 'solution,' both in the concrete (liquid) and abstract sense" (191). In other words, Coetzee associates the euthanasia of animals (and, by extension, the treatment of blacks under apartheid) with the Holocaust.

13 For a similar idea, see Laurens van der Post's "Our Mother Which Art in Earth" (10–11).

14 Laura Wright notes that "Lucy's banjo [was] an instrument created and first played by black Africans" (94). Her source is Cecelia Conway's chapter in the Works Cited (135). Brian Macaskill notes that the banjo "directly descended from the three-stringed African akonting and its close relatives" (172).

15 The idea that the composing process is active imagination is supported by Laurence Wright's comment that the "chamber opera ... thins to a duet, a musical dialogue, between Teresa in her fifties and the shade of the dead Byron, and finally to a one-sided, all-absorbing 'inner duet' in which Lurie hears only the music of Teresa" (161). Colleen M. Sheils considers the opera's significance for Lurie's "inner psyche," his unconscious, "in both its private and public domains" (38), reading his retreat into art as his surrender of ego and a journey into the heart (40, 44). Byron's refusal to respond to Teresa's call to return from the dead resonates ambiguously with Lurie's wishes regarding the world (47), but Sheils too negatively evaluates the outcome. Although Lurie gives up Byron and leaves the opera incomplete, he *has* engaged with the unconscious, and that is progress in itself.

16 Attridge rightly points out that Lurie's feelings for the abandoned bulldog parallel "his feeling of affinity with the widowed and loverless Teresa Guiccioli" (n.p.).

17 Van der Merwe and Gobodo-Madikizela state that "Petrus's name suggests that he is reliable as a rock" in his protection of Lucy (86); however, he is also complicit in the robbery and rape. They further suggest that Lucy's agricultural activities and the rise of Petrus "oppose the conventions of the traditional farm novel (*plaasroman*)" (88).

18 For example, Sarvan states that Lurie "achieves moral regeneration and tranquility" (n.p.).

19 Boito's opera premiered on March 5, 1868 at La Scala, Milan ("Arrigo Boito" 90). *Faust* was written between 1798 and 1800.

20 This is one of the lines that Boito imports directly from Goethe. Mephistopheles identifies himself as "[p]art of that force which would / Do ever evil, and does ever good" (*Faust*, lines 1335–36).

21 Laurence Wright's article on "Lurie's Learning" provides a more general overview of the meaning behind his three monographs.

22 Lurie originally believes that his relation to his opera, *Byron in Italy*, will be "between a yearning to prolong the summer of the passionate body and a reluctant recall from the long sleep of oblivion"; however, instead "he is held in the music itself" (184).

23 Kevin O'Neill's analysis of the novel resonates meaningfully with Jung's point about modernity. O'Neill observes that "Lurie has 'descended' to the world of the animals" and that he "becomes a true dog-man" (225, 222). In Jungian terms, Lurie experiences *enantiodromia*, a swing from intellection as a professor to affirmation of the body in his role as dog psychopomp. It is somewhat difficult, however, to reconcile O'Neill's notion of a complete descent to dogdom with the creation of an opera.

24 Jung's translator glosses Mephistopheles's name as follows: "From L. *mephitis*, a noxious exhalation from the earth" (*CW* 13, par. 295, n. 8). Edinger states that the name means "lover of the sulphurous fumes of hell" (29). A note in the text of *Faust* cites the Hebrew *Mephistoph*, "destroyer of the good" (7, n. 4).

25 Keats mentions negative capability in his December 21–27, 1817 letter to George and Tom Keats (1276). Note that Rosalind mentions "Grace" by mistake when thinking of Lucy's partner Helen (187). Hayes points out that Coetzee views the body as having

"the same place in his outlook as the concept of 'grace' in Christian theology"; specifically, the body's ability "to overwhelm the understanding and reform the desires . . . is akin to the working of grace" (105, 108).

26 Jung's main description of the stages of eroticism appears in *CW* 16, par. 361. See also *CW* 15, par. 211.

27 Lucy's pregnancy resonates with Coetzee's mention in 1987 of South Africa's laws against miscegenation. See Patrick Hayes (97).

28 Jung associates Helen with Henry Rider Haggard's Ayesha (*CW* 10, par. 75).

29 In the background no doubt is Shakespeare's Rosalind in *As You Like It* who gives relational advice to the lovesick Orlando. Both Rosalinds challenge people's illusions.

30 Sutcliffe identifies the German phrase as a direct borrowing from *Faust*, line 12,110 (176). One may take issue, however, with her idea that Faust's paying court to Helen parallels Lurie's beginning anew on Lucy's farm (179). As Jung's schema suggests, Helen and Lucy represent different stages in Lurie's experience of the feminine. Helen is to anima possession as Lucy is to good advice (Sophia). In addition, a passage from Boito's opera is relevant: Sophia's presence in an old proverb that Mefistofele quotes, "That wives with wise heads are rarely straying" (12), echoes Faust's "craving for all-wisdom" (4), though the former means common sense and virtue, while the latter refers to Faust's thirst for knowledge.

31 *CW* 12, par. 243 references "that strange Faustian figure who bursts into flame three times." See also Jung's January 18, 1941 letter to Karl Kerényi: "What chiefly fascinates me is the figure of the Homunculus, who appears in threefold form in Part II. First the Boy Charioteer, then Homunculus, and finally Euphorion. They all end in fire" (*Letters* 1.291). Laurence Wright links Euphorion and Lurie in terms of "errant sexuality" and notes that "Euphorion dies like Icarus" (153).

32 Other quaternities in the novel are equally problematic. The three thugs and Lucy produce life that will forever be a child of rape. Also, Lucy, Rosalind, Bev, and Lurie are a massive knot of (familial) dysfunction.

33 Edinger contrasts "despair and psychological bankruptcy" in Part I with "a similar condition on the collective or transpersonal level" in Part II (46).

7

"THE EYES IN THE TREES ARE WATCHING"

The Dissociated Anima and African Agency in Barbara Kingsolver's *The Poisonwood Bible*

During his Bugishu Psychological Expedition, C. G. Jung not only studied the African people but also examined the impact that the environment had on himself. In effect, his own psyche was as important an object of study as the dreams of the people he interviewed. To his credit, he understood that Africa was not a *tabula rasa* where the civilized could etch their will upon the primitive but instead an active agent capable of powerfully affecting Western visitors. Just as Jung's BPU was partly about Africa's influence on the European psychologist, Barbara Kingsolver's *The Poisonwood Bible* concerns Africa's impact on an American missionary family.[1] Her use of eye imagery illustrates the point. On the one hand, Orleanna Price's phrase "the eyes in the trees" seems at first to refer to the reader's eyes, but the eyes are more properly the eyes of Africa's people (their *nommo*, or life force, can be "pulled into trees" [210]), as well as the eyes of her deceased (and favorite) daughter, Ruth May, who merges with the spirit of Africa in the final book. On the other, the image implies that Africa is not only an observing eye but also an acting subject, an "I" with its own agency. Like Kingsolver's missionary Nathan Price, Westerners ignore its power at their peril, a point that is central to the novel's postcolonial message.

Nathan has few things in common with the male protagonists discussed in previous chapters, but the eye-related parallels are illuminating. Like Doris Lessing's Charles Watkins, he served in World War II. When hit in the head by a shell fragment, Nathan suffered a concussion and permanent damage to his left eye, which becomes inflamed in Africa by exposure to the poisonwood tree. The "eyepatch" (196) he wore during the war is more reminiscent of the one-eyed terrorist in Laurens van der Post's *A Far-Off Place* than J. M. Coetzee's David Lurie, who emerges from his chrysalis-like bandages a better, though still deeply flawed, person. Like these previously discussed images, however, Nathan's physical injury has psychological resonance. The eye wound signifies not only a monocular devotion to preaching the gospel but also, as Jeanna Fuston White points out, "his own spiritual and psychological damage and the larger colonialist oppression of Africa by white men who could not see past their own self interest [sic]" (132). More significantly, since the left side, as Leah points out, is feminine ("*right* and *left*: the man hand and the woman hand" [113]), injury to the left eye implies that war has affected Nathan's ability to connect with his own feminine side, the anima. In addition, he has survivor guilt, for just as Watkins lost all his comrades (twice), Nathan hid in a pig shed while the Japanese rounded up his comrades, all of whom died on the Bataan Death March as he recuperated in a hospital. When postcolonial upheaval of the sort described by van der Post and Coetzee afflicts the Congo, Nathan apparently attempts to atone for abandoning his unit by remaining in an African jungle because he did not remain in a Philippine jungle. Ironically, whereas his war-related guilt is unjustified, his single vision renders him genuinely culpable for abandoning his wife and their daughters after Ruth May's death. His attempt to save more souls than he lost in the Pacific theater results in both the failure of his ministry and the loss of his family.

Although Nathan's experience in the Army links him to Lessing's character, he is the intellectual and sexual anti-type of Watkins and Lurie, who are both brilliant, promiscuous academics. Nathan, though not highly educated, knows one system of thought well, Christianity, but lacks intellectual curiosity even about properly nuanced interpretation of scripture. The world must adapt to his views, which are right because his reading of the Bible is right. Sexually, too, Nathan contrasts with Watkins (the adulterer) and Lurie (the womanizer). He reportedly regrets the fact that Orleanna has a vagina, is embarrassed by her pregnancies (198), and considers his wife and their four daughters to be "dull-witted, bovine females" (73), though most of them, like Lucy Lurie, have much to teach him.

Because Nathan's brushes with collective shadow during the war have rendered inner work difficult and perhaps impossible (in the course of the novel, he lurches from neurosis to insanity), he is unable to individuate and remains a flat, static character. For example, unlike Watkins and Lurie, Nathan experiences no *nekyia*. Such descent into the unconscious is present in *The Poisonwood Bible* only in Leah's hovering between life and death because of malaria. Instead Nathan projects the shadow onto others in order to stave off the feminine, which could otherwise provide a bridge to the unconscious and foster psychological wholeness. The fact that Kingsolver tells his story not from his point of view but instead from the multiple perspectives of his female family members underscores his lack of roundness and psychological potential. The novel's multiple female narrators thus offer an opportunity to discuss the anima from the outside in.

Chapter 7 provides a psychological complement to the feminist and postcolonial emphases in the previous criticism. It enables a fuller understanding of the novel's relationship to Joseph Conrad's *Heart of Darkness* and argues that Nathan Price is dissociated from the anima in ways that Jung lays out in *Two Essays in Analytical Psychology* in a chapter entitled "Anima and Animus" (*CW* 7, par. 296–340). Nathan's encounter with the collective shadow during the war has stunted his individuation process, and from this psychic wound proceed many of the symptoms of dissociation that Jung discusses. Like Goethe's Faust, Nathan's individual case illustrates, more broadly, the fundamental split that Jung perceived within the psyche of modern persons. *The Poisonwood Bible* responds to these diagnoses, however, with a prescription for psychological balance, a middle ground for cultural accommodation, and an affirmation that Africa is not just an observing eye but also an "I," an acting subject with meaningful agency of its own.

Kingsolver's *Heart of Darkness*

Much of the previous criticism emphasizes postcolonial approaches to *The Poisonwood Bible*.[2] There is very little psychological criticism of the novel, but we may begin moving in a psychological direction by examining its relationship to one of the texts in its bibliography: Joseph Conrad's *Heart of Darkness*. Considering *The Poisonwood Bible* a revision of Conrad's novel is a logical approach that has already received some attention. Héloïse Meire provides a feminist reading, arguing that Kingsolver "creatively answered the feminist call for a departure from Conrad's masculinist conventions" (84–85), particularly by using female narration. Meire notes various similarities between Kurtz and Nathan: violence, rhetoric, madness, and references to both men as Jove.[3] Pamela H. Demory begins by emphasizing that the two works are similar in plot, narrative point of view, portrayal of whites as "soulless and corrupt," and depiction of Africa as "seductive and dangerous" (par. 1).[4] In her view, the Price females' narrations correspond to Marlow's; Axelroot resembles Conrad's Station Manager, brickmaker, and faithless "pilgrims"; and Nathan stands in for Kurtz. Demory considers *The Poisonwood Bible* to revise "what it means for a white man to go crazy in the heart of Africa" (par. 16), properly noting that whereas Kurtz abandons his European ideals in order to practice "unspeakable rites," Nathan never abandons his intention to baptize children in crocodile-infested waters (par. 15). Therefore, DeMarr inaccurately asserts that "[l]ike Kurtz in *Heart of Darkness*, Nathan Price becomes sucked into the mystery and is ultimately destroyed by it" (122).[5] Had Kurtz gone mad trying to apply European values beyond all hope of relevance, he and Nathan would be alike in madness. Nathan is at fault precisely because he is oblivious to the mystery of Africa and certainly does not get "sucked into" it. Even in the face of nature's extremes he fulfills his missionary role. For example, he preaches "a sermon about the Pharaoh's army and the plagues" during the ants' attack and "knew nothing about the children" he baptizes in the rain (307, 374).[6] The latter parodies Jesus's call, "Let the children come to me" (Matt. 19.14), and both episodes suggest that Nathan's ministry is a veneer of pure formalism that privileges the letter of missionary duties over the true spirit of Christianity. He preaches even when it is risible to do so because he is a hack fulfilling a role and therefore a hollow man, like Kurtz and the "soulless, empty men" who overthrow the Congo's newly elected prime minister, Patrice Lumumba (323). Until his bitter end, Nathan is to religion what Lumumba's successor, Joseph Mobutu, is to politics—an agent of American imperialism.

There is still more to say, however, about Kingsolver's use of *Heart of Darkness*, including unnoticed parallels. To begin with, Nathan and Rachel, his eldest daughter, are opposites in the same way that Kurtz and the Accountant are foils. If Nathan succumbs to madness, Rachel does everything she can to ward it off, and like the white-suited Accountant she "stroll[s] through" The Equatorial in a bikini, showing off her gorgeous figure and "platinum-blonde hair" to her male patrons (462). Her strategy for dealing with Africa is basically the Accountant's, and it is complete with one of her frequent malapropisms:

> The way I see Africa, you don't have to like it but you sure have to admit it's out there. You have your way of thinking and it has its, and never the train ye shall meet! You just don't let it influence our mind. If there's ugly things going on out there, well, you put a good stout lock on your door and check it twice before you go to sleep. You focus on getting your own one little place set up perfect, as I have done, and you'll see. Other people's worries do not necessarily have to drag you down.
>
> (516)

Rachel's approach to living in Africa deconstructs The Equatorial's implication of a borderland between black and white, African and European. It is a whites-only establishment where she carefully monitors the black servants to prevent theft.

Rachel's deceased sister, Ruth May, also corresponds to a Conradian character, Marlow's helmsman, who takes a spear through the chest as the steamboat chugs up the river. The detail echoes the fate of Virgil's Palinurus, who falls overboard in a sacrifice that ensures the Trojans' safe passage. Virgil writes that "one single life shall be offered to save many" (Ahl trans.; Book 5, line 815). In the same way, Ruth May dies, her body becoming part of the African soil, so that the other Price women can escape in their various ways, though like Marlow they are changed by their experience. Her life is the *price* that must be paid for the others' safe passage.

One of Conrad's most damning statements involves the deconstruction of European morality, which has a corresponding motif in *The Poisonwood Bible*. Europeans are assumed to be paragons of enlightenment and self-restraint, yet the pilgrims spray the jungle with bullets, whereas the native Africans, though ravenously hungry, show admirable restraint in not eating their white masters. Remarkably, the savages are more civilized than the Europeans on the steamboat. Kingsolver introduces a similar detail in Nathan's physical abuse of his wife and critiques it in the words of Brother Fowles, the novel's wise old man. "In my six years here I saw the practice of wife beating fall into great disfavor," he tells Nathan (257–58). As Mary Ellen Snodgrass states, "To spread Christian practice, he debated husband-wife relations with Tata Ndu so thoroughly that village wife-beating declined" (83). The Baptist minister who strikes his wife is more of a savage than the natives to whom he ministers, just as the Catholic priest on whom he blames his own difficulties is the more successful missionary.

An image common to both *Heart of Darkness* and *The Poisonwood Bible* furthers the point about Nathan's extremism. Marlow states that because he "had peeped over the edge" himself he understands Kurtz who "had made that last stride" and "had stepped over the edge"; Marlow, in contrast, "had been permitted to draw back [his] hesitating foot" (86–87). The statement is similar in intent to Ishmael's "Look not too long in the face of the fire, O man" (Melville 404; chapter 96); *but do look* is the clear implication. In *The Poisonwood Bible* the corresponding images describe Orleanna's marriage—her "long, long fall" from "the edge of another narrow precipice"—and the "precipice" Adah "teetered upon when entering the first grade" (90, 406). Edge and precipice therefore invite application to the family's reaction to the heart of darkness. One can be inured to the darkness like the Accountant and Station Manager or like Rachel and Axelroot (whose similarity adds to the logic of their fake engagement). One can fall off the edge like Kurtz and Nathan. The proper orientation, however, is achieved by Leah and Adah, and it is more constructive than Marlow's use of rivets to occupy his conscious mind. Leah is to the teaching of nutrition, sanitation, and agriculture in Angola (523) as Adah is to scientific research in the United States: the middle sisters achieve a middle way akin to the reformed cave dweller in Plato's allegory who returns to help those in shackles move up to the light. The actual productive assistance that Leah and Adah provide belies the hollow formalism of Nathan's ministry and illustrates the fruitful balance he cannot achieve. Not only have they looked over the edge of the precipice and not fallen; they also bring light to the darkness in their respective ways.

With *Heart of Darkness* in mind, it is possible to defend Kingsolver to a degree against her critics. William F. Purcell criticizes her for treating Africa "as an undifferentiated cultural monolith" ("Essentializing," par. 4), and Brad S. Born critiques the use of Nathan as a caricature of fatherhood, fatherland, and Christianity and of Africa as a mere backdrop for Kingsolver's "good-hearted morality tale" (n.p.). Quoting Chinua Achebe's "An Image of Africa: Racism in Conrad's *Heart of Darkness*," Born takes similar aim at Conrad's use of "Africa as setting and backdrop which eliminates the African as human factor" in order to ridicule Europeans (Achebe 12). However, the idea that Africa is a flat backdrop in each novel is inaccurate. That Kingsolver means to criticize American foreign policy is indisputable, but she takes pains to depict the life and hardships that African people face, as well as the complexity and resonance of the Kikongo language. If Africa were purely a flat backdrop, Kingsolver would not have written words like Tata Ndu's to Nathan:

> "Á, Tata Price," he said in his deep, sighing voice. "You believe we are *mwana*, your children, who knew nothing until you came here. Tata Price, I am an old man who learned from other old men. I could tell you the name of the great chief who instructed my father, and all the ones before him, but you would have to know how to sit down and listen. There are one hundred twenty-two. Since the time of our *mankulu* [ancestors] we have made our laws without help from white men."
>
> (333)

Brother Fowles anticipates this depth of characterization in stating that the chief "is a man of surprising resources" to whom he wants to pay his respects (257, 250).

Whereas Ndu is an actual human being looking back at Nathan, Conrad provides no such native figure in *Heart of Darkness*. Although Kingsolver's tendency to essentialism is a genuine issue, her depiction of Africa is more developed and fair-minded than Conrad's.

Finally, Nathan and Kurtz may both be measured according to the precept that "the tree is known by its fruit" (Matt. 12.33). Both men employ unsound methods in an attempt to achieve a culturally imperialistic goal, but even though Nathan is a caricature his psychic situation has one concession to roundness. Because his experience of the collective shadow in World War II renders him incapable of making progress with the anima, he remains unable even to achieve the "apprentice-piece" with other men (*CW* 9i, par. 61) so that intellectual empathy eludes him. As a result, the qualities of the five amazing females in his own home go totally unnoticed, especially the fact that his wife, in Adah's words, is "an entire botanical garden waiting to happen" (410). Instead, Nathan's psyche is like Orleanna's china plate, which he breaks—a round object that signifies the wholeness of the Self now lies in useless pieces. Since he cannot heal in others what is broken in himself, his ministry in Kilanga bears no more fruit than the sterile vegetable garden. Kurtz is to Nathan, then, as rapacious effectiveness and the ruin of a district are to a ministry that has only marginal impact on a native community. Kurtz acts; Nathan appears.

Nathan and the dissociated anima

Those who see Kingsolver's *The Poisonwood Bible* through the lens of Conrad's *Heart of Darkness* emphasize Kurtz's insanity and see the same in Nathan, especially when Leah sees him as "a small, befuddled stranger" and years later admits to having been "scared of seeing him as a crazy person" (80, 488). A Conradian approach still emphasizes the novel's political allegory, but Nathan also participates in psychological allegory that aligns almost perfectly with C. G. Jung's statements about the anima. Jung would diagnose Nathan's problem as dissociation from the anima, which therefore cannot provide a bridge to the unconscious.[7] Jung states that the

> man who identifies himself absolutely with his reason and his spirituality
> . . . is in danger of becoming *dissociated* from his anima and thus losing
> touch altogether with the compensating powers of the unconscious. In a
> case like this the unconscious usually responds with violent emotions,
> irritability, lack of control, arrogance, feeling of inferiority, moods,
> depression, outbursts of rage, etc., coupled with lack of self-criticism and
> the misjudgments, mistakes, and delusions which this entails.
>
> (*CW* 13 par. 454; emphasis added)

Nathan matches this definition with great specificity, for he identifies most with reason and spirituality. As Leah says, "My father believes in enlightenment," and she goes on to identify that quality with his learning to read "parts of the Bible in Hebrew" (42). His dissociation from the anima registers in his disdain for his five females—he does not realize that they are all girl guides, psychopomps, pearls of great price, who could help him get to know the anima.[8] The final part of Jung's statement fits Nathan precisely—"Father's escalating rage" (219), physical violence against his family members, an arrogant assumption that he is right about everything, and multiple mistakes rooted in cultural centrism.

According to "Anima and Animus," the first step in a male's journey with the unconscious is the mother's role as a "safeguard against the unconscious" (*CW* 7, par. 316). Jung notes that it is problematic for a male to pass from mother to wife without the mediating influence of the "men's house" (*CW* 7, par. 314), which provides separation from the mother and the opportunity to do shadow work, the first step in the individuation process. What happens to Nathan Price? As Orleanna's retrospective narrative indicates, his wartime experience with the collective shadow was so traumatic that he is incapable of doing anima work properly. He does not move beyond the shadow stage and has been irrevocably altered by his experience in the Philippines. Orleanna notes, for example, that his "cheerful V-mail letter" from a hospital on Corregidor Island "was the last I would ever hear from the man I'd married" (196). The young preacher she had known is gone, and he returns to her with diminished sight in his left eye, which signals that his connection to the anima has been permanently disabled, like a burned-out circuit that can no longer carry electrical current. Since he is fixed in his need for shadow work, the anima remains dissociated and cannot provide a bridge to the unconscious (*CW* 7, par. 339). Its energy instead manifests negatively in Nathan's relationship with Orleanna, as Jung describes:

> The modern civilized man has to forgo this primitive but nonetheless admirable system of education [the men's house]. The consequence is that the anima, in the form of the mother-imago, is transferred to the wife; and the man, as soon as he marries, becomes childish, sentimental, dependent, and subservient, or else truculent, tyrannical, hypersensitive, always thinking about the prestige of his superior masculinity.
>
> (*CW* 7, par. 316)

Nathan has not forgone his experience with other men; it has simply rendered him incapable of doing anima work in proper ways. Orleanna does not stand in for the mother whom Kingsolver never mentions, but "truculent, tyrannical, hypersensitive, always thinking about the prestige of his superior [religious system]" is an apt description of Nathan in Kilanga where he doubles down on his convictions. As Adah puts it, "Only Nahtan [the spelling is one of her palindromes] remains essentially himself, the same man however you look at him. The others of us have two sides" (276). That he is "steady as a stump" (39) seems admirable to Leah in the beginning, but steadiness devolves into intransigence and insanity as the novel progresses.

Jung describes how the repression of the anima is directly proportional to the strength of the persona. Kingsolver too understands that repressed content becomes a nemesis. In the novel's most Jungian statement, Nelson points out, "Leba [Leah], the gods you do not pay are the ones that can curse you best" (208). Jung would affirm this principle, which "The Gospel of Thomas" articulates more eloquently: "If you bring forth what is within you, what you bring forth will save you. If you do not bring forth what is within you, what you do not bring forth will destroy you" (verse 70).[9] This principle applies to Nathan because his minister persona rests upon a foundation of repressed anima. As Jung states, "Society expects, and indeed must expect, every individual to play the part assigned to him as perfectly as possible, so that *a man who is a parson* must not only carry out his official functions objectively, but must at all times and in all circumstances play *the role of parson* in a flawless manner" (*CW* 7, par. 305; emphases added). By identifying his ego with his professional role, Nathan "becomes one with his persona" (*CW* 7, par. 306), believing that he is who he pretends to be and developing a blindness "to the existence of inner realities" (*CW* 7, par. 319). He *is* the surface he projects, which defines his flatness and renders him a caricature.

Nathan's positive inflation shores up his dysfunction. Kingsolver implies that he sees himself as akin to Jesus whose gospel he preaches. Orleanna's comment about his letter from Corregidor mentions "his salvation by the grace of God and a Jap hog manger" (196). He is not born in a manger, but his psychic life is recast in one. After a period of itinerant preaching, the Prices settle in *Bethlehem*, Georgia, where Adah has developed the habit of referring to Nathan as "Our Father," two words that reflect and mock his inflation by echoing of the start of the Lord's Prayer. In addition, he presumes to be able to minister to the folk of Kilanga without knowing their native language and without receiving any training in overseas mission work. Therefore, it is apt that Brother Fowles gets him to recite a warning, via Romans 12.3, "not to think of himself more highly than he ought to think" (253). The priest knows, and Nathan must learn, that inner work requires frank self-assessment.

Repressing the anima, projecting to the world a mere face or mask, and inflating the ego have psychological consequences in private life. As Jung puts it, "Whoever builds up too good a persona for himself naturally has to pay for it with irritability." Jung adds: "What goes on behind the mask is then called 'private life.' This painfully familiar division of consciousness into two figures, often preposterously different, is an incisive psychological operation that is bound to have repercussions on the unconscious" (*CW* 7, par. 305). And a bit later: "Take, for example, the 'spotless' man of honour and public benefactor [missionary preacher], whose tantrums and explosive moodiness terrify his wife and children. What is the anima doing here?" (par. 319). The answer is that the persona/ego nexus represses the anima, which does not manifest as a bridge to the unconscious but instead sparks Nathan's growing rage. It is little wonder that his ministry in Kilanga never flourishes because he cannot bring spiritual fruition to others when his own psychic garden is infertile. He cannot successfully minister to the public when "a vacuum" of estrangement surrounds him at home (*CW* 7, par. 320).

Kingsolver builds other forms of compensation into Nathan's story as well. Jung makes clear that "a compensatory relationship exists between persona and anima" (*CW* 7, par. 304) so that, as the persona strengthens its repressive hold on the unconscious, the push-back from the anima increases. Elsewhere, Jung notes: "Intellect and feeling . . . are difficult to put into one harness—they conflict with one another by definition. Whoever identifies with an intellectual standpoint [as Nathan does with Christianity] will occasionally find his feeling confronting him like an enemy in the guise of the anima" (*CW* 9ii, par. 58). Life in Georgia does not prove sufficient to connect him to the anima, so psyche ups the ante by transporting him to a continent that personifies the feminine heart of darkness. As Jung says, "[t]he anima [like Africa], being of feminine gender, is exclusively a figure that compensates the masculine consciousness" (*CW* 7, par. 328). As Adah puts it, "*Congo* was a woman in shadows, dark-hearted, moving to a drumbeat" (495). The point is that, if one does not individuate, life's lessons reappear in more powerful form. Jung describes this dynamic as follows:

> Our model case [Nathan] behaves, in the world, like a modern European [who thinks himself superior, more civilized]; but in the world of spirits [with respect to the unconscious] he is the child of a troglodyte [a rank beginner who lacks individuation]. He must therefore submit to living in a kind of prehistoric kindergarten [African village] until he has got the right idea of the powers and factors [archetypes] which rule that other world.
>
> (*CW* 7, par. 322)

That kindergarten, one supposes, exists in psychological space; but Kilanga, its geographical equivalent, increases the intensity of the lesson, offering Nathan a chance to do shadow work the right way, in a kind of men's house, with Tata Ndu, Tata Kuvudundu, Brother Fowles, and perhaps Eeben Axelroot. Kingsolver even implies that Kilanga is a place where Nathan could get in touch with the ancient natural man within him by having his daughters mention Pygmies (95, 106, 119, and 137). He might also get in touch with nature itself by learning from Brother Fowles the ability to see God's word in the Creation (248).[10] Africa compensates for Nathan's repression, offering him a chance to individuate; but because the author made him a caricature instead of a round character, the intensification that the setting brings only increases the feedback loop between persona and repression until he devolves into a mad obsession with baptism.

A byproduct of the persona/repression nexus is projection of fault onto others. As Jung notes, the repression of feminine traits leads "contrasexual demands to accumulate in the unconscious," which leads in turn to projection. In other words, what is repressed tries to attract one's attention in the form of projections (*CW* 7, par. 297). More precisely, "So long as the anima is unconscious she is always projected, for everything unconscious is projected" (*CW* 7, par. 314). Nathan has five female family members on whom he can project his dissociated anima, as when he lashes out at Orleanna for idolatry and poor cooking (134) instead of acknowledging that he has not contributed to feeding the family and cannot convert the local people from their false beliefs. Ruth May notes, "Father said, 'They are living in darkness. Broken in body and soul, and don't even see how they could be healed'" (53). His statement is an apt self-description. Fuel for seeing others' faults lies in his belief that his God does too. As Leah states, "And no God, in any heart on this earth, was ever more on the lookout for human failing" (393). She also realizes that he is "always the first to spot flaws and transgressions" (41). Rachel notes, "Usually he can see insults as big as a speck when they're hiding under a rock in the next county over" (164). The biblical allusion—one sees the speck in another person's eye rather than the plank in one's own (Matt. 7.3 and Luke 6.41)—nicely encapsulates the projection process. In addition, Orleanna remembers that he "is quick to blame others for his mistakes" (198). Adah states, for example, that he blames his predecessor for his lack of success, "frequently tak[ing] the name of Brother Fowles in vain, feeling certain now that all the stones in his path were laid by this deluded purveyor of Christian malpractice [Catholicism]" (259). The Prices are clearly aware of Nathan's projection-making. As a result, Rachel notes that "Father would sooner watch us all perish one by one than listen to anybody but himself" (169). This attitude directly opposes Jung's prescription for the dissociated anima, namely active imagination, "the art of conversing with oneself in the setting provided by an affect, as though the affect itself were speaking without regard to our rational criticism" (*CW* 7, par. 323). Nathan could begin to do so simply by not censuring his females and, like Brother Fowles, by trying to understand the native people on their own terms. By not doing so, Nathan is unlike his biblical namesake who tells David of the covenant God is making with him but later rightly reprimands him for committing adultery with Bathsheba (2 Sam. 7 and 12). Kingsolver's Nathan convinces the Congolese of no such covenant and faults others unjustly. Whereas Jung would suggest that he do inner work by "objectivat[ing] the effects of the anima and then try[ing] to understand what contexts underlie those effects" (*CW* 7, par. 327), he remains a caricature, with his projected thoughts creating a one-sided reality in which sin abides in others but not in himself.

Some of Jung's statements in "Anima and Animus" highlight Nathan's lack of depth because they do *not* apply. To begin with, whereas Jung supposes that a man with a dissociated anima "comes under the heel of his wife's slipper" (*CW* 7, par. 309), Orleanna's coming increasingly under Nathan's heel highlights his brutality. Moreover, he never realizes the detrimental feedback loop between developing the persona and repressing the anima. Jung writes: "when a man recognizes that his ideal persona is responsible for his anything but ideal anima, his ideals are shattered, the world becomes ambiguous, he becomes ambiguous even to himself. He is seized by doubts about goodness, and what is worse, he doubts his own good intentions" (*CW* 7, par. 310). Nathan never suffers such doubt because his flatness and inflation do not allow it. Nor does he illustrate this statement: "Then follow remorse, reconciliation, oblivion, repression, and, in next to no time, a new explosion. Clearly, the anima is trying to enforce a separation. This tendency is in nobody's interest. The anima comes between them like a jealous mistress who tries to alienate the man from his family" (*CW* 7, par. 320). For Nathan, there is no such cycle of reconciliation and relapse because he is a never-wavering caricature, even in the bedroom. Jung is of two minds as regards the sexual life of the anima-dissociated man. On the one hand, he suggests that sexual fantasies compensate for his social mask and that "the wives of such men would have a pretty tale to tell" (*CW* 7, par. 307). On the other, Jung's suggestion that compensation can take the form of "limp sexuality" (par. 308) is more in sync with Orleanna's recollection that "Nathan was made feverish by sex, and trembled afterward, praying aloud and blaming me for my wantonness" (198). Because Nathan is unable to connect emotionally and sexually with his wife (denying nature itself), his sexuality compensates allegorically by taking one of his daughters. Ruth May is bitten by a phallic-shaped green mamba, in which "the diabolic genius of nature has attained the highest degree of perfection" (362).

Kingsolver's *via media*

Although much of Jung's theory in "Anima and Animus" is eerily prescient of Nathan's situation in *The Poisonwood Bible*, one statement seems unusually obtuse. "Unfortunately," he writes, "our Western mind . . . has never yet devised a concept, nor even a name, for the *union of opposites through the middle path*, that most funda-mental item of inward experience, which would respectably be set against the Chinese concept of Tao" (*CW* 7, par. 327). The *via media*, or middle way, may be the term that Jung is grasping for, and Kingsolver calls it simply "balance," a word that resonates throughout the text and means both outer accommodation and inner development. The present section demonstrates, first, that *The Poisonwood Bible* uses Nathan's *imbalance* to depict the same split that Jung locates in modern man and, second, that the novel offers, as a moral, a culturally relative and anima-driven "*union of opposites through the middle path*" such as Jung advocates.

Karen Blixen makes a statement in *Out of Africa* that encapsulates Jung's dichotomy: "perhaps the white men of the past, indeed of any past, would have been in better understanding and sympathy with the coloured races than we, of our industrial age, shall ever be. When the first steam engine was constructed, the roads of the races of the world parted, and we have never found one another since" (186). Technology, science, industry, rationalism, Christianity—such are the forces that steer modern persons away from "the coloured races" that live closer to nature and the archetypes. *The Poisonwood Bible* starkly illustrates this dichotomy. Not only does Nathan Price illustrate the dissociated anima; in a larger context, he also embodies the Western culturally centric attitude that the novel criticizes. Rachel calls him "the Father Knows Best of all times" (131), which suggests that he personifies Western patriarchy. Within the family, he dominates his females unjustly, especially by being "in full possession of the country once known as Orleanna Wharton" (200). His unjust criticism of his wife resembles Joakim's treatment of Susanna in Daniel 13 (71), a story that Adah invokes presumably because Nathan, a proponent of the Apocrypha, has exposed her to it. Ironically he does not understand that *he* is a Joakim figure or that Chapter 13 is a Catholic addition, which he ought to despise on principle. Nathan's domination of his family suggests a further parallel to colonial forces personified by the American president and the Belgian king, who seek to promote democracy and to exploit the country's resources, respectively. The fact that Orleanna has a photograph of President Dwight D. Eisenhower in her cooking hut reinforces the connection between familial and political domination. Nathan, of course, is hegemonic in his missionary efforts, promoting Western systems such as Light, the Word, Christianity, and salvation. But in actuality he is to his parishioners as big-game hunters are to their prey: he seeks to convert souls the way hunters seek "the mounted heads of rhinoceros and cheetah" (317–18). His wrong-headed approaches are summed up in his redneck use of dynamite to kill fish in the river: he provides a huge feast (an emblem perhaps of Western wastefulness), but most of the harvested fish putrefy on the banks (69–70), just as he alienates more souls than he converts. Cartesian dualism characterizes his attitude toward natural resources: nature is there to be consumed, and humans are separate from it. For Kingsolver, all of these details add up to the idea that Nathan and his ministry are poisonwood.

In opposition to the Western male values just adumbrated are the feminine qualities assigned to Africa. It is no coincidence that Kingsolver opposes "Father Knows Best" with "Mother May I?," a game that Ruth May uses to break the ice with the native children (111). Instead of Christianity, paganism and idolatry occupy the natives, and even Orleanna acknowledges "the beautiful heathen girl in me" who once flourished (200). Instead of mind/father/law there is the idea that "[a] wife is the earth itself, changing hands, bearing scars" (89). Western medicine yields to throwing the bones (360), colonialism to independent home rule, exploitation to sustainability. Instead of the Christian Word there is word, *nommo*, "the force that makes things live as what they are: man or tree or animal" (209). This life force can migrate from humans to other forms of life so that a tree can be *muntu*, a person (210). Consequently, nonhuman forms of life are respected; the Congolese people have "great feelings for the living world around them" and are "very humble in their debts to nature" (252). In other words, nature is "something precious and dear" (276), the other meaning of "poisonwood." Ultimately, the binaries in the novel coalesce around the dual meanings of that word: the negative sense for the Western/male and the positive sense for the African/female.

The Poisonwood Bible's moral is that a mean between these two extremes, a unity of the best of both the West and Africa, is a desirable and appropriate goal. Kingsolver is advocating much the same point of view that Jung took in his interaction with the Africans whom he encountered on his BPE—respectful curiosity, cultural accommodation, and a willingness to learn from a native people. How, then, does Kingsolver create a *via media*? Halfway between Nathan-as-missionary and Kuvudundu-as-witchdoctor is, of course, Brother Fowles with a name that represents birds, a policy of accommodating Christianity to native ways, and a gift for seeing God's handiwork in nature. He understands that the Bible is sometimes faulty in English translation, that its provenance is culturally relative (247), and that its imagery emphasizes balance between God and nature (252). Under his leadership, church services started with Congolese fertility songs. That the native people do everything "with one eye to the spirit" has not escaped him (246), and he knows that Western missionaries have lessons to learn from their African brethren. Brother Fowles's being fired for "consorting with the natives too much" (249) is a positive credential from Kingsolver's point of view. Relieved of his responsibility to the church in Kilanga, he travels by boat with his English-fluent Congolese wife Celine and their children, dispensing medicine and giving aid in ways that reverse the colonial mission of Kurtz in *Heart of Darkness*: Brother Fowles *gives back* rather than *taking from*.

The marriage of Leah to Anatole provides a parallel image of cultural accommodation. Anatole, the local school teacher, speaks English and French, just as Leah later becomes "passably fluent in Lingala" (420). Their marriage bed—he calls it "the New Republic of Connubia" (519)—and the mixed-race children produced there, like the Fowles children, are images of cultural accommodation and integration. Since Anatole's nickname for her is "*béene-béene*," which means "as true as the truth can be" (286–87), he is married to the truth that Nathan rejects when he no longer even stoops to punish his defiantly assertive daughter. Allegorically, Anatole is properly attuned to the anima. For her part, Leah sets out to help the native people by teaching the women of Angola, much as the Fowles family helps people along the riverbank. The two couples, then, are situated between Nathan and Kuvudundu, who are locked in a zero-sum game, each man seeking to perpetuate his own system by diminishing the other's.

Some of the minor characters also suggest a type of accommodation. Mama Tataba and Methuselah, for example, are culturally liminal figures—one is an African woman who speaks a bit of English and attempts to help the Price family adapt to life in Africa, the other a bird that speaks English words. Losing her services is a setback for the Price family that they never fully overcome, and the parrot's death on Congolese Independence Day is a bad omen not only for the new state but also for the family. If "Hope is a thing with feathers," as Emily Dickinson tells us via Adah (185), then the parrot's death foreshadows failure and despair for both the country and the family. Even the despicable Eeben Axelroot (axle, machinery; root, vegetation) suggests a kind of synthesis by flying his plane to primitive places. But, in his case, a nascent sense of synthetic accommodation winks out because "ax" is also in his name. Reflecting on the American government's intervention, Orleanna remembers "[w]aiting for the ax to fall" in the Congo and in her marriage (323). In actuality, Axelroot is a diamond smuggler, an exploiter of those whose goods he transports, and a mercenary for the American government who helps topple Patrice Lumumba. Axelroot's first name is the more accurate descriptor: "Eben" is Hebrew for stone, which links him to the unaccommodated Nathan and Orleanna who both "turned to stone," though in different ways (393). Nathan, in particular, is "reborn, with a stone in place of his heart" (97).

One may imagine, then, a chart with three columns: Nathan, the colonialists, and the West are on the left; Kuvudundu, his fellow Kilangans, and Africa are on the far right. Even Rachel understands that these categories represent "two opposite worlds crashing into each other" (465). However, in a middle column for cultural liminality, accommodation, and balance are Brother Fowles, Leah, and their two families. The word "balance" is characteristic of that area and appears in many of Leah's chapters because she is cultural accommodation's greatest proponent and voice in the novel. At first it is used ironically when she is unreasonably optimistic about the family's journey as "a great enterprise of balance," and Nathan signals a similar naïve hopefulness in the success of his mission when he asserts that God's world is a system of "work and rewards" that exists "on a big balanced scale" (19, 37). Much later, she ironically proves to be her father's daughter in stating, "Maybe I'll never get over my grappling for balance, never stop believing life is going to be *fair*" (504)—she wishes that she were rewarded in proportion to her efforts. Balance is even a part of her malaria-induced fever dreams: when "the river is miles below [her, she stretches] out over the water, making that endless crossing, reaching for balance" (526). Leah also describes the African people and biosphere in terms of balance. Most literally, she notes that "[t]he Congolese sense of balance is spectacular" (107) when she sees the women of Kilanga bearing supplies on their heads. Without using the word, she describes the native people's balanced relationship with nature before the Europeans arrived: "The Portuguese peered through the trees and saw that the well-dressed, articulate Kongo [sic] did not buy or sell or transport their crops, but merely lived in place and ate what they had, like the beasts of the forest" (522). There is also balance in nature's equilibrium: "Central Africa is a rowdy society of flora and fauna that have managed to balance together on a trembling geologic plate for ten million years: when you clear off part of the plate, the whole slides into ruin. Stop clearing, and the balance slowly returns" (525). The word "balance" receives its most psychological use, however, in Adah's concluding chapters when she observes that "[t]he power is in the balance: we are our injuries, as much as we are our successes" and that "[w]e are the balance of our damage and our transgressions" (496, 533). In this description of life as a balanced distribution of good deeds, wounds, and errors, perhaps Kingsolver echoes a comment in William Shakespeare in *All's Well That End's Well*: "The web of our life is of a mingled yarn, good and ill together. Our virtues would be proud if our faults whipped them not; and our crimes would despair if they were not cherished by our virtues" (4.3.70–73). Such frank self-assessment characterizes the middle column, a liminal state of cultural accommodation versus Nathan's attitude that it is "a mistake to bend his will, in any way, to Africa" (97).

In order to situate themselves in the middle, Westerners must acknowledge that Africa and Africans have active agency, a point that Kingsolver supports by using the word "eye" throughout the novel. To begin with, Jung understood the importance of point of view in the perceptual process: "Whatever we look at, and however we look at it, we see only through our own eyes" (*CW* 6, par. 936). But feminine intuition can provide important assistance in seeing more clearly: "Woman, with her very dissimilar psychology, is and always has been a source of information about things for which man has no eyes" (*CW* 7, par. 296). Nathan's problem is that he sees his mission only through his own eyes, ignoring what he might learn from the females around him and from the anima. Originally, Orleanna shares his myopia, stating that the Price family "stepped down there on a place we believed unformed, where only darkness moved on the face of the waters" (10). The image from Genesis 1.2 implies that in his missionary position Nathan will be a co-creator with God, etching his will on the land and its people.

The notion that Westerners are acting subjects and Africa merely a receiving object is a fundamental misconception that Kingsolver's eye imagery begins to correct. It is not a coincidence, for example, that Orleanna's father, Dr. Bud Wharton, was an eye doctor (193) because she quickly sees the family's situation accurately. As she states in her conclusion, "From the first moment I set foot in the Congo, I could see we were not in charge" (516). In fact, impaired vision and its correction become a frequent repetition in the novel. Mama Tataba, blind in one eye, looks at the family with "her acute monocular beam" (39). Tata Ndu "wears glasses with no glass in them," which seems risible at first but later "did not seem ridiculous" (130, 333). Lumumba "wore real eyeglasses," and Anatole purchases "a pair of spectacles . . . good lenses that magnify things" (182, 279). Meanwhile, Tata Kuvudundu "gave off the evil eye" at the meeting to determine whether Leah may join the fire hunt (340), and he is a purveyor of "evil-eye fetishes" (208). Thus, it is not just that the eyes in the trees are watching. As readers, we watch Kingsolver watching the Price family watch the natives watch them back. As this process unfolds, Nathan remains like the "foreign glass eyes" that watch over the destruction of Patrice Lumumba and the destruction of the Congolese biosphere (318). But when his ill-conceived ministry descends on Kilanga, its citizens—far from being a *tabula rasa*—cast their intelligent gaze upon him. The inescapable interpretation of all the eye imagery is that Kingsolver, contrary to Born's reading of the continent as a mere backdrop, creates Africa with agency of its own. As Brother Fowles elegantly puts it, Westerners are like branches grafted onto the good tree of Africa, which sustains them (252, 258), an echo of Paul's statement that "it is not you [the grafted branch] that support[s] the root, but the root that supports you" (Rom. 11.18). Or as Leah says, "In Congo, it seems the land owns the people" (283). Even the obtuse Rachel gets it right: "You can't just sashay into the jungle aiming to change it all over to the Christian style, without expecting the jungle to change you right back" (515).

Conclusion

Balance, accommodation, and proper seeing form a mutually supportive relationship with Jungian individuation so that a cultural middle ground is the prerequisite and result of inner work. Whereas Nathan's individuation is blocked because his experience of the collective shadow makes him see faults in everyone but himself, Adah conveys the importance of engaging with the shadow in her allusions to Robert Louis Stevenson. "We go to bed ourselves and like poor Dr. Jekyll we wake up changed," and "[l]ike Jekyll I crave that particular darkness curled up within me" (276, 492). When the shadow is befriended so that its energy is in sync with the individuation process ("apprentice-piece"), it provides a proper foundation for work with the anima ("master-piece") (*CW* 9, par. 61). Recognizing Nathan's shortcomings signifies the daughters' acknowledgement of the shadow in themselves. As a result, they make progress with the animus through constructive relationships of various sorts with their partners and their work. The book's description of "self," however, differs markedly from Jung's understanding of the Self as the archetype of wholeness. Adah notes that "[t]he Bantu speak of 'self' as a vision residing inside, peering out through the eyeholes of the body, waiting for whatever happens next" (342). Here the self is consciousness waiting to be acted upon, not the archetype of wholeness. Yet *The Poisonwood Bible* does provide an image of the Self in a counterpoint to the "shattered plate" (212): the globe that Leah fashions for her husband. Whereas the china plate is two-dimensional, the globe's three dimensions signify the greater potential for wholeness when man and woman achieve a successful partnership. And when Leah states, "Anatole has even kept the globe I gave him for a wedding present" (503), the very Jungian implication is that the wholeness they have achieved in their psyches and in their marriage is a first step toward forging wholeness within the global community.

Notes

1 For a study of the novel's place within the Kingsolver oeuvre, see Chapter 8, "*The Poisonwood Bible* as Apex," in Linda Wagner-Martin's *Barbara Kingsolver's World*.

2 For a helpful summary of the history of colonial intervention in the Congo, see Diane Kunz who "supplies the missing links between the political events that Kingsolver recounts" (295) and offers a small amount of interpretation. For example, Brother Fowles and Eeben Axelroot "represent the polar opposites of American intervention," the idealist and the evil doer; and Leah is "as guilty of American hubris as Nathan" for her self-assertion in the hunt, which leads to Ruth May's death (286–87). Kunz concludes that Kingsolver's anti-interventionist stance is "touchingly naïve" (296). Another study that deals with the novel's anti-imperialism is Elaine R. Ognibene's "The Missionary Position: Barbara Kingsolver's *The Poisonwood Bible*." Ognibene points out that religion and politics were "a powerful combined force" in the Congo (20) and discusses the parallels among imperialism, missionary work, and family dynamics. Similarly, Mary Jean DeMarr stresses that the novel "is concerned with issues of truth, justice, colonial occupation, and genocide" (118).

3 Kurtz "came to them [the Africans] with thunder and lightning" (Conrad 71), and Nathan at one point seems "fixing to send down the thunderbolts and the lightning" (26).

4 See also J. U. Jacobs's article.

5 DeMarr incorrectly states that Nathan was a Japanese prisoner during World War II (125). Accuracy is also a problem for Wagner-Martin who conflates Tata Ndu and Tata Kuvudunu (*Reader's Guide* 39).

6 Ognibene points out that, during the rainstorm, "Nathan appears like Lear, a mad father abandoned by his daughters, wandering in the wilderness and speaking in words that few can understand" (26).

7 See Daphne Dodson's Jungian reading, "Rebirthing Biblical Myth: *The Poisonwood Bible* as Visionary Art," on the Works Cited list.

8 Kingsolver never uses the phrase "pearl of great price," but the family name is Price; Orleanna grew up "in a scrubby settlement called Pearl" in Mississippi (193); the bombing of Pearl Harbor is mentioned (195); Adah quotes *The Tempest*: "Those are pearls that were his eyes" (482, 491); and Rachel wears a string of pearls (491).

9 "The Gospel of Thomas" was discovered fourteen years before the Prices moved to the Congo. That Nathan does not see the relevance of its principle to his own psychic life deepens the irony of his interest in promoting apocryphal writings.

10 See Purcell's discussion of pantheism ("all is God") and panentheism ("all is in God") ("Gospel" 98).

8

MOTHER IS NOT SUPREME

The Anima and (Post)Colonial Strife in Chinua Achebe's *Things Fall Apart* and Nadine Gordimer's *July's People*

It is clear for at least three reasons that *The Poisonwood Bible* reflects Barbara Kingsolver's understanding of Chinua Achebe's *Things Fall Apart* (1958), which Kwame Anthony Appiah calls "the archetypal modern African novel in English" (ix). Achebe's novel is on her bibliography, she borrows from it the idea that twins are abandoned in the bush after birth, and at one point Rachel Price says that "things fall apart" (483). Kingsolver may also have transferred the masculine intransigence of Achebe's Okonkwo to her own Nathan Price. One character is a black African native, the other a white American missionary, but they share a dysfunctional relationship with the anima, which manifests in abusive relationships with their wives and children. Whereas there is tragedy for Okonkwo, Gordimer's Smales family suffers a geographical displacement but undergoes no lasting change. Despite being set in the bush, which symbolizes the collective unconscious, *July's People* (1981) depicts no significant exploration of the inner life on the part of Bamford and Maureen Smales. The difference between the portrayals by Achebe and Gordimer, then, is intransigence and a steady psychological decline versus indifference and a failure to engage, respectively. However, Gordimer adds the sense that hope lies with the younger generation: Gina Smales, who like Kingsolver's Ruth May makes friends with a native boy named Nyiko, accommodates a little bit to the native village; and even her brother, the materialistic Victor, offers a native gesture of obeisance when July gives him some "real plastic fishing-line" (157).

The two novels are an appropriate pairing because they mirror each other quite precisely. *Things Fall Apart* concerns what happens when white civilization imposes itself on native Nigerian culture, and *July's People* describes the fate of the white middle class when an insurrection erupts against the South African government. Both novels present a commingling of cultures, but whites are dominant in Achebe's vision, whereas blacks hold the upper hand in Gordimer's. In each case there is a challenge to the status quo. In Achebe, Okonkwo's good friend Obierika notes that "we have fallen apart"; the narrator states that the clan is "breaking up and falling apart" and that the "[t]imes . . . had altered unaccountably"; native tradition is ignored, and the clan is abandoned and "broken" (152, 157, 165, 168–69, and 174). Okonkwo, like the old medicine man whom Jung encountered in Africa, "was the living embodiment of the spreading disintegration of an undermined, outmoded, unrestorable world" (*MDR* 265). In the novel, the agents of decay are white institutions—Christianity, government, education, and the local store. In *July's People*, however, "a destroyed white society" leads to the Smales family's "[s]ubmission to the elements" in a primitive village (51, 57). Moreover, whereas Achebe depicts the demise of native civilization, Gordimer imagines what happens to a family from the white bourgeois class when blacks seize power by violence. In Shakespearean terms, Okonkwo, like Caliban, is a native who unsuccessfully defends his way of life against Western intruders; there are also the *kotma* (court messengers) who work for the white colonialists and, like Ariel, are "correspondent to command" (*Temp*. 1.2.299). Gordimer adds a third category of natives who successfully use force to topple the white hegemony.[1]

Political correctness and post-Jungian thought tell us to be careful about associating women with femininity and men with masculinity, yet traditional gender categories are on clear display in the two novels. For example, as Abdul R. JanMohamed notes, in *Things Fall Apart* the distinction is between language, ritual, art, manners, and religion (feminine) and "material success and courage in battle" (masculine) (*Manichean* 168). In addition, *July's People* distinguishes between masculine roles (working, driving, hunting, building) and feminine pursuits (mothering, cooking, dancing), though here the roles are complicated by the employer-employee relationship. Although nurture rather than biology is the predominant driver in Achebe and economics plays a role in Gordimer, Jung's essentialist system unpacks the gender bifurcation in both works: masculine and feminine—mother earth and father politics—are still relevant categories. Chapter 8, then, suggests that black-white political strife impedes progress with the feminine, and vice versa, so that the anima, especially its maternal stage, is undervalued and thwarted—mother is not supreme. Insofar as a lack of anima integration leads to strife that blocks psychological integration, (post)colonial politics and the anima are depicted as a zero-sum game and a vicious circle.[2]

Psychological principles in *Things Fall Apart*

Colonialism moves the African villagers in *Things Fall Apart* away from unity with mother earth toward domination by Western patriarchy. A societal *enantiodromia* from one system that respects the maternal to one that does not is crucially important, as Appiah points out in a comment regarding "Ani, the earth goddess," who seems to personify the anima.[3] He writes: "And it is a reflection of Okonkwo's failure to seek balance between the manly virtues and the womanly virtues as understood in Umuofia, that each of the disasters that afflicts him can be seen as a crime against the earth. . . . And it is through this flaw that he is destroyed" (xiv).[4] Okonkwo transgresses both the clan's earth-centered justice system and the white man's patriarchal judiciary. Jungian psychological principles help to chart his decline.

Things Fall Apart opens by describing, in positive terms, a native culture untouched by the white man and associated with the *participation mystique* and the connection to the earth that Jung observed on his Bugishu Psychological Expedition. A mentality characterized by *participation mystique* is not so much "primitive" as it is "archaic" or "undifferentiated," and in this case it simply means that the people of Umuofia attribute agency to inanimate objects. For example, there is mention of "magic" and the conflation of *agadi-nwayi* (old woman) and medicine so that *war* medicine becomes "an old woman with one leg" (9).[5] More to the point is the *iyi-uwa*, "a smooth pebble" that links an *ogbanje* (reincarnated child) and the spirit world (70). The latter is a clear example of *participation mystique* because an object is assumed to perform the role of psychopomp, which Jung assigns to the anima. In addition, Umuofia worships Ani who is "the owner of all land," "the earth goddess," "Mother Earth," and "the source of all fertility," with "all" presumably referring to fertility that is physical, psychological, and agricultural (14, 25, 160, and 31). As "the ultimate judge of morality and conduct," she also plays a role similar to the *ogbanje*'s by being "in close communion with the departed fathers of the clan whose bodies had been committed to the earth" (31). Not surprisingly, the earth in *Things Fall Apart* has some of the qualities that Jung associates with the anima, as in Nwoye's mother's story of a quarrel between Mother Earth and Father Sky: Earth sends a vulture to ask for mercy and pity, the kind of softening that Okonkwo never allows himself to embrace. This closeness to myth, along with a magical mentality and a proper orientation to the earth, illustrates the kind of closeness to nature that Jung believes modern man has lost.

The novel also comments positively on the feminine principle by invoking some aspects of the feminine that *Anima and Africa* has traced and by introducing the expression "Mother is Supreme" (116). Okonkwo has three wives and daughters (Eve or biological motherhood and its prospect); the oracle's priestess, Chielo, calls to mind both Mary (spiritual motherhood) and Sophia (wisdom); but there is no Helen figure. Although Okonkwo is abusive to his women, the presence of the three positive stages of eroticism and the absence of the one negative female type signal the potential for individuation in traditional Igbo life. This positive potential, however, remains unachieved because lessons are not learned. Following the accidental killing of a teenager, Okonkwo is exiled to his motherland, Mbanta, where he is asked the significance of the phrase "Mother is Supreme," a common name for girls (142). He does not know that mother is supreme because in times of tribulation one seeks maternal assistance, as he himself does in returning to Mbanta. The answer points to the need for psychological balance through integration of the feminine, which would curb his hyper-masculinity. Although he names his first daughter born in exile Nneka (mother is supreme), he simply rebuilds his old life in a new place and then returns to Umuofia without learning, in A. G. Stock's words, "man's need of the tender and consoling qualities which are the woman's side of his nature" (89). After all, in Igbo culture mother is actually not supreme—*father* is supreme. Then, by superseding the male-dominated native culture, Western colonial patriarchy provides further evidence that the feminine is not integrated. Unlike the American intervention in *The Poisonwood Bible*, the interference here is by the United Kingdom, ruled until 1901 by Queen Victoria. Perhaps the novel's greatest irony is that the queen really *is* supreme in overseeing a colonial and very patriarchal empire. A consequence of colonial intervention is that the men of Umuofia experience a disadvantaged position not unlike the one they impose on their women, yet the men still do not see the need to cultivate the feminine. Suffering at the hands of white men only promotes further intransigence, for they—and especially Okonkwo—erroneously believe that hardness is all that matters.

A further indicator of the potential for individuation is an enigmatic episode that occurs about halfway through *Things Fall Apart*. Chielo, the priestess of the god Agbala and "the Oracle of the Hills and Caves" (94), comes in the night and takes Okonkwo and Ekwefi's daughter Ezinma, claiming that Agbala wants to see the girl. The parents disobey Chielo's warning not to follow lest Agbala be angry with them. Ekwefi follows the god-possessed Chielo at a distance in the moonlight until they reach the god's shrine, "a circular ring" formed by the surrounding hills. There Chielo descends with Ezinma into "underground caves" (95). After apparently falling asleep by the entrance, Ekwefi awakes to find that Okonkwo is with her, carrying a machete. Together they watch and wait. Eventually Chielo crawls out with Ezinma on her back and returns the girl to her bed in Ekwefi's hut. Nothing more is ever said about the incident, and the narrator provides no clues regarding its significance.[6] The episode, however, is perhaps a little allegory of the possibility for psychological progress that the anima offers to Okonkwo. The female priestess of the god Agbala (the word *agbala*, in lower case, means woman or title-less man like Unoka [11]), represents the anima's function as a bridge between masculine consciousness (the hut) and the feminine unconscious (the darkness, the caves, the hills).[7] Chielo stands for Okonkwo's repressed but powerful feminine side. The encounter of Okonkwo and Ekwefi at the cave mouth signals the potential for syzygy consciousness and perhaps *coniunctio*, as does the relationship between Agbala and Chielo. But the fact that nothing comes of the night journey is consistent with Okonkwo's inability to diverge from the hyper-masculinist course (the useless machete) that his ego has charted.[8] The fact that Ezinma—another emblem of the feminine within Okonkwo—is asleep at the end of the episode implies that the dormant potential he could begin to access simply by being a little kinder to his family is never realized.

Unfortunately, whereas the potential for individuation lies in harmony with the earth and access to the unconscious, the values that the anima represents do not make one a great man in an African village. Bad psychological habits drive Okonkwo's hyper-masculinity and obviate any possibility of inner work. The first of these is his lifelong repression of the feminine. Of his younger years he states, "I began to fend for myself at an age when most people still suck at their mothers' breasts" (18). Presently he shows no emotion except anger, for showing anything else is a sign of weakness. Appropriately, his nickname is "Roaring Flame" or "a flaming fire" (133), suggesting that he is a powerful, destructive force.[9] His repression of the feminine appears most prominently in his disappointment regarding the feminine qualities he perceives in (and projects onto) his father Unoka and his son Nwoye. Since they are the carriers of his feminine principle (the objects of his anima projection), and he is full of disdain for their lack of initiative, responsibility, and masculine strength, the three generations of males in Okonkwo's family learn nothing from each other. Moreover, the masculine ideal that he fosters within his own psyche has various equivalents on the communal level. In Umuofia masculinity is defined by the titles one earns, and Okonkwo is on his way to being one of the most highly titled men before his exile.[10] Another measure of a man involves controlling his women and children, which shuts down the inner work they could help him do. Okonkwo is similarly critical of "a lot of effeminate men clucking like old hens" who flock to the Christian church (133), and the village ostracizes the converts, even using violence to bar the Christian women from the stream. In summary, the repression of the feminine that occurs within Okonkwo's psyche takes place within his family and is mirrored in their community. His libido, especially the sexual kind, is instead channeled into violence: "He trembled with the desire to conquer and subdue. It was like the desire for woman" (36–37). Lost on him is the wisdom of the Tortoise in Ekwefi's story in Chapter 11. Tortoise says, "I have learned that a man who makes trouble for others is also making it for himself" (85).[11] Since there is a direct correspondence between inner and outer, it is equally true that he who represses the anima will also cause trouble for others.

Repression, projection, and displacement of psychic material naturally result in compensatory behavior. The image of the charioteer in Plato's *Phaedrus* (starting at section 254a) is relevant here. As a charioteer's horses must all pull in the same direction, consciousness and the unconscious must align. Something similar obtains in *Things Fall Apart* with respect to the word "*chi*," which means "personal god" (*TFA* 14, 180); "a soul or spiritual double" (Carroll 29); "the individual manifestation of the Supreme Creator (Chukwu)" (Sarma 67); and "god, guardian angel, personal spirit, soul, spirit double, etc." (Achebe, "Chi" 159).[12] Thus, the word emphasizes the importance of harmony within the psyche and fulfills the compensatory role of the personal unconscious. Achebe is quite clear about compensation:

> It is important to stress what I said earlier: the central place in Igbo thought of the notion of duality. Wherever Something stands, Something Else will stand beside it. Nothing is absolute. . . . The world in which we live has its double and counterpart in the realm of spirits. A man lives here and his chi [sic] there. Indeed the human being is only one half (and the weaker half at that) of a person. There is a complementary spirit being, chi.
>
> ("Chi" 161–62)

In psychological terms, the "spirit being" (archetype) is to "the realm of spirits" (the unconscious) as the "human being" is to ego/consciousness, and the former pair is vastly more powerful, as a story attests. A great wrestler decides to wrestle in the spirit world and there is successful until his own *chi* "lifts him clear off the ground with his little finger and smashes him to death" ("Chi" 163). Whatever additional meanings *chi* possesses, it certainly seems to stand in for the personal unconscious in *Things Fall Apart*.[13]

According to the narrator, "the Ibo people have a proverb that when a man says yes his *chi* says yes also" (23).[14] Elsewhere, "[a] man could not rise beyond the destiny of his *chi*. The saying of the elders was not true—that if a man said yea his *chi* also affirmed" (114). The proverb expresses the idea that conscious volition and the personal unconscious should ideally be in sync, as they are within a well-integrated psyche. The second statement offers a more realistic portrait in which a man and his personal unconscious want different things. If one follows the ego's dictates and ignores psyche's deeper imperatives, compensatory behavior results, as a tiny allegory illustrates. Ezinma's appetite for eggs increases when Okonkwo forbids her to eat them. Repression begets compensation; making an object taboo leads one to fear the consequences of possessing it but strengthens one's desire to attain it. As in Okonkwo's father-daughter relationship, so it is for him in Umuofia more generally. He even wonders if "his *chi* might now be making amends [compensating] for the past disaster" (147). After all, "[t]here was a saying in Umuofia that as a man danced so the drums were beaten for him. [The missionary] Mr. Smith danced a furious step and so the drums went mad" (159). The phrase "as a man danced" refers not only to action but also to psyche: Mr. Smith's psyche and actions lead to consequences, and Okonkwo is no different. A man who represses his feminine side, who personifies a roaring fire, is likely to see his unacknowledged qualities in others. Okonkwo and Mr. Smith are alike in extremism, as their attendant metaphors suggest: one man is a roaring fire, the other a smith who uses fire to bend iron to his will. In this way, Mr. Smith is an example of the compensation that psyche brings when Okonkwo fosters anger and hyper-masculinity but refuses to engage with the anima. In other words, Mr. Smith is the *consequence* of Okonkwo's psychic imbalance, which is what his enemies in Umuofia mean when "[t]hey called him the little bird *nza* who so far forgot himself after a heavy meal that he challenged his *chi*" (26). They mean that he emphasizes his persona, which is prideful and unrepentant, over his true feelings. As Jung well knew, however, if feelings are not integrated, they manifest as an outer force in defiance of conscious intention.

As Okonkwo's masculine repression increases, outer events provide increasingly forceful reminders that mother is not yet supreme—that the anima needs to be honored and integrated. In fact, his life allegorizes psyche's futile attempts to turn him toward the feminine. The key events all reflect his separation from the earth and lack of psychic integration. His greatest early accomplishment is throwing the wrestler Amalinze the Cat. "He was called the Cat because his back would never touch the earth" (1). Allegorically, to throw an opponent who is never pinned implies that Okonkwo is even more disconnected from the earth than his opponent. Also as a young man, he becomes a successful warrior, taking his first head in war, an image that reflects separation of the head from the heart, masculine from feminine, and perhaps consciousness from the unconscious. After Okonkwo beats his first wife Ojiugo during the Week of Peace, he receives a visit from the priest Ezeani who informs him that his action is a crime against the earth goddess Ani. Okonkwo also beats his second wife Ekwefi for cutting a few leaves from a banana tree; and a bit later he shoots at her with his "old rusty gun" (33). He misses, but the bullet is an image of the projection of his unacknowledged feminine principle. Trying to kill the carrier of his own femininity signals not only repression but also an attempt to eradicate the potential for an inner life.

Next, fearing the appearance of weakness, Okonkwo commits the judicial murder of Ikemefuna, who has lived with him for three years as a foster son.[15] It is unclear from the narrator's statement that "Okonkwo drew his machete and cut him down" (53) whether the boy is beheaded, but the reader suspects a decapitation. If this suspicion is accurate, then the killing echoes his earlier victory in war: now he has not killed an enemy in combat; he has executed a virtual family member. In Rinda West's view, the murder of Ikemefuna shows "Okonkwo's acting out his shadow," which is "his fear of being seen as soft" (64). Obierika says: "What you have done will not please the Earth. It is the kind of action for which the goddess wipes out whole families" (58). Damian U. Opata argues that Okonkwo's murder of his son does not constitute an offense against the earth because the Oracle orders it (90–91). In any case, this action is certainly a crime against the anima, which is trying hard to get his attention. In other words, because the feminine has not been integrated, psyche increases the intensity of the compensation, and Okonkwo's action is very serious indeed. It is little wonder, as C. L. Innes states, that the murder of Ikemefuna "connotes the murder of the clan's potential" and its "inability to maintain a harmonious balance between male and female principles" (*Chinua Achebe* 29). But the immediate consequence is more personal. After the execution, the anima cries out to Okonkwo: he is deeply affected and cannot eat or sleep for two days. The narrator speaks of how such affect can be avoided: "If only he could find some work to do he would be able to forget" (56). Something similar appears in *Heart of Darkness* when Charlie Marlow emphasizes the role of work in keeping the unconscious at bay: "rivets were what really Mr. Kurtz wanted, if he had only known it" (Conrad 43). Eventually Okonkwo buries his feelings and moves on, ironically, only after the anima figure Ekwefi feeds him roasted plantains—a reconnection to the earth and a small encounter with the feminine principle that he continues to reject. Whereas Robert M. Wren emphasizes Okonkwo's "wholly feminine" reaction to the killing of his foster son (44–45), it appears that the feminine is what brings Okonkwo out of a state of negative inflation.

Then Okonkwo kills another boy with a fragment from his exploding gun. Although it is a female killing (an accident) rather than a masculine killing (willful murder), "[i]t was [still] a crime against the earth goddess to kill a clansman" (110). Finally, after his seven-year exile in his motherland, Okonkwo and his fellow leaders are briefly imprisoned, causing him to swear vengeance, which he takes by decapitating a court official. Since his act is a masculine offense this time, he knows that there is no way out for him and, in a final "offense against the Earth," hangs himself (178). He is to be "buried like a dog" (179) in the Evil Forest, his father's resting place. Despite all his attempts to distance himself from Unoka, father and son share a shameful death. Okonkwo's life, then, is a series of acts against the earth: prowess in athletics and in war, spousal abuse, the killing of a son figure, accidental homicide, first-degree murder, and self-murder. Each is more serious than what precedes it because as his masculinity tightens its hold on his psyche, the compensatory behavior increases its intensity. *Things Fall Apart* is a tragedy because he never recognizes the anima's attempts to get his attention, never reconsiders his behavior, and allows his anger and masculinity to dominate and fracture his psyche.

Ironically, the Christian missionaries make inroads into Igbo culture because their approach, contrary to Okonkwo's lack of individuation, recognizes on the cultural level the Jungian principle that acknowledging the shadow is the beginning of wholeness. During Okonkwo's exile, a Christian missionary in Mbanta named Mr. Kiaga challenges the natives' *participation mystique* by stating "that they worshipped false gods, gods of wood and stone" (125). Christianity undermines native belief and, for Nwoye, has a feminine appeal of its own: "It was the poetry of the new religion, something felt in the marrow" (128).[16] Insofar as Christianity speaks to the unconscious or the whole person, it is a more effective agent of the Self than the pagan beliefs that it challenges. Meanwhile, Obierika informs Okonkwo that the church in Umuofia is recruiting "*efulefu*, worthless, empty men . . . the excrement of the clan," and the *osu* (outcasts) (124, 136). Similarly, the church in Mbanta is built in the Evil Forest, which is "alive with sinister forces and powers of darkness" (129).[17] The community represses its worthless element the way Okonkwo represses the feminine; but by recruiting the empty and the outcast, as well as by placing the church in the Evil Forest, the Christians incorporate the communal "shadow," a task that Okonkwo does not achieve within his own psyche.[18]

Integration on the psychic level also corresponds to cultural accommodation, for which Umuofia's missionary, Mr. Brown, is noted. His name combines white and black, and he accepts "a carved elephant tusk" (153), much as Kingsolver's Brother Fowles allows native culture in his services. Like Nathan Price, however, Mr. Brown's successor, Mr. Smith, "condemned openly Mr. Brown's policy of compromise and accommodation" (158). After the spirit of accommodation opens the door to more forceful types of Western imperialism, the damage begins in earnest. Mr. Brown's school, Mr. Smith's hard-line approach, the trade store, and the judicial system—Western religion, education, capitalism, and government—all invade Igbo culture and collaborate with each other. For example, the converts shave their heads, much as Okonkwo and his fellow prisoners have their heads shaved in prison, which signifies that the Christian converts and those subject to the white man's laws are alike in being colonized subjects. The native Christians may be initially attracted to the feminine element in Christianity (the outcasts flee to the church as Okonkwo, himself an outcast, flees to his motherland), but they are merely exchanging one patriarchal system for another. As a result, Christianity's seeming appeal to individual persons' desire for wholeness ultimately leads to the destruction of cultural wholeness in the wider community.

In Umuofia repression and hyper-masculinity result in compensatory forces on which Christianity can prey, and then the harsher ways of white government lead to a cultural *enantiodromia*—a swing from the natives' hardness to the white man's. The first part of the novel describes Umuofia's justice system and warrior culture, Okonkwo as its masculine ideal, and reverence for Mother Earth, though human mothers are far from supreme and are generally oppressed. The unacknowledged feminine in Okonkwo and others surfaces as softness in Unoka, Nwoye, Okonkwo's wives, and the outcasts. For some of these, Christianity at first provides a merging of African and Western, as in Mr. Brown's policy of accommodation. Okonkwo errs greatly, however, in thinking that Westerners are womanly countertypes to native masculinity when they are, in fact, agents of an even more powerful form of patriarchy. Soon Mr. Smith takes a hard-line approach to ministry, which leads to economic domination and judicial control (torture, financial penalty, consumerism, hanging). Consequently, things fall apart in the sense that they transform into their opposite, and the white man's repression compensates for the natives'. The deeper irony, though, is that England, the colonial/patriarchal power, is headed by a woman, Queen Victoria. Only in that sense is "mother" really supreme.

Economics and psychology in *July's People*

Gordimer's *July's People* is important to discuss in connection with *Things Fall Apart* for several reasons. To begin with, the novels are mirror images. For example, in Achebe, whites perpetrate violence against blacks; in Gordimer, blacks are killing whites. Okonkwo is subject to the white man's justice, and the Smales family flees the black uprising in Johannesburg and while in exile pays its respects to a village chief. In addition, *July's People* further illustrates the zero-sum relationship between anima integration and (post)colonial strife simply by not being a deeply psychological novel. Although Okonkwo misses numerous opportunities to foster self-understanding and achieve some degree of individuation, his tale resonates meaningfully with depth psychology. Since the Smales family inhabits the veneer of consciousness, their exile to July's village does not promote any lasting personal growth. Whereas Okonkwo defies the imperatives of psyche in spite of the anima's many warnings, Bam and Maureen experience geographical displacement and economic leveling—now they live in a tribal hut (July's mother's, as it turns out)—but never question their ego-centered bourgeois assumptions, which anchor them to consciousness. While the country itself is experiencing a *nekyia* of violence and strife, which will effect a transition to a more egalitarian form of government, Bam and Maureen, though they go to a different place, remain fundamentally unchanged.

A Marxist economic reading of *July's People* is actually a good place to begin because Mr. and Mrs. Smales are part of the bourgeoisie. Maureen, the daughter of a mine worker, rose by marriage from the proletariat, and the family owns a large house with a swimming pool and a master bedroom that apparently has an "*en suite*" bathroom (103). As an architect, Bam has designed homes like their own and other structures that are part of South Africa's economic superstructure. Whereas Achebe connects Christianity, education, consumerism, and government, Gordimer emphasizes the links among sex, race, and money. The phrase "master bedrooms" repeats numerous times throughout the novel (master, economics; bedroom, sex). A telling passage from Maureen's point of view concerns

> the sacred power and rights of sexual love as formulated in master bedrooms, and motels with false names in the register. Here, the sacred power and rights of sexual love are as formulated in a wife's hut, and a backyard room in a city. The balance between desire and duty is—has to be—maintained quite differently in accordance with the differences in the lovers' place in the economy. These alter the way of dealing with the experience, and so the experience itself. The *absolute nature* she and her kind were scrupulously just in granting to everybody was no more than the price of the master bedroom and the clandestine hotel tariff.
>
> (65)

The location of these sacred rights (not rites) depends on money. Maureen's later appeal to Bam not to "transpose" their "suburban adulteries" (103) suggests that they and their lovers may have registered in motels under false names, but primarily they have enjoyed each other in their master bedroom. Therefore, "the blowing up of the Union Buildings and the burning of master bedrooms" (117) challenge both the white man's economic power and his sexual potency. In contrast to Bam and Maureen, July, who is economically disadvantaged, has sex with Martha in her "wife's hut" when he is home on leave and with Ellen in "a backyard room" when he is in Johannesburg. Then the narrator gets to the point. Twice before in the same paragraph the phrase "the absolute nature of intimate relationships" appears. Apparently Maureen believes that sexual intimacy should involve total commitment ("sacred power and rights") and that "she and her kind" have the right to impose their attitudes toward sex on everyone else. But the reality is that sex is a mere economic transaction, especially for those who are less well-off. No doubt as a result, women are objectified, as in another statement that links sex and money: "[t]he vehicle [the bakkie] was bought for pleasure, as some women are said to be made for pleasure" (6). A different type of sexual currency surfaces during the family's exile. Bam and Maureen make love only once in the novel—after he kills two small warthogs on which the village feasts. Bam the Boer shoots birdshot from the bore of his gun in order to kill two wild boars. Although the punning is probably unintentional, the incident establishes his credentials as a provider of meat; sex is his reward for masculine prowess, as it is in Hemingway's story when Margot fornicates with the hunting guide on his double cot.

The frequent references to consumerism also reinforce the sense that Gordimer is more interested in economics than psychology. July states that "African people like money," which the narrator identifies as "the lowest category of understanding" (71). Later July adds, "*Everybody he's like money*," which the narrator identifies as

"Shylock's gesture" (110). The importance of money is common ground between July and Bam, who cultivates "the male role of initiative and reassurance—something he always had on him, a credit card or cheque-book" (59). It is the Smales children, however, who are the most blatantly addicted to consumerism. They take pride in their possessions such as T-shirts with their names on them from "suburban malls" (125). "Nothing made them [the Smales children] so happy as buying things; they had no interest in feeding rabbits" in July's village (6). Son Victor is egregiously addicted to consumerism, brings his "electric racing-car track" with him to a native village with no electricity because he wants to show it off (13), and later wants Bam to buy "an old car radiator grid whose honey comb was welded with rust" during the visit to the chief (114). The parents believe that the chief is going to ask them to leave (serious), and Victor wants a souvenir (trivial). The inveterate synergy of sex, race, and money—"white privilege" (8)—can only be altered by violence. *July's People* tells the story of one family's escape from that violence and their consequent fall from enjoying their bourgeois status to depending on a proletarian for food, shelter, and safety.

Probably because of the emphasis on economics, the novel's psychological elements are fairly elementary. Unlike Okonkwo, the Smales family lives in a universe where "[t]here is no music of the spheres[;] science killed that along with all other myths" (124). Whereas *Things Fall Apart* includes various myths handed down orally for many generations, there is no equivalent in *July's People*. The result is the situation of modern man that Jung criticizes: lack of access to nature and the unconscious. The natural world ought to provide an alternative avenue for experiencing the psyche, but it does not. July's village is located hundreds of kilometers from Johannesburg where nature is as it had been in the time of "ancient migrations" (26). In addition, the bush, a symbol of the unconscious, is referred to as "the boundlessness" and "that immensity" (27, 43). But except for the hunting episode and the visit to the chief's home, the family does not explore outside the village and does not fully "go native." Maureen's major concession to her surroundings is to drown kittens herself rather than having a black person do it: spaying is a suburban solution, drowning the native way. Bam, Maureen, and the children do, of course, experience the subaltern way of life—Okonkwo's experience is colonial, theirs postcolonial; but no one in the white family ever explores the unconscious, which corresponds to the immensity that surrounds them.

The psychological references in *July's People* are a mixture of Freudian and Jungian terminology, but they reinforce the sense that the unconscious is not ever genuinely encountered. Sleep is an avenue for experiencing the deeper parts of the psyche, but in the novel the unconscious is something to be shaken off as soon as possible. "Bam got up and had the menacing aspect of maleness a man has before the superego has gained control of his body, come out of sleep" (39). This quotation is Gordimer's most explicit reference to the unconscious mind, but the morality principle overcomes any possibility that Bam could connect to the archaic man within him. Maureen has a similar experience in a Jungian vein during an encounter with July. She senses "an archetypal sensation between them . . . a feeling brutally shared." This feeling "did not exist before Pizarro deluded Atahualpa; it was there in Dingane and Piet Retief" (62). Since the latter reference is to King Dingane whose Zulu tribesmen kill the Boer leader Piet Retief and his men, the imaginary black uprising in Johannesburg, as well as the miniature contest of wills between July and Maureen, participates in an archetypal pattern of racial hatred, discord, and violence. A similar moment occurs a bit later when July pounds his fist on his chest to threaten Maureen, as if embracing the ancient strength that Bam shakes off when he awakens. As the narrator observes, "[s]he was not his mother, his wife, his sister, his friend, his people" (152), a statement that critiques the relationship between the employers and their employee. She and Bam believe that they have treated July well, but he has been more servile than they realize. "July" is a nickname; they do not know his real name (Mwawate [120]). He has been allowed to visit his wife only once every two years; he speaks badly broken English despite having been present in their home for fifteen years; she and July are strangers, as he demonstrates when he switches from English into his native language. In summary, the minor conflicts between Maureen and July have an archetypal resonance, and there is a subtle shift of agency in favor of July that parallels South Africa's movement toward a more just form of government. Bam and Maureen, however, remain the same bland suburbanites they were back home.

What Bam experiences in the course of the novel is not a *nekyia* or even a *nigredo* but debasement and humiliation. Little allegories suggest his decline. First, he constructs a water tank for July's village, but Victor (a miniature Pizarro) objects when the blacks start using the water (62–63). The incident represents South Africa's situation: Bam's emphasis on sharing resources must supersede Victor's thoughtless zeal for exclusivism. Along with Bam's success with the water tank, however, come experiences in the village that signal and effect his debasement. Early on, for example, he handles the radio with "the baffled obstinacy of a sad, intelligent primate fingering the lock on his bars" (50). The phrase does not signal an anti-evolutionary return to a pre-human stage; it simply means that Bam seems inept in a situation he is powerless to manage effectively. Later his minimal prowess as a hunter of baby pigs is undercut when the chief's request for an alternative weapon indicts his sexual authority: "You not got another kind, revolver?—The kind white men are known to keep in their bedrooms" (120). He does not have one, and soon his shotgun is stolen. Much as the car keys transfer from Bam to July, the shotgun transfers from Bam to Daniel, a milkman. As the pastoral villager puts on an epic mantle, Bam and his family descend into "total dependency" (155). Maureen knows that here in the bush he is merely "an architect lying on a bed in a mud hut, a man without a vehicle"; "she had gone on a long trip and left him behind in the master bedroom: what was here, with her, was some botched imagining of his presence in circumstances outside those the marriage was contracted for" (98). In her eyes, he is simply "the man who had been left behind," unable to protect his family (126). Inept, he cannot even fix a simple machine. So as July's authority grows, Bam's decreases; now he hides out with his family in his former servant's *mother's* hut (perhaps a faint parody of Okonkwo's exile to his motherland). Maureen herself is reduced too, at least in the eyes of Martha, who thinks that her white guest knows nothing. These details—uncomfortable circumstances, a debasement, an inconvenience—are not a productive descent into the unconscious, much less a way to integrate the anima.

The Smaleses' psychological shallowness and failure to individuate can be illuminated by Jung's stages of eroticism. July's "town woman" (16), Ellen, is the only Helen figure (as the Ellen/Helen pun suggests); but she is also an Eve, a biological mother like Maureen and Martha. Bam has experienced a wide spectrum of Maureen's other roles, as a long passage emphasizes: wife, daughter, girl, consort, woman, cook, and legal partner (104–05). Mary is present but corrupted in Maureen's imagination in a way that underscores the absence of spiritual motherhood. "She saw Martha securely petrified, Madonna drawing snuff into one nostril above a baby's head, *pietà* with a machine-gunned son across her lap" (146). The image condenses the virgin mother cradling the dead body of Jesus, the black woman's baby in her lap, and the possible fate of a black child in South Africa. As the imagery suggests, mother is not supreme. Even worse, the most important stage, Sophia, is not present in the novel because the violence in Johannesburg and the absence of the anima's wisdom are mutually reinforcing.

Conclusion

The main characters' failure to achieve individuation in *Things Fall Apart* and *July's People* is reflected in the remoteness or inadequacy of symbols of the Self. Achebe provides three such images: wrestling takes place in "a huge circle" (40); the oracle's shrine, surrounded by "a circular ring of hills" (95), features a round hole so that visiting the oracle is like a reverse birth—people who crawl through it "found themselves in a dark, endless space in the presence of Agbala" (13); and the Christian church is located in a circular clearing in the Evil Forest. As a younger man, Okonkwo must have bested Amalinze the Cat in that very ring; however, he is distanced from the spiritual possibilities of the oracle and the church. Gordimer provides only one image of the Self, and it is a hollow one: the bakkie's steering wheel sports a "mock leopard-skin" (109) so that the novel's sole image of wholeness is clad in fakeness and implies a disconnection from the earth. These four images point to the potential for, and the limits of, individuation in general and anima work in particular in a (post)colonial situation.

Achebe and Gordimer also underscore their characters' lack of psychological growth by emphasizing their status as textual place-holders. That fictional characters are merely textual to begin with is obvious, but the two novels imply that the native way of life, which Jung found important and interesting, is dying out and will soon be accessible only in the media. Such diminishment illustrates Edward Said's reminder that "a complex Orient [here Africa] suitable for study in the academy, for display in the museum, for reconstruction in the colonial office, for theoretical illustration in anthropological, biological, linguistic, racial, and historical theses about mankind and the universe" (7) enables Westerners to create and maintain a hegemonic view of the African people. The best example is that Okonkwo's life, richly chronicled in *Things Fall Apart*, will receive a mere paragraph in the District Commissioner book, *The Pacification of the Primitive Tribes of the Lower Niger*.[19] The title's key word—pacification—furthers this chapter's argument that Okonkwo's repression of the feminine leads to a compensatory response to him and his people by the white man: he ultimately becomes the receiving object of someone else's narration. Native culture is similarly diminished in *July's People* where textual references proliferate. Maureen remembers that a photo of herself as a girl with her family's black servant Lydia appears in a book. She views the people in July's village in terms of "dioramas of primitive civilizations in a national history museum" (24). When standing naked in the rain, she thinks of herself as "some caricature of a titillating photograph in a porn magazine, or—yes, more like—a woman in the Toulouse-Lautrec brothel drawings they had seen together in Europe" (52). Similarly, Bam views the village in textual terms when the "utility structure" (108) they see during their visit to the chief reminds him of a paper he once gave at an architectural conference. The final example appears near the end of the family's ordeal: "At this moment in its span, its seasons, the village coincides with the generic moment of the photographer's village seen from afar, its circles encircled by the landscape, held in the pantheistic hand, the single community of man-and-nature-in-Africa reproduced by skilled photogravure processes in Holland or Switzerland" (156). Far from helping Bam, Maureen, and their children to integrate the unconscious, the village becomes an object of Western photographic processing. Its actual qualities are obscured in favor of an ideal, idyllic, and almost air-brushed version for consumption by the European viewer. In other words, textuality affects the way Bam and Maureen experience the bush, separating them from Africa as surely as consciousness keeps them from exploring the unconscious. In both novels, then, textuality underscores the (post)colonial forces that vitiate inner work, especially work with the feminine.

Shortly after Maureen's musing about photography, the sound of an approaching helicopter implies that the family is about to be either rescued and returned to civilization by South African soldiers or slaughtered by freedom fighters. Either way, Bam and Maureen Smales will avoid the slow tragic decline that Okonkwo experiences, but their stay in the bush amounts to nothing. It is a nuisance and a debasement rather than a *nigredo* or a *nekyia*.

Notes

1 The analogy between *The Tempest* and Africa is more fully explored by Octave Mannoni in *Prospero and Caliban: The Psychology of Colonization*. Prospero (97–109) is said to be a father figure to Caliban, and Ariel is parallel to Friday in *Robinson Crusoe*. Later on, Mannoni quotes Jung's *The Relation of the Ego to the Unconscious* (*CW* 7) on Europeans' projection of their instinct onto Africans to support the contention that colonial conflict has its roots in the European psyche (197).

2 The thesis is in sync with Rinda West's Jungian reading of *Things Fall Apart* in *Out of the Shadow* (57–66). Whereas she argues that Okonkwo's tragedy is due to the repression of his feminine qualities into his shadow, this chapter focuses on the anima's independent

agency. Other than West's book, the only Jung-like study of *Things Fall Apart* in the MLA Bibliography is Thomas J. Lynn's article, which argues that Tortoise and Parrot in Ekwefi's tale (Chapter 11) allegorically satirize "British colonial authority and methods" (58) and foreshadow the construction of a new society through a dialogic exchange between cultures. MLA does not list any Jungian studies of *July's People*, but studies by the following authors were consulted: Stephen Clingman, Robert F. Haugh, Dominic Head, Abdul R. JanMohamed (*Manichean*), Rowland Smith, and Barbara Temple-Thurston.

3 The setting aligns with the maternal/natural, for as F. Abiola Irele points out, Umuofia means "people of the forest" (121). Robert M. Wren translates the name as "children of the forest" (9). A cultural *enantiodromia*, or a major shift in orientation, is what W. B. Yeats's "The Second Coming" describes, and it is from this poem that Achebe takes the novel's title. C. L. Innes helpfully notes "that Yeats' theory of the cycles of history ignores African history, as does European thought generally" (*Chinua Achebe* 35). See also A. G. Stock's article.

4 Appiah's point is articulated at greater length by Nwando Achebe and by Christopher Anyokwu. For Nwando Achebe, the novel depicts the feminine principle (in Igbo society and in the spiritual realm) as a source of social cohesion. He does not mention the anima, the female principle within the psyche of men, but his reading is compatible with the one presented here. Anyokwu argues that Obierika embodies the proper balance between masculine and feminine. Irele agrees, regarding Obierika as a foil to Okonkwo (130); however, later calling Obierika "the manifest antithesis of Okonkwo" (147) is inaccurate, for Unoka and Nwoye serve that function. The relationship between Ndulue and his wife Ozoemena provides a foil for Okonkwo's attitude toward his wives and an image of male/female balance: "He [Ndulue] could not do anything without telling her" (C. Achebe 60). Finally, Kalu Ogbaa notes that Uchendu's name means "Thought of Life" (67); therefore, advising Okonkwo in his exile makes Uchendu another foil.

5 Colonizers used the primitive-as-magic to justify enlightened intervention. Primitivism lies at the heart of Wole Soyinka's calling Jung the "begetter of so many racist distortions of the structure of the human psyche" (34). JanMohamed deals with another aspect of primitive culture in "Sophisticated Primitivism": African culture's transition from orality to chirography.

6 West supposes that the visit to the cave relates to the healing of Ekwefi's illness in Chapter 9 and speculates that "[e]ntering the womb of all life, enveloped by a great power, the worshipper receives the wisdom of the earth and the ancestors through the agency of the priestess" (58). For Remi Akujobi, "[t]he fact that Ezimma [sic] is restored after the encounter with Chielo says a lot about Chielo's spiritual power in agbala [sic]" (378). It seems more likely, however, that the tea Okonkwo prepares for his daughter at the end of Chapter 9 has taken effect. As Kalu Ogbaa points out, Ezinma is sick with *iba* (malaria) (31), and Wren describes her illness as "the jaundice-like fever that accompanies a malarial attack" (51). Apparently Agbala wants to make Ezinma Chielo's successor (Anyokwu 26, Wren 42) in order to restore the girl "to a realm of feminine mysticism from which she is beginning to be separated by Okonkwo's projection upon her of a male essence" (Irele 131). Finally, Corley considers Chielo to embody "an archetypal femininity" that makes her akin to female African characters in Henry Rider Haggard's *She* and Joseph Conrad's *Heart of Darkness* (206). Florence Straton states "that Chielo is a latter-day descendant, following Conrad's 'savage and superb' African woman in *Heart of Darkness* . . . of the female figure in Haggard's *She*" and that the episode allegorizes Achebe's distrust of the irrationality of female power (30–31). The fact that Chielo "crawl[s] out of the shrine on her belly like a snake" (Achebe 97) is an unnoticed parallel to Ayesha, who is frequently described as a snake. Straton's characterization of Chielo as "a psychological archetype" and "a demonic parody of powerful men" (37) are further links to *She*.

7 The deity, according to Wren, is female but is referred to as masculine in order to balance Ani, the Earth Mother (41). Roselyne M. Jua identifies a tension between the novel's positive emphasis on motherhood/womanhood and the "duplicity" of "Agbala/*agbala*, which [not only] names a god and means a woman" but also suggests that "[t]he woman therefore is worthless" (201).

8 For a study of this theme, see Íde Corley's article. Bu-Buakei Jabbi refers to Okonkwo's "manliness complex" (135).

9 For a study of fire, see Jabbi's article. An additional point not made by Jabbi is that, although Okonkwo is not directly responsible, the destruction of the church in Umuofia by arson is in sync with his nickname.

10 According to David Carroll, these titles "are acquired in a certain order of prestige by the payment of initiation fees which are then shared among existing members" (28).

11 Ogbaa deals with "Igbo Trickster Tales" on 156–60.

12 Achebe points out that the name Chukwu comes from "Chi Ukwu," which means "Great Chi" ("Chi" 168–69). Richard N. Henderson, author of *The King in Every Man*, the definitive study of Igbo culture, identifies three meanings of *chi*: "The general meaning: animate, purposeful essence"; an "unmarked narrow meaning: underlying essence of the individual self"; and a "marked narrow meaning: underlying essence of the universe" (109, fig. 14). Wren discusses *chi* in its cultural context (42–45). See also Harold Scheub's article. Kalu Ogbaa sums up *chi* by stating that it means, "variously, a personal god or spirit, guardian angel, soul, or spirit double" (15).

13 Ogbaa's claim that "*chi* is an individual ego or initiative" (16) is inaccurate because ego is not synonymous with the personal unconscious.

14 "Ibo" is a misspelling of "Igbo." Therefore, Achebe's use of "Ibo" in *Things Fall Apart* reflects the influence of British colonialism.

15 For a discussion of the execution, see Solomon O. Iyasere, "Okonkwo's Participation in the Killing of His 'Son' in Chinua Achebe's *Things Fall Apart*: A Study of Ignoble Decisiveness"; and Damian U. Opata, "Eternal Sacred Order versus Conventional Wisdom: A Consideration of Moral Culpability in the Killing of Ikemefuna in *Things Fall Apart*."

16 Wren states that Christianity appeals to Nwoye because it offers relief from the "repression of the feminine part of the universal duality" (59). Nwoye begins to turn away from Okonkwo and native ways because of the execution of Ikemefuna. When Nwoye becomes a Christian he takes the name Isaac, making Okonkwo parallel to Abraham. For a discussion of the biblical parallel, see Cobbam 25; and Innes, *Chinua Achebe* 35 and 176 (n. 6). Irele states that taking the name Isaac "enacts a symbolic reversal of the killing of Ikemefuna" (134).

17 The church's thriving in the Evil Forest shows that the natives' belief about sinister forces is false. The same thing happens when rescued pairs of twins survive without consequence.

18 This reading is in sync with West's point that an Evil Forest is the location of "cultural shadow" (60–01).

19 Wren deals with the historical realities of pacification in Nigeria on 26–32.

9

THE ANIMA AND SHADOW DYNAMICS IN APHRA BEHN'S *OROONOKO*

Chapter 9 caps off *Anima and Africa* with a brief analysis of Aphra Behn's *Oroonoko*, but we begin in conclusion mode by summarizing the points that have emerged regarding Africa and Jungian psychology in the preceding chapters.

In fiction, features of Africa's topography represent the female body or the collective unconscious. These connections are present, for example, in Henry Rider Haggard's sexualized rendering of hills and caves, and in depictions of the jungle in the works of Joseph Conrad, Laurens van der Post, and Nadine Gordimer. In addition, the personification of Africa's feminine nature in Kurtz's native mistress and *She*'s Ayesha allegorizes Western man's encounter with the dangerous feminine. Africa also facilitates his access to the shadow and/or the archaic. Francis Macomber, François Joubert, and David Lurie all experience some combination of these qualities. Black Africans and criminals of whatever race are often the objects of shadow projection, which may provide an occasion for protagonists like Lurie and Charles Watkins to do inner work.

A trip to Africa such as a journey up the Congo River puts a Western man more in touch with the archetypes because simply being there promotes an *abaissement du niveau mental*. Specific psychological experiences—*nigredo, nekyia*, dream, vision—also facilitate the lowering process. Since individuation depends on the archetypes being made conscious, opposite traps like projection and *enantiodromia* should be avoided. Van der Post, who rightly suggests that modern persons must find a middle ground between Western and native African, would have approved of the *via media* illustrated by the marriages and careers of Leah Price and Brother Fowles. Such middle ground between Western and African is of course not achieved in Chinua Achebe's novel, which is why native culture falls apart. Colonization's hegemonic forces—the religion, trade, education, and government seen in numerous works—degrade native culture and thwart individuation.

Other traps involve the shadow and the anima more specifically. Attempting to do anima work before doing shadow work guarantees a troubled contrasexual relationship. Along with having this problem, Francis Macomber projects conflicting aspects of the anima onto his wife. Even worse, becoming possessed by the shadow because of traumatizing experiences with the collective shadow in war can cause dissociation from the anima, as it does for Nathan Price, with spousal abuse and rigid adherence to Christian ideology as further results. As works by van der Post and Barbara Kingsolver illustrate, dissociation from the anima may also undergird terrorism and political dictatorship.

In an African setting the anima has agency, compensates for the persona, and acts as a psychopomp by providing the ego with a bridge or means of communicating with the deeper parts of the psyche. This communication process can be psychic (dreams in Hemingway and Schreiner, François's intuition, Xhabbo's "tapping," Watkins's vision, Lurie's inner work); or it can be communal (Chielo's role as priestess and translator for Agbala). Finally, the anima may be not only the multifaceted archetype of the feminine and a psychopomp/bridge but also a field greater than the collective unconscious or even the *unus mundus*. As James Hillman proposes, perhaps we are within the anima rather than vice versa (*Anima* 81).

Anima and Africa thus demonstrates the helpfulness of Jungian psychology for a study of fiction that intersects with the "dark" continent, whether that intersection is through authorship, characters, or setting. Jung's system of thought, however, is not without flaws that reflect his cultural assumptions. Although the archaic is a helpful transracial concept, the primitive is racist because it is based on the assumption that Westerners are higher on the Great Chain of Being in terms of the privileging of reason over instinct and intuition. Yet it appears that the primitive, despite its serious shortcomings, is sometimes useful in the analysis of fiction. For example, in the novels by Haggard, van der Post, Kingsolver, and Achebe, the primitive characterizes either the natives in their *participation mystique*, the Western characters' assumptions about their native counterparts, or a combination of both.

Aphra Behn's *Oroonoko* adds slavery to the toxic combination of colonial influences that has been observed in *The Poisonwood Bible* and *Things Fall Apart*. Moreover, the novel employs the concept of syzygy through its pairing of Oroonoko and Imoinda (Caesar and Clemene), Adam and Eve, Mars and Venus. The Western assumption is that the natives in the West Indies are like "our first parents before the Fall" (11), but Oroonoko and Imoinda are more like the exiled couple in the wilderness east of Eden. Or as Mars (the god of war) and Venus are caught in a net by Vulcan, Oroonoko (a martial leader) and Imoinda are found out by the old king who has claimed her. In the title character's attraction to Imoinda, the anima— "some new and till then unknown power [that] instructed his heart and tongue in the language of love" (17)—is clearly being projected, which is bad enough. Even worse, essentialism, Jung's problematic attribution of gender characteristics to biological sex, infects syzygy consciousness but provides a way of accessing the text because the narrator, who is based on Behn herself, holds similar assumptions about gender. Thus, *Anima and Africa* comes to a close with another example of how Jung is useful in literary analysis because his flaws align with the cultural assumptions that imbue a literary work.

Jung writes "that the manifestations of the collective unconscious [in literature] are compensatory to the conscious attitude, so that they have the effect of bringing a one-sided, unadapted, or dangerous state of consciousness back into equilibrium" (*CW* 15, par. 152). This compensatory feature of literature is present in *Oroonoko*, for the novel reflects and critiques the psychological disequilibrium that fosters slavery. Rather than being properly integrated, the shadow of various male characters, mainly William Byam, is projected onto Oroonoko and manifests as extreme brutality, while the anima is projected onto women, mainly Imoinda and the narrator. These twin projections are complementary. The male psyche attributes fault to (and brutalizes) a male Other partly *because* it wrongly attributes virtue and the feminine to various female Others, rather than genuinely fostering those qualities in itself. Behn links these two projection processes in important passages where the worst actions are perpetrated in the absence of women, as though women, if they *were* present, would have a tempering influence. In this fashion, the novel enacts the essentialist fallacy that characterizes Jung's attribution of gender to biological sex over three centuries later. The purpose of Chapter 9, then, is to examine Behn's essentialism in *Oroonoko* in order to understand the tragic impulse that results when the anima and the shadow are projected rather than integrated.

Jung's few comments on slavery in *The Collected Works* deal with it in a classical rather than an African or a New World context, but his comments on European experience are relevant and helpful in an approach to *Oroonoko*. His statement in "Crime and the Soul" exactly describes the psychic compartmentalization that takes place in the novel: "A very large number of criminals lead a thoroughly middle-class existence and commit their crimes, as it were, through their second selves. Few criminals succeed in attaining a complete severance between their liking for middle-class respectability, on the one hand, and their instinct for crime on the other" (*CW* 18, par. 800). This remark characterizes some of the whites in Behn's novel, especially slave owners and managers who, the narrator tells us, "consisted of such notorious villains as Newgate never transported, and possibly originally were such, who understood neither the laws of God or man, and had no sort of principles to make them worthy the name of men" (69; see Ferguson 48). Of course, the novel's most notorious *non*criminal is William Byam, Surinam's lieutenant governor, whose brutality masquerades as legal authority. He is what Jung calls the "so-called civilized man . . . [who] never suspects that his own hidden and apparently harmless shadow has qualities whose dangerousness exceeds his wildest dreams. As soon as people get together in masses and submerge the individual, the shadow is mobilized, and, as history shows, may even be personified and incarnated" (*CW* 9i, par. 478). Institutional slavery is such an aggregate, and Byam is its statutory personification.

Jung's further insights do not square precisely with Behn's depictions, but shadow projection is a crucial concept for understanding *Oroonoko*. Jung is especially critical of how national socialism "splits off the conscious from the unconscious man more and more menacingly" (*CW* 9i, par. 453; 10, par. 559). Like communism, it "threatens our freedom with tyranny and *slavery*"; "the State became all-powerful and claimed its *slaves* body and soul" (*CW* 10, par. 818; 18, par. 1324; emphases added). Although Jung does not address modern slavery directly, he does describe life in a repressive regime *as* slavery. Like the political systems that he mentions, a state that tolerates slavery provides a context for male shadow projection to manifest as brutality. For Behn, although collectivity does mobilize the shadow under the guise of state authority, the target is not the state's own citizens but the Other in remote locations like Africa and Surinam. As in *Heart of Darkness*, Europe's shadow is largely displaced onto a wilderness where the nonintegrated shadow is indeed "personified and incarnated." Rinda West's comment on *Heart of Darkness* is relevant here: "The imperial conquerors' image of themselves as the great civilizers required that they deny their own brutal impulses. They projected these dangerous qualities onto those they were brutalizing, casting Africans and Indians, along with their land, as 'savage'" (35–36). Instead of doing inner work, the whites, who are driven by the profit motive, project their negativity onto Oroonoko and punish him for it. The more unconscious one is, the more powerful the projection becomes. In Jung's words, "Everyone carries a shadow, and the less it is embodied in the individual's conscious life, the blacker and denser it is" (*CW* 11, par. 131). There is no "blacker and denser" object of projection in the novel than Oroonoko himself, whose blackness is "not of that brown, rusty black which most of that nation are, but a perfect ebony or polished jet" (15). As a result, the blackest of slaves is a likely target for the most brutal kind of male shadow projection.

Rather than dealing directly with shadow projection, however, the criticism focuses on such issues as the novel's historical, biographical, narrative, and feminist underpinnings. Nevertheless, various critics do notice that violence is perpetrated in the absence of women, and the commentary focuses on the female narrator's absence at crucial moments.[1] Critics are more interested, however, in what this pattern augurs for the absent narrator's complicity with colonial authority than in the psychology of the male victim and his victimizers. As the novel eventually bears out, the narrator, whether present or absent, is unlikely to prevent brutality because projection of the anima onto a woman is not inner work. In particular, a female character's absence symbolizes men's lack of anima integration and highlights the need for genuine anima integration, not an external woman, to temper a man's actions. The point is not that the narrator, however well-intentioned, could change the outcome if she were present but that change must arise from greater integration within the male psyche.

The essentialism that subtly underlies these implications is encapsulated in a couplet from the poem "Virtue and Charm" by medieval German poet Walter Von Der Vogelweide: "He who good woman's love doth heed / Will blush to do an evil deed" (32). A good woman's presence, the poet believes, discourages a man from doing bad deeds perhaps because anima projection momentarily quells the shadow's violent manifestations. The couplet's further implication—and Jung's, as Susan Rowland observes—is a gender bifurcation in which *Logos*/reason is the province of men, whereas women are embodiments of *eros*/relatedness (*Literary*

Theory 14). According to Rowland, Jung turned "his own unconscious anima" into psychological theory and women into animas, though he did locate "plurality and androgyny in the unconscious" (*Feminist Revision* 19, 45; *Literary Theory* 191).

Behn's female narrator is essentialist in believing that her mere presence prevents the potential for male violence. The implicit gender bifurcation and the attendant projection drive the novel away from individuation and toward tragedy. In other words, the flaws in Jungian theory, sans feminist revision, directly parallel and can helpfully illuminate the psychological forces that afflict the main characters. The essentialist comments of Robert Johnson, for example, sum up almost precisely the kind of shadow dynamics that Behn's novel enacts. The feminine, he states, relates to "qualities that bring meaning into life: relatedness to other human beings, the ability to soften power with love, awareness of our inner feelings and values, respect for our earthly environment, a delight in earth's beauty, and the introspective quest for inner wisdom" (19–20). But Johnson adds that the masculine, if it is isolated from the feminine, pursues "power, production, prestige, and 'accomplishment'"; thinks "only of empire building, accumulation of territory and wealth, and domination of the environment at any cost"; and achieves power through brutality and destruction at the expense of "love, feeling, and human values" (21–23). Johnson further states:

> *No aspect of the human psyche can live in a healthy state unless it is balanced by its complementary opposite.* If the masculine mind tries to live without its "other half," the feminine soul, then the masculine becomes unbalanced, sick, and finally monstrous. Power without love becomes brutality. . . . When one side of human nature grows out of balance with the other, it becomes a tyranny in the soul.
>
> (23)

The words "monstrous" and "brutality," as we shall see a bit later, have particular resonance with *Oroonoko*, as does Johnson's comment on the sword image: without the feminine harp, the sword, which "symbolizes the sharp, aggressive wielding of masculine power . . . is reduced to egotistical brute force" (29–30). The sword may even, as in *Oroonoko*, be turned against the projection of a man's own feminine side. As with Jung, so with Johnson: the bifurcation of masculine and feminine is a flawed theory; but a man's psyche, in order to be healthy, must consciously integrate masculinity and femininity into the wholeness of the Self. That much is true; and Johnson's prescription, because of its essentialist flaws, is a helpful lens for viewing a novel that subscribes to the same fallacy. On the surface, Behn's portrayal of male brutality in the absence of females supports the essentialist notion that, for males, the nonintegrated shadow becomes brutality without a mitigating female presence. The absent feminine, however, is significant not only in itself but also as a symbolic image of the male psyche: the outer landscape of characters is actually an inscape of archetypes.

A troubling passage illustrates the close relationship between essentialism and projection by depicting Oroonoko's unawareness that he is projecting his own anima and shadow. The narrator says of Imoinda's effect on Oroonoko's psyche that "the awfulness [awe] wherewith she received him, and the sweetness of her words and behavior while he stayed, gained perfect conquest over his fierce heart. So that having made his first compliments and presented her a hundred and fifty slaves in fetters, he told her with his eyes, that he was not insensible of her charms" (16). Like Behn and her narrator, neither Oroonoko nor Imoinda opposes slavery per se; they are merely opposed to the enslavement of upper-class persons, especially royalty. For them, there is no contradiction: Oroonoko can heed a good woman's love and still enslave lower-class Africans because the latter act is not considered an evil deed. At a minimum, his ironic complicity in the slavery that he later suffers suggests a morally relative ground where relationship with a woman and injustice to others can coexist. After all, in Behn's century slavery was customary in Africa and legal in the new world. In Africa, enslaving others (an evil deed) and enjoying a woman's love are not in binary opposition; one furthers the other and lends dramatic logic to Oroonoko's own enslavement. He reaps what he sows. In psychological terms, however, enslaving others and loving Imoinda are complementary acts of projection (of the shadow and the anima, respectively). Locating the feminine in Imoinda takes the place of realizing and integrating the anima within himself, and shadow projection (enslaving others) appears as an unconscious byproduct. In other words, anima projection prevents anima integration, and Oroonoko treats his fellow Africans as Others in much the same way that his white enslavers will regard him.

The essentialism and anima projection continue in the new world when Imoinda has an even more salutary effect on men, both whites and blacks, as though "[h]er power saps men's strength, rendering the most eminent submissive in her presence" (Sussman 121). In the first half of the novel, the narrator's comment anticipates Imoinda's effect on the men in Surinam: "I have seen an hundred white men sighing after her and making a thousand vows at her feet, all vain and unsuccessful" (16). Later Trefry notes "that all the white beauties he had seen, never charmed him so absolutely as this fine creature had done; and that no man of any nation ever beheld her that did not fall in love with her, and that she had all the slaves perpetually at her feet, and the whole country resounded with the fame of Clemene" (45). Focused on Imoinda, the slaves are unlikely to revolt; only Oroonoko's masculine agency foments a rebellion later in the narrative. For now, the lovers experience "joy and pleasure" in each other's presence so that "even fetters and slavery were soft and easy" (47). In love with a good woman, Oroonoko does not yet have rebellion on his mind, and Imoinda's love enables him to tolerate an evil institution. The feminine prevents masculine brutality in Trefry's case as well: he has contemplated raping her but notes that "*she disarms me with that modesty and weeping so tender and so moving that I retire, and thank my stars she overcame me*" (46). Statements such as these indicate that characters fail to distinguish between their own inner feminine principle and outer women. The anima is projected rather than being properly integrated, though this process for the present forestalls shadow projection.

Like the teenaged Imoinda, the narrator (not many years her senior) has a similar, though not sexualized, effect on Oroonoko. She describes how she "was obliged . . .

to discourse with Caesar when he becomes more impatient for the promised liberty. She "entertained him with the lives of the Romans" and with Christian theology—discussions that distract him from his concerns. She is clearly complicit in his captivity because a female presence mollifies and, for the moment, defuses a potentially brutal masculine agent by gently informing him that he will be confined if he attacks those on whom he projects his shadow. He then admits what the reader already knows—he has "suffered slavery so long" because of "love alone" (49); that is, he attributes his passivity-in-captivity to the tempering influence of his beloved Imoinda (49). The admission is ominous, however, because when the hero's psychic content is repressed rather than integrated, the shadow festers.

Worse than projecting the anima onto a woman is to fight a symbolic image of it, which is what happens next. Since Oroonoko's spirit remains "rough and fierce" (50), he needs more action than the narrator's conversations can supply. As a result, the Europeans engage him as their guide on various excursions into the jungle where he kills two tigers. The gender shifts in the narrator's description of the tiger slayings provide a key to the way in which these episodes further a point about shadow projection in the form of brutality. When the first beast comes at the party because they have been playing with its cub, Oroonoko

> ran his sword quite through *his* breast, down to *his* very heart, home to the hilt of the sword. The dying beast stretched forth *her* paw, and going to grasp his thigh, surprised with death in that very moment, did him no other harm than fixing *her* long nails in his flesh very deep, feebly wounded him, but could not grasp the flesh to tear off any.
>
> (53; emphases added)

Whereas this first tiger is male but becomes female in the killing, the second (a female) becomes male as it dies. Oroonoko

> shot *her* just into the eye; and the arrow was sent with so good a will and so sure a hand that it struck in *her* brain and made *her* caper and become mad for a moment or two, but being seconded by another arrow, *he* fell dead upon the prey. Caesar cut *him* open with a knife, to see where those wounds were that had been reported to him, and why *he* did not die of them . . . but when the heart of this courageous animal was taken out, there were seven bullets of lead in it, and the wounds seamed up with great scars, and *she* lived with the bullets a great while, for it was long since they were shot.
>
> (54; emphases added)

In one reading, the eye and heart signal essentialism: eye/head/*Logos*/reason versus heart/*eros*/relatedness/emotion. But these images also relate to Jung's link between animals and the feminine: "The anima also has affinities with animals, which symbolize her characteristics. Thus she can appear as a snake or a tiger or a bird"

(*CW* 9i, par. 358). Eric Miller emphasizes the same point in stating, "Pliny's tiger emphatically belongs to the female sex: the archetypal tiger is a 'she,' and a reproductive 'she' at that" (56–57). So the tigers, however their genders may shift, appear to represent the anima; and Johnson's view of the sword and the harp is relevant to Oroonoko's actions. Masculine images (the sword, the arrow) are not balanced with anything feminine; instead, they penetrate the feminine heart and eye, perhaps with Othello's reference to Desdemona's "precious eye" in the background (*Oth.* 4.3.68). As Miller also notes, the word "eye," the ocular organ, is a pun on "I," the first-person pronoun, so that Oroonoko's attack on the tiger represents his own inner dysfunction (64). Therefore, the tiger episodes suggest not only that gender is bifurcated in the novel but also that the masculine is attacking and slaying the feminine, the loss of which ultimately causes Oroonoko's psychic disintegration. In other words, fighting the tigers allegorizes Oroonoko's unconsciousness of his own feminine aspect and his losing battle for inner wholeness.

There is a still-deeper dimension of the projection process in the tiger slayings. It is especially significant that Oroonoko's sword pierces the tiger's heart in the first case and that he removes the bullet-ridden heart of the second tiger, for both hearts anticipate his murder of Imoinda, on whom he projects his heart and soul. The tigers' hearts may be "the heart of female Nature," as Robert A. Erickson suggests (210), but they also represent Oroonoko's own heart, emotional life, and well-being. In Africa, love talk has the following effect: "She [Imoinda] was touched with what he said, and returned it all in such answers as went to his very *heart*, with a pleasure unknown before" (17; emphasis added here and below). In Surinam, "Her griefs were so many darts in the great *heart* of Caesar" (61). As the narrator notes after the trip on which the tigers are slain, "his *heart* . . . took part with his charming Imoinda" (70–71). He believes that she is not only his heart but also his soul, and the latter association etymologically reinforces her role as a projection of his anima. As the narrator states,

> they spoke so well and so effectually, as Imoinda no longer doubted but she was the only delight and the darling of that *soul* she found pleading in them its right of love, which none was more willing to resign than she. And it was this powerful language alone that in an instant conveyed all the thoughts of their *souls* to each other, that they both found there wanted but opportunity to make them both entirely happy.
>
> (23)

Even more directly, she is later called "this treasure of his soul" (71). Since the anima/soul provides a bridge to the collective unconscious, Oroonoko's relationship with Imoinda does not connect him with the unconscious and provide a context for inner work. Rather, he projects onto her his feminine principle and his feminine soul. For him, she becomes the keeper and embodiment of these qualities; he does not welcome them into the wholeness of the Self. When he destroys her, even anima projection ceases, and psychic integration is no longer possible because murdering his beloved represents the forcible disconnection with the anima.

In summary, the novel moves beyond a stage in the projection process where women are said to prevent brutality by keeping the nonintegrated male shadow in check to a stage where the male hero brutally attacks wild animals who represent his own masculinity and femininity. Oroonoko's psyche is at war with itself, and shifting gender pronouns signal a lack of psychic integration: male, then female; female, then male; complementarity to be sure but never a healthy unity of both. The masculine attacks the feminine, and the feminine attacks back, sinking its claws into the hero, only to be permanently banished in the killing of Imoinda. Thus, by representing the unintegrated anima, the tiger slayings foreshadow the disintegration of Oroonoko's psyche.

Following the tiger episodes, Oroonoko, realizing that the white people's promises are hollow, organizes a slave rebellion, which fizzles in a way that illustrates the essentialist assumption that the presence of a woman obviates the need for inner work—that an outer complement stands in for genuine integration. The men are dissuaded from their course because they have wives and children (62). As Charlotte Sussman notes, "the sentimental attachments between husbands, wives, and children work to keep the slaves in captivity" (224). As with Oroonoko's love of Imoinda earlier in the book, women's love makes men *forgo* a good deed (in this case, resisting an evil institution). The hero is baited back into captivity by phony paperwork and is then brutally whipped, after which "Indian pepper" is rubbed into his wounds (67). This brutality is reported to the narrator because the fear that he would cut everyone's throats "made all the females of us fly down the river to be secured, and while we were away they [the men] acted this cruelty" (68). What she says next is crucially important: "For I suppose I had authority and interest enough there, had I suspected any such thing to have prevented it" (68). The narrator believes that a feminine presence could curb the shadow and prevent male brutality if, in fear and complicity, the women had not fled. But the more significant point is that curbing manifestations of the masculine shadow would be a repressive act that is not equivalent to integrating either the shadow or the anima. We are still in the realm of essentialism—women's presence may activate anima projection, which thwarts the individuation process.

The narrative moves swiftly to Oroonoko's decapitation of the pregnant Imoinda or, in psychological terms, the ultimate disunity with his own feminine side. The resulting psychic disintegration renders him unable to execute the desired revenge on his captors. Now "his grief swelled up to rage; he tore, he raved, he roared like some monster of the wood, calling on the loved name of Imoinda." The whites even say, "*O monster! that hast murdered thy wife*" (73). The two statements may echo Shakespeare's phrase, "some monster in thy thought," a fairly clear expression of the shadow in *Othello*, a play about another wife-murderer (3.3.119). In Behn's novel, the shadow manifests in Oroonoko's vow "to finish the great work" of his revenge, but he only kills one man after ripping out his own entrails, which "recalls that he has just effectively aborted Imoinda's child" (Sussman 220). When he heals from his self-inflicted wound, the whites execute him. The narrator is absent on this occasion as well, as are the somewhat-virtuous white men (Colonel Martin and Trefry); she hears the details of Oroonoko's death from her mother and sister who, in an echo of the crucifixion, "were by him all the while but not suffered to save him" from the executioner, "one Banister, a wild Irishman and one of the council, a fellow of absolute barbarity" (75–76).[2] In this final scene, even the presence of women no longer has a tempering effect on male brutality—the women are impotent spectators. The complicit narrator is absent; the women who *are* present can merely watch in horror. As Jacqueline Pearson emphasizes with italics, female authority fails: "The maleness of those who betray and torture Oroonoko is remorselessly stressed. . . . It is a 'Bold English*man*' and a 'wild Irish*man*' . . . who ultimately kill Oroonoko" (137). The male shadow is now so strongly projected that it overcomes the mitigating influence of anima projection; and the final fate of the hero's body, being cut into quarters, is a reverse quaternity image that reinforces the sense of disunity and anti-individuation.

The fact that much of the novel's violence takes place in the absence of women suggests not only an inappropriately bifurcated sense of gender but also a lack of integration and a projection of the shadow and the anima. The novel, however, deconstructs its own essentialist stance on male violence and female goodness in several ways. First, Imoinda is a warrior, a woman whose projected blind spots stand in the way of the shadow work that she herself needs to do. During the rebellion, she becomes a type of Amazon who shoots Byam in the shoulder, much as Oroonoko shoots the tiger through the eye. Imoinda's martial effort manifests a version of Behn's male characters' violence against the Other, and this parallelism shows the narrator's essentialism to be grounded in seventeenth-century European culture rather than in psychological reality. Second, the narrator may be complicit in the violence perpetrated by men, as Laura Brown acknowledges in observing "a perverse connection between the female narrator and Oroonoko's brutal executioners" (196). Third, there are male characters like Trefry who, though decent, support the institutional evils of slavery. In other words, although the novel does present examples of female benignity and extreme male violence, there is a middle ground where men are neither brutes nor saints, where the feminine principle (projected or not) has some impact, but where the ideology of slavery corrupts both sexes. Whether in real life or in Behn's fiction, humans' violence against other humans is not completely reducible to an ironclad axiom; but her depiction of the projection process, which enables slavery and impels the novel toward tragedy, does provide a compensatory critique of slave culture. That is, the novel critiques slavery to the exact degree that the characters reinforce and uphold it through the presence of projection and the lack of individuation. In the final analysis, the absence of women provides an occasion for the nonintegrated shadow to manifest brutally against Oroonoko, a key to understanding the shadow's role in the disintegration of his psyche, and a fable of male brutality that is still relevant to the cultural situation in the present day.

Notes

1   See Robert L. Chibka (523), Moira Ferguson (28, 38, and 48), Stephanie Athey and Daniel Cooper Alarcón (38–39), Jane Spencer (192), and Jacqueline Pearson (135).
2   See Erickson (213), Richard Kroll (576), and John 19.25.

WORKS CITED

Achebe, Chinua. "Chi in Igbo Cosmology." *Morning Yet on Creation Day*. Garden City: Anchor/Doubleday, 1975. 159–75.

——. "An Image of Africa: Racism in Conrad's *Heart of Darkness*." *Hopes and Impediments: Selected Essays*. New York: Doubleday, 1988. 1–20.

——. *Things Fall Apart*. 1958. New York: Knopf, 1992.

Achebe, Nwando. "Balancing Male and Female Principles: Teaching about Gender in Chinua Achebe's *Things Fall Apart*." *Ufahamu: A Journal of African Studies* 29.1 (2002): 121–43.

Adams, Michael Vannoy. *The Multicultural Imagination: "Race", Color, and the Unconscious*. New York: Routledge, 1996.

Akujobi, Remi. "African Literatures and Cultures and the Universal Motherhood." *Companion to Comparative Literature, World Literatures, and Comparative Cultural Studies*. Ed. Steven Tötösy de Zepetnek and Tutun Mukherjee. New Delhi: Foundation, 2013. 371–81.

Anyokwu, Christopher. "Re-Imagining Gender in Chinua Achebe's *Things Fall Apart*." *Interdisciplinary Literary Studies: A Journal of Criticism and Theory* 12.2 (2011): 16–31.

"Apocatastasis." *The Cambridge Dictionary of Philosophy*. *Credo Reference*. Web. 28 July 2014.

Appiah, Kwame Anthony. Introduction. *Things Fall Apart*. By Chinua Achebe. ix–xvii.

Arnold, Matthew. "Dover Beach." *Victorian Poetry and Prose*. Ed. Lionel Trilling and Harold Bloom. New York: Oxford UP, 1973. 593–94.

"Arrigo Boito, *Mefistofele*." *The New Kobbé's Opera Book*. Ed. The Earl of Harewood and Antony Peattie. New York: G. P. Putnam's Sons, 1997. 90–01.

Athey, Stephanie, and Daniel Cooper Alarcón. "*Oroonoko*'s Gendered Economies of Honor/ Horror: Reframing Colonial Discourse Studies in the Americas." *Subjects & Citizens: Nation, Race, and Gender from* Oroonoko *to* Anita Hill. Ed. Michael Moon and Cathy N. Davidson. Durham: Duke UP, 1995. 27–55.

Attridge, Derek. "Age of Bronze, State of Grace: Music and Dogs in Coetzee's *Disgrace*." *Novel: A Forum on Fiction* 34.1 (2000): n.p. *MLA International Bibliography*. Web. 18 Aug. 2015.

Austin, Sue. "Desire, Fascination and the Other: Some Thoughts on Jung's Interest in Rider Haggard's 'She' and on the Nature of Archetypes." *Harvest: International Journal for Jungian*

Studies 50.2 (2004): n.p. Rpt. in *Reflections on Psychology, Culture and Life: The Jung Page.* Web. 30 Mar. 2014.

Barash, Carol. Introduction. *An Olive Schreiner Reader: Writing on Women and South Africa.* Ed. Carol Barash. New York: Pandora, 1987. 1–20.

——. "Virile Womanhood: Olive Schreiner's Narratives of a Master Race." *Speaking of Gender.* Ed. Elaine Showalter. New York: Routledge, 1989. 269–81.

Barnard, Alan. "The Lost World of Laurens van der Post?" *Current Anthropology* 30.1 (1989): 104–14. *JSTOR.* Web. 7 Aug. 2014.

Baym, Nina. "Feminist Perspective: 'Actually I Felt Sorry for the Lion.'" Krstovic 115–20.

Beard, Margo. "Lessons from the Dead Masters: Wordsworth and Byron in J. M. Coetzee's *Disgrace.*" *English in Africa* 34.1 (2007): n.p. *Literature Resource Center.* Web. 25 Sept. 2015.

Behn, Aphra. *Oroonoko, or the Royal Slave: A True History.* 1688. Ed. Janet Todd. New York: Penguin, 2003.

Bender, Bert. "Margot Macomber's Gimlet." Krstovic 92–97.

Berkman, Joyce Avrech. *The Healing Imagination of Olive Schreiner.* Amherst: U of Massachusetts P, 1989.

Bevington, David, ed. *The Complete Works of Shakespeare.* 4th ed. New York: HarperCollins, 1992.

Blake, Kathleen. *Love and the Woman Question in Victorian Literature: The Art of Self-Postponement.* Totowa: Barnes & Noble, 1983.

Blake, William. "Auguries of Innocence." Perkins 150–52.

——. *The Marriage of Heaven and Hell.* Perkins 103–10.

——. "To Tirzah." Perkins 96–97.

Bleek, W. H. I., and L. C. Lloyd, ed. and comp. *Specimens of Bushman Folklore.* London: George Allen, 1911.

Blixen, Karen. *Out of Africa.* New York: Penguin, 1937.

Bohm, David. *Wholeness and the Implicate Order.* New York: Routledge, 1980.

Boito, Arrigo. *Libretto of* Mefistofele. *Opera in Four Acts.* Trans. Theodore T. Barker. Boston: Oliver Ditson, 1880.

Bolling, Douglas. "Structure and Theme in *Briefing For A Descent Into Hell.*" *Contemporary Literature* 14.4 (1973): 550–64. *JSTOR.* Web. 1 June 2015.

Born, Brad S. "Kingsolver's Gospel for Africa: (Western White Female) Heart of Goodness." *Mennonite Life* 56.1 (2001): n.p. Web. 4 Dec. 2015.

Brandon, Ruth. *The New Women and the Old Men: Love, Sex and the Woman Question.* New York: Norton, 1990.

Brantlinger, Patrick. *Rule of Darkness: British Literature and Imperialism, 1830–1914.* Ithaca: Cornell UP, 1988.

Breuer, Horst. "Hemingway's 'Francis Macomber' in Pirandellian and Freudian Perspective." Krstovic 190–97.

Bristow, Joseph. Introduction. *The Story of an African Farm.* By Olive Schreiner. vii–xxix.

Brodersen, Elizabeth, and Michael Glock, eds. *Jungian Perspectives on Rebirth and Renewal: Phoenix Rising.* New York: Routledge, 2017.

Brontë, Charlotte. Jane Eyre: *Authoritative Text, Backgrounds, Criticism.* Ed. Richard J. Dunn. 2nd ed. New York: Norton, 1987. 1–398. Norton Critical Edition.

Brown, David Maughan. "The Noble Savage in Anglo-Saxon Colonial Ideology, 1950–1980: 'Masai' and "Bushmen' in popular fiction." *English in Africa* 10.2 (1983): 55–77.

Brown, Laura. "The Romance of Empire: *Oroonoko* and the Trade in Slaves." Todd 180–208.

Browne, Sir Thomas. *Religio Medici. The Broadview Anthology of Seventeenth-Century Verse & Prose.* Ed. Alan Rudrum et al. Peterborough, Can.: Broadview, 2000. 465–88.

Brunner, Cornelia. *Anima as Fate*. Ed. David Scott May. Trans. Julius Heuscher. Dallas: Spring, 1986.

Burdett, Carolyn. *Olive Schreiner and the Progress of Feminism*. New York: Palgrave, 2001.

Burke, Colleen. "Joseph Conrad's *Heart of Darkness*: A Metaphor of Jungian Psychology." 1996. Web. 19 May 2016.

Burleson, Blake W. *Jung in Africa*. New York: Continuum, 2005.

Byron, George Gordon, Lord. "So, We'll go No More A-Roving." Perkins 896.

Campbell, Joseph. *The Hero with a Thousand Faces*. Princeton: Princeton UP, 1949.

Carpenter, Frederic I. *Laurens van der Post*. New York: Twayne, 1969.

Carroll, David. *Chinua Achebe*. New York: Twayne, 1970.

Cederstrom, Lorelei. *Fine-Tuning the Feminine Psyche: Jungian Patterns in the Novels of Doris Lessing*. New York: Peter Lang, 1990.

Cheatham, George. "The Unhappy Life of Robert Wilson." Krstovic 112–14.

Chibka, Robert L. "'Oh! Do Not Fear a Woman's Invention': Truth, Falsehood, and Fiction in Aphra Behn's *Oroonoko*." *Texas Studies in Literature and Language* 30 (1988): 510–37.

Clayton, Cherry. "Olive (Emilie Albertina) Schreiner." *South African Writers*. Ed. Paul A. Scanlon. *Dictionary of Literary Biography*. Vol. 225. Detroit: Gale, 2000. n.p. *Literature Resource Center*. Web. 30 May 2014.

——. *Olive Schreiner*. New York: Twayne, 1997.

Clingman, Stephen. *The Novels of Nadine Gordimer*. 2nd ed. Amherst: U of Massachusetts P, 1992. E-book.

Cobbam, Rhonda. "Problems of Gender and History in the Teaching of *Things Fall Apart*." *Modern Critical Interpretations of Chinua Achebe's* Things Fall Apart. Ed. Harold Bloom. Philadelphia: Chelsea, 2003. 19–30.

Coetzee, J. M. *Disgrace*. London: Vintage, 1999.

——. *White Writing: On the Culture of Letters in South Africa*. New Haven: Yale UP, 1988.

Cohen, Morton. *Rider Haggard: His Life and Works*. London: Hutchinson, 1960.

Coleridge, Samuel Taylor. *Biographia Literaria*. Perkins 563–607.

Conrad, Joseph. Heart of Darkness: *Case Studies in Contemporary Criticism*. Ed. Ross C. Murfin. New York: St. Martin's, 1989. 17–94.

Conway, Cecilia. "The Banjo-Song Genre: A Study of 'High Sheriff,' Dink Roberts's Man-against-the-Law Song." *Arts in Earnest: North Carolina Folklife*. Ed. Daniel W. Patterson and Charles G. Zug III. Durham: Duke UP, 1990. 135–46.

Corley, Íde. "Conjuncture, Hypermasculinity and Disavowal in *Things Fall Apart*." *Interventions: International Journal of Postcolonial Studies* 11.2 (2009): 203–11.

Cott, Jonathan. *Isis and Osiris: Exploring the Goddess Myth*. New York: Doubleday, 1994.

Crawford, Claudia. "*She*." *SubStance: A Review of Theory & Literary Criticism* 9.29 (1980): 83–96. *JSTOR*. Web. 21 Aug. 2013.

DeFalco, Joseph. *The Hero in Hemingway's Short Stories*. Pittsburgh: U of Pittsburgh P, 1963.

DeMarr, Mary Jean. *Barbara Kingsolver: A Critical Companion*. Westport: Greenwood, 1999.

Demory, Pamela H. "Into the Heart of Light: Barbara Kingsolver Rereads *Heart of Darkness*." *Conradiana: A Journal of Joseph Conrad Studies* 34.3 (2002): 181–93. *Academic One File*. Web. 23 Nov. 2015.

Dickinson, Philip. "Feeling, Affect, Exposure: Ethical (In)capacity, the Sympathetic Imagination, and J. M. Coetzee's *Disgrace*." *Mosaic* 46.4 (2013): n.p. *Literature Resource Center*. Web. 25 Sept. 2015.

Didion, Joan. "Review of *Briefing for a Descent into Hell*." Sprague and Tiger 192–96.

Dodson, Daphne. "Rebirthing Biblical Myth: *The Poisonwood Bible* as Visionary Art." Brodersen and Glock 74–85.

Drob, Sanford L. *Reading* The Red Book: *An Interpretive Guide to C. G. Jung's* Liber Novus. New Orleans: Spring Journal, 2012.

DuPlessis, Rachel Blau. *Writing beyond the Ending: Narrative Strategies of Twentieth-Century Women Writers*. Bloomington: Indiana UP, 1985.

Easton, Kai. "Coetzee's *Disgrace*: Byron in Italy and the Eastern Cape c. 1820." *Journal of Commonwealth Literature* 42.3 (2007): 113–30.

Eby, Carl P. *Hemingway's Fetishism: Psychoanalysis and the Mirror of Manhood*. Albany: State U of New York P, 1999.

Eby, Cecil D. "Hemingway's 'The Short Happy Life of Francis Macomber.'" Krstovic 133.

Edinger, Edward F. *Goethe's* Faust: *Notes for a Jungian Commentary*. Toronto: Inner City, 1990.

———. *Melville's* Moby-Dick: *An American* Nekyia. Toronto: Inner City, 1995.

Eliot, T. S. "The Love Song of J. Alfred Prufrock." *Modern British Literature*. Ed. Frank Kermode and John Hollander. New York: Oxford UP, 1973. 464–68.

———. "*Ulysses*, Order, and Myth." *Selected Prose of T. S. Eliot*. Ed. Frank Kermode. New York: Farrar, 1975. 175–78.

Ellis, Peter Berresford. *H. Rider Haggard: A Voice from the Infinite*. London: Routledge & Kegan Paul,1978.

Emerson, Ralph Waldo. "Self-Reliance." *Selections from Ralph Waldo Emerson*. Ed. Stephen E. Whicher. Boston: Houghton, 1957. 147–68.

En-nehas, Jamal. "Laurens van der Post's Ventures to the Interior: A Study in Travel, Cultural Quests, and Self-Exploration." Diss. U of New Brunswick, 1995.

Erickson, Robert A. "Mrs. A. Behn and the Myth of Oroonoko-Imoinda." *Eighteenth-Century Fiction* 3 (1993): 201–16.

Esty, Jed. "The Colonial Bildungsroman: *The Story of an African Farm* and the Ghost of Goethe." *Victorian Studies: An Interdisciplinary Journal of Social, Political, and Cultural Studies* 49 (2007): 407–30.

Etherington, Norman. *Rider Haggard*. Boston: Twayne, 1984.

———, ed. *The Annotated "She": A Critical Edition of H. Rider Haggard's Victorian Romance with Introduction and Notes*. Bloomington: Indiana UP, 1991.

Evans, Robert O. "Conrad's Underworld." *Modern Fiction Studies* 2 (1956): 56–62.

Fantina, Richard. *Ernest Hemingway: Machismo and Machoism*. New York: Palgrave Macmillan, 2005.

Farrell, Marcia K. "Poster Children: Laurens van der Post's Imperial Propaganda in *A Far-Off Place*." *Ariel: A Review of International English Literature* 42.3–4 (2011): 315–32. *Literature Resource Center*. Web. 7 Aug. 2014.

Feder, Lillian. "Marlow's Descent into Hell." *Nineteenth-Century Fiction* 9 (1955): 280–92.

Ferguson, Moira. *Subject to Others: British Women Writers and Colonial Slavery, 1670–1834*. New York: Routledge, 1992.

Fike, Matthew A. *A Jungian Study of Shakespeare: The Visionary Mode*. New York: Palgrave Macmillan, 2009.

———. *The One Mind: C. G. Jung and the Future of Literary Criticism*. New York: Routledge, 2014.

———. "Time Is Not an Arrow: Anima and History in H. Rider Haggard's *She*." *ANQ: A Quarterly Journal of Short Articles, Notes and Reviews* 28.2 (2015): 105–09.

———. "Visionary and Psychological: Jung's 1925 Seminar and H. Rider Haggard's *She*." Brodersen and Glock 245–57.

First, Ruth, and Ann Scott. *Olive Schreiner: A Biography*. New Brunswick: Rutgers UP, 1980.

Fishburn, Katherine. *The Unexpected Universe of Doris Lessing: A Study in Narrative Technique*. Westport: Greenwood, 1985.

Flora, Joseph M. *Ernest Hemingway: A Study of the Short Fiction*. Boston: Twayne, 1989.

Franssen, Paul J. C. M. "Pollux in Coetzee's *Disgrace*." *Notes and Queries* 57.2 (2010): 240–43.

Gaillard, Theodore L., Jr. "The Critical Menagerie in 'The Short Happy Life of Francis Macomber." *English Journal* 60.1 (1971): 31–35. *National Council of Teachers of English*. Web. 13 Mar. 2013.

Gardner, Martin. "Ernest Hemingway and Jane." Krstovic 187–90.

Gilbert, Sandra M. "Rider Haggard's Heart of Darkness." *Reading* Fin de Siècle *Fictions*. Ed. Lyn Pykett. New York: Longman, 1996. 39–46.

Gilbert, Sandra M., and Susan Gubar. *No Man's Land: The Place of the Woman Writer in the Twentieth Century*. Vol. 2. New Haven: Yale UP, 1989.

Giles, Jana María. "Of Gods and Dogs: The Postcolonial Sublime in Coetzee's Disgrace, or, David Lurie's Aesthetic Education." *Sublime Today: Contemporary Readings in the Aesthetic*. Ed. Gillian Pierce. Newcastle-upon-Tyne: Cambridge Scholars, 2012. 13–48.

Goethe, Johann Wolfgang von. *Faust*. Ed. Cyrus Hamlin. Trans. Walter Arndt. New York: Norton, 1976. Norton Critical Edition.

Gold, Barri J. "Embracing the Corpse: Discursive Recycling in H. Rider Haggard's *She*." *English Literature in Transition, 1880–1920* 38.3 (1995): 305–27.

Golden, Kenneth L. "Joseph Conrad's Mr. Kurtz and Jungian *Enantiodromia*." *Interpretations* 13.1 (1981): 31–38.

Gordimer, Nadine. *July's People*. New York: Viking, 1981.

"The Gospel of Thomas." Trans. Thomas O. Lambdin, B. P. Grenfell, and A. S. Hunt. Commentary by Craig Schenk. Web. 23 Dec. 2015. <www.sacred-texts.com/chr/thomas.html>.

Gray, Stephen. *Southern African Literature: An Introduction*. Cape Town: David Philip, 1979.

Grayson, Erik. "'Moderated Bliss': Coetzee's *Disgrace* as Existential Maturation." *Journal of African Literature and Culture* (2006): 177–88.

Haggard, H. Rider. *Ayesha, the Return of She*. N.p.: CreateSpace, 2012.

——. *She: A History of Adventure*. 1886. Ed. Andrew M. Stauffer. Peterborough, Can.: Broadview, 2006.

Hallock, John W. M. "H(enry) Rider Haggard." *British Travel Writers, 1876–1909*. Ed. Barbara Brothers and Julia Marie Gergits. *Dictionary of Literary Biography*. Vol. 174. Detroit: Gale Research, 1997. *Literature Resource Center*. Web. 16 July 2013.

Hämäläinen, Nora. "The Personal Pilgrimage of David Lurie—or Why Coetzee's *Disgrace* Should and Should Not Be Read in Terms of an Ethics of Perception." *Partial Answers* 11.2 (2013): 233–55.

Hannah, Barbara. *Jung: His Life and Work: A Biographical Memoir*. New York: Putnam's, 1976.

Hardin, Nancy Shields. "Doris Lessing and the Sufi Way." *Contemporary Literature* 14.4 (1973): 565–81. *JSTOR*. Web. 18 May 2015.

Hardy, Donald E. "Strategic Politeness in Hemingway's 'The Short Happy Life of Francis Macomber.'" Krstovic 122–32.

Harper Study Bible: Revised Standard Version. Ed. Harold Lindsell. Rev. ed. Grand Rapids: Zondervan, 1971.

Harrington, Gary. "'A Plague of All Cowards': 'Macomber' and *Henry IV*." Krstovic 151–56.

Harrow, Kenneth W. "Gordimer *contre* Hemingway: Crossing back through the Mirror That Subtends All Speculation." Krstovic 167–75.

Harvey, Melinda. "Re-educating the Romantic: Sex and the Nature-Poet in J. M. Coetzee's *Disgrace*." *Sydney Studies in English* 31 (2005): 94–108.

Haugh, Robert F. *Nadine Gordimer*. New York: Twayne, 1974.

Hayes, Patrick. "'In the heart of the labyrinth': J. M. Coetzee and Political Emotions." *Critical Insights: Political Fiction*. Ed. Mark Levene. Amenia: Grey House, 2014. 97–115.

Hayman, Ronald. *A Life of Jung*. New York: Norton, 1999.

Head, Dominic. *Nadine Gordimer*. New York: Cambridge UP, 1994. Cambridge Studies in African and Caribbean Literature.

Heaney, Claire. "Emotional Intelligence: Literature, Ethics and Affective Cognition in J. M. Coetzee's *Disgrace*." *Understanding Knowledge Creation: Intellectuals in Academia, the Public Sphere and the Arts*. Ed. Nikita Basov and Oleksandra Nenko. Amsterdam: Rodopi, 2012. 141–66.

Heller, Tamar. "The Unbearable Hybridity of Female Sexuality: Racial Ambiguity and the Gothic in Rider Haggard's *She*." *Horrifying Sex: Essays on Sexual Difference in Gothic Literature*. Ed. Ruth Bienstock Anolik. Jefferson: McFarland, 2007. 55–66.

Hemingway, Ernest. *Death in the Afternoon*. 1932. New York: Scribner's, 1955.

——. *A Farewell to Arms*. 1929. New York: Scribner's, 1969.

——. *Green Hills of Africa*. New York: Scribner's, 1935.

——. "The Short Happy Life of Francis Macomber." *The Complete Short Stories of Ernest Hemingway*. The Finca Vigía Edition. New York: Scribner's, 1987. 5–28.

Henderson, Richard N. *The King in Every Man: Evolutionary Trends in Onitsha Ibo Society and Culture*. New Haven: Yale UP, 1972.

Herbert, George. "The Pulley." Hollander and Kermode 672.

Hill, Michael Ortiz. "C. G. Jung in the Heart of Darkness." *Spring: A Journal of Archetype and Culture* 61 (1997): 125–33.

Hillman, James. *Anima: An Anatomy of a Personified Notion*. Dallas: Spring, 1985.

——. *The Dream and the Underworld*. New York: Harper, 1979.

Hinz, Evelyn J. "Rider Haggard's *She*: An Archetypal 'History of Adventure.'" *Studies in the Novel* 4.3 (1972): 416–31.

Hollander, John, and Frank Kermode, eds. *The Literature of Renaissance England*. New York: Oxford UP, 1973.

Hopkins, Gerard Manley. "No Worst, There Is None." *The Oxford Anthology of English Literature*. Ed. Lionel Trilling and Harold Bloom. New York: Oxford UP, 1973. 686.

Hovey, Richard B. *Hemingway: The Inward Terrain*. Seattle: U of Washington P, 1968.

Howe, Florence. "A Conversation with Doris Lessing (1966)." *Contemporary Literature* 14.4 (1973): 418–36. *JSTOR*. Web. 18 May 2015.

Howell, John M. *Hemingway's African Stories: The Stories, Their Sources, Their Critics*. New York: Scribner's, 1969.

Hutton, Virgil. "The Short Happy Life of Macomber." *The Short Stories of Ernest Hemingway: Critical Essays*. Ed. Jackson J. Benson. Durham: Duke UP, 1975. 239–50.

Innes, C. L. *Chinua Achebe*. New York: Cambridge UP, 1990. Cambridge Studies in African and Caribbean Literature.

Innes, C. L., and Bernth Lindfors, eds. *Critical Perspectives on Chinua Achebe*. Washington, DC: Three Continents, 1978.

Irele, F. Abiola. *The African Imagination: Literature in Africa & the Black Diaspora*. New York: Oxford UP, 2001. E-book.

"Ivan Ribar." *Wikipedia*. 8 June 2015. Web. 7 July 2015.

Iyasere, Solomon O. "Okonkwo's Participation in the Killing of His 'Son' in Chinua Achebe's *Things Fall Apart*: A Study of Ignoble Decisiveness." Iyasere 129–40.

——, ed. *Understanding* Things Fall Apart: *Selected Essays and Criticism*. Troy: Whitston, 1998.

Jabbi, Bu-Buakei. "Fire and Transition in *Things Fall Apart*." Innes and Lindfors 135–47.

Jacobs, J. U. "Translating the 'Heart of Darkness': Cross-Cultural Discourse in the Contemporary Congo Book." *Current Writing: Text and Reception in South Africa* 14.2 (2002): 104–17.

JanMohamed, Abdul R. *Manichean Aesthetics: The Politics of Literature in Colonial Africa.* Amherst: U of Massachusetts P, 1983.

——. "Sophisticated Primitivism: The Syncretism of Oral and Literate Modes in Achebe's *Things Fall Apart*." Iyasere 86–105.

Johnson, Robert A. *We: Understanding the Psychology of Romantic Love.* New York: Harper, 1983.

Jones, J. D. F. *Teller of Many Tales: The Lives of Laurens van der Post.* New York: Carroll & Graf, 2001.

Jua, Roselyne M. "*Things Fall Apart* and Achebe's Search for Manhood." *Interventions: International Journal of Postcolonial Studies* 11.2 (2009): 199–202.

Jung, Carl G. *Analytical Psychology: Notes of the Seminar Given in 1925 by C. G. Jung.* Ed. William McGuire. Princeton: Princeton UP, 1989. Bollingen Ser. 99.

——. *The Collected Works of C. G. Jung.* Ed Sir Herbert Read et al. Trans. R. F. C. Hull. 20 vols. Princeton: Princeton UP, 1953–1979. Bollingen Ser. 10.

——. *Letters.* Ed. Gerhard Adler and Aniela Jaffé. Trans. R. F. C. Hull. 2 vols. Princeton: Princeton UP, 1973–1975. Bollingen Ser. 95.

——. *Memories, Dreams, Reflections.* Ed. Aniela Jaffé. Trans. Richard and Clara Winston. New York: Vintage, 1989.

——. *The Red Book:* Liber Novus. Ed. Sonu Shamdasani. Trans. Mark Kyburz, John Peck, and Sonu Shamdasani. New York: Norton, 2009.

——. *Visions: Notes of the Seminar Given in 1930–1934 by C. G. Jung.* Ed. Claire Douglas. 2 vols. Princeton: Princeton UP, 1997. Bollingen Ser. 99.

Kast, Verena. "Anima/animus." Trans. Bobbi Whitcombe. *The Handbook of Jungian Psychology: Theory, Practice and Applications.* Ed. Renos K. Papadopoulos. New York: Routledge, 2006. 113–29.

Kates, Bonnie R. "Novels of Individuation: Jungian Readings in Fiction." Diss. U of Massachusetts, 1978.

Katz, Wendy R. *Rider Haggard and the Fiction of Empire: A Critical Study of British Imperial Fiction.* New York: Cambridge, UP, 1987.

Keats, John. "Ode on a Grecian Urn." Perkins 1252–53.

——. "To George and Tom Keats." 12–27 Dec. 1817. Letter. Perkins 1275–76.

Keynes, Geoffrey, ed. *The Letters of William Blake.* New York: Macmillan, 1956.

Kingsolver, Barbara. *The Poisonwood Bible.* 1998. New York: Harper Perennial Modern Classics, 2005.

Klein, Carole. *Doris Lessing: A Biography.* New York: Carrol & Graf, 2000.

Klopper, Dirk. "In Pursuit of the Primitive: Van der Post's Lost World." *Current Writing* 20.1 (2008): 38–53.

Kravitz, Bennett. "'She Loves Me, She Loves Me Not': The Short Happy Symbiotic Marriage of Margot and Francis Macomber." *Journal of American Culture* 21.3 (1998): 83–87.

Kroll, Richard. "Tales of Love and Gallantry." *Ariel: A Review of International English Literature* 67 (2004): 573–604.

Krstovic, Jelena, ed. "'The Short Happy Life of Francis Macomber.'" *Short Story Criticism.* Vol. 137. Detroit: Gale, Censage Learning, 2010. 90–237. *Literary Criticism Online.* Web. 3 Jan. 2013.

Kruminiene, Jadvyga, and Arturas Cechanovicius. "On Some Jungian Archetypes Reflected in Joseph Conrad's *Heart of Darkness*." *Respectus Philologicus* 20.25 (2011): 107–21.

Kucich, John. *Imperial Masochism: British Fiction, Fantasy, and Social Class*. Princeton: Princeton UP, 2007.

Kunz, Diane. "White Men in Africa: On Barbara Kingsolver's *The Poisonwood Bible*." *Novel History: Historians and Novelists Confront America's Past (and Each Other)*. Ed. Mark C. Carnes. New York: Simon, 2001. 285–97.

Laing, R. D. *The Politics of Experience*. New York: Pantheon, 1967.

Lane, Christopher. "'Gregory's Womanhood' in Schreiner's *The Story of an African Farm*." *The Burdens of Intimacy: Psychoanalysis and Victorian Masculinity*. Chicago: U of Chicago P, 1999. 93–18. Rpt. in *Twentieth-Century Literary Criticism*. Ed. Lawrence J. Trudeau. Vol. 235. Detroit: Gale, 2010. *Literature Resource Center*. Web. 30 May 2014.

Larson, Kelli A. "On Safari with Hemingway: Tracking the Most Recent Scholarship." *Hemingway in Africa*. Ed. Miriam B. Mandel. Rochester: Camden, 2011. 323–83.

Lessing, Doris. *Briefing for a Descent into Hell*. London: Jonathan Cape, 1971.

——. "Hunger." *The Sun Between Their Feet*. Frogmore: Triad/Panther, 1979. 208–331.

——. Introduction. *Learning How To Learn*. By Idries Shah. San Francisco: Harper, 1981. n.p.

——. *Shikasta*. New York: Knopf, 1979.

——. "The Temptation of Jack Orkney." *The Temptation of Jack Orkney & Other Stories* New York: Knopf, 1972. 231–308.

——. *Under My Skin: Volume One of My Autobiography to 1949*. New York: HarperCollins, 1994.

——. *Walking in the Shade: Volume Two of My Autobiography, 1949–1962*. New York: HarperCollins, 1997.

Lewis, C. S. *A Preface to* Paradise Lost. New York: Oxford UP, 1961.

Libby, Andrew. "Revisiting the Sublime: Terrible Women and the Aesthetics of Misogyny in H. Rider Haggard's *King Solomon's Mines* and *She*." *CEA Critic* 67.1 (2004): 1–14.

Lloyd, D. W. "Beyond the Colonial Novel: The Last Novels of Laurens van der Post." *Literature & Theology* 13.4 (1999): 323–32.

Lynn, Kenneth S. *Hemingway*. New York: Simon, 1987.

Lynn, Thomas J. "Trickster and Carnival in *Things Fall Apart*." *Publications of the Arkansas Philological Association* 23.1 (1997): 49–70.

Macaskill, Brian. "Entr'acte: Cannibalism, Semiophagy, and the *Plunk-Plink-Plonk* of Banjo Strings in J. M. Coetzee's *Disgrace*." *African Cultures and Literatures: A Miscellany*. Ed. Gordon Collier. Amsterdam: Rodopi, 2012. 137–81.

Mannoni, Octave. *Prospero and Caliban: The Psychology of Colonization*. Trans. Pamela Powesland. New York: Praeger, 1964.

Marchino, Lois A. "The Search for Self in the Novels of Doris Lessing." *Studies in the Novel* 4.2 (1972): 252–61.

Marlowe, Christopher. *Doctor Faustus*. Hollander and Kermode 348–99.

Mazlish, Bruce. "A Triptych: Freud's *The Interpretation of Dreams*, Rider Haggard's *She,* and Bulwer-Lytton's *The Coming Race*." *Comparative Studies in Society and History* 35.4 (1993): 726–45. *JSTOR*. Web. 16 Aug. 2013.

Mazzanti, Roberta. "Lyndall's Sphinx: Images of Female Sexuality and Roles in *The Story of an African Farm*." *The Flawed Diamond: Essays on Olive Schreiner*. Ed. Itala Vivan. Sydney: Dangaroo, 1991. 121–34.

McDonald, William E., ed. *Encountering* Disgrace: *Reading and Teaching Coetzee's Novel*. Rochester: Camden, 2009.

McGuckin, John A. *St Gregory of Nazianus: An Intellectual Biography*. Crestland: St. Vladimir's Seminary, 2001.

McKenna, John J., and Marvin V. Peterson. "More Muddy Water: Wilson's Shakespeare in 'The Short Happy Life of Francis Macomber." Krstovic 97–99.

McLaughlan, Robbie. *Re-imagining the 'Dark Continent' in* fin de siècle *Literature*. Edinburgh: Edinburgh UP, 2012.

McLean, Adam. *The Triple Goddess: An Exploration of the Archetypal Feminine*. Grand Rapids: Phanes, 1989. Hermetic Research Ser. Number 1.

McNeal, Nancy. "Joseph Conrad's Voice in the *Heart of Darkness*: A Jungian Approach." *Journal of Evolutionary Psychology* 1.1 (1979): 1–12.

Meire, Héloïse. "Women, a Dark Continent? *The Poisonwood Bible* as a Feminist Response to Conrad's *Heart of Darkness*." *Seeds of Change: Critical Essays on Barbara Kingsolver*. Ed. Priscilla Leder. Knoxville: U of Tennessee P, 2010. 71–86.

Mellard, James. "Myth and Archetype in 'Heart of Darkness.'" *Tennessee Studies in Literature* 13 (1968): 1–15.

Melville, Herman. *Moby-Dick; or The White Whale*. 1851. New York: Signet Classic, 1961.

Miller, Eric. "Aphra Behn's Tigers." *Dalhousie Review* 81.1 (2001): 47–65.

Milton, John. *Paradise Lost*. *The Riverside Milton*. Ed. Roy Flannagan. Boston: Houghton, 1998. 349–710.

Monsman, Gerald. *Olive Schreiner's Fiction: Landscape and Power*. New Brunswick: Rutgers UP, 1991.

Moss, John G. "Three Motifs in Haggard's *She*." *English Literature in Transition* 16.1 (1973): 27–34.

Murphy, Patricia. *Time Is of the Essence: Temporality, Gender, and the New Woman*. Albany: SU of New York P, 2001.

Myers, Jeffrey. *Hemingway: Life into Art*. New York: Cooper Square, 2000.

Newman, John Henry Cardinal. *Essays and Sketches*. Ed. Charles Frederick Harrold. Vol. 3. New York: Longmans, 1948.

O'Connor, Robert. "Beauty of Truth: Ayesha's Faustian Dilemma in H. Rider Haggard's *She*." *Lamar Journal of the Humanities* 36.1 (2011): 43–55.

Ogbaa, Kalu. *Gods, Oracles and Divination: Folkways in Chinua Achebe's Novels*. Trenton: Africa World, 1992.

Ognibene, Elaine R. "The Missionary Position: Barbara Kingsolver's *The Poisonwood Bible*." *College Literature* 30.3 (2003): 19–36.

Okpewho, Isidore, ed. *Chinua Achebe's* Things Fall Apart*: A Casebook*. New York: Oxford UP, 2003.

Oliver, Charles M. *Ernest Hemingway: A Literary Reference to His Life and Work*. New York: Facts on File, 2007.

O'Neill, Kevin. "The Dispossession of David Lurie." McDonald 202–29.

Opata, Damian U. "Eternal Sacred Order versus Conventional Wisdom: A Consideration of Moral Culpability in the Killing of Ikemefuna in *Things Fall Apart*." Okpewho 83–94.

Parkin-Gounelas, Ruth. *Fictions of the Female Self: Charlotte Brontë, Olive Schreiner, Katherine Mansfield*. London: Macmillan, 1991.

Paxton, Nancy L. "*The Story of an African Farm* and the Dynamics of Woman-to-Woman Influence." *Texas Studies in Literature and Language* 30.4 (1988): 652–82.

Pearson, Jacqueline. "Gender and Narrative in the Fiction of Aphra Behn." Todd 111–42.

Perkins, David, ed. *English Romantic Writers*. 2nd ed. New York: Harcourt, 1995.

Perrakis, Phyllis Sternberg. "Sufism, Jung and the Myth of the Kore: Revisionist Politics in Lessing's *Marriages*." *Mosaic: A Journal for the Interdisciplinary Study of Literature* 25.3 (1992): 99–120.

Pickrell, Alan. "Rider Haggard's Female Characters: From Goddess of the Cave to Goddess of the Screen." *Dime Novel Round-up* 67.1 (1998): 18–26.

Plato. *Phaedrus. The Collected Dialogues of Plato Including the Letters.* Ed. Edith Hamilton and Huntington Cairns. Princeton: Princeton UP, 1961. 475–525. Bollingen Ser. 71.

"Portrait of an ENFJ." personalitypage.com. Web. 19 Mar. 2013.

"Portrait of an ISTP." personalitypage.com. Web. 19 Mar. 2013.

Pratt, Annis V. *Archetypal Patterns in Women's Fiction.* Bloomington: Indiana UP, 1981.

———. "Spinning Among Fields: Jung, Frye, Lévi-Strauss, and Feminist Archetypal Theory." *Jungian Literary Criticism.* Ed. Richard P. Sugg. Evanston: Northwestern UP, 1992. 153–66.

Purcell, William F. "Barbara Kingsolver's *The Poisonwood Bible* and the Essentializing of Africa: A Critical Double Standard?" *Notes on Contemporary Literature* 37.5 (2007): 2–4. *Literature Resource Center.* Web. 23 Nov. 2015.

———. "The Gospel According to Barbara Kingsolver: Brother Fowles and St. Francis of Assisi in *The Poisonwood Bible.*" *Logos* 12.1 (2009): 93–116.

Raskin, Johan. "Doris Lessing at Stony Brook: An Interview by Johan Raskin." *A Small Personal Voice: Doris Lessing Essays, Reviews, Interviews.* Ed. Paul Schlueter. New York: Knopf, 1974. 61–76.

Robb, Kenneth A. "Laurens (Jan) van der Post." *British Travel Writers, 1940–1997.* Ed. Barbara Brothers and Julia Marie Gergits. *Dictionary of Literary Biography.* Vol. 204. Detroit: Gale, 1997. Web. 28 July 2014.

Rodgers, Terence. "Restless Desire: Rider Haggard, Orientalism and the New Woman." *Women: A Cultural Review* 10.1 (1999): 35–46.

Rosenthal, M. L., ed. *Selected Poems and Two Plays of William Butler Yeats.* Updated ed. New York: Collier, 1962.

Rowe, Margaret Moan. *Doris Lessing.* New York: St. Martin's, 1994.

Rowland, Susan. *C. G. Jung and Literary Theory.* New York: Palgrave, 1999.

———. *Jung: A Feminist Revision.* Cambridge, UK: Polity, 2002.

Rubenstein, Roberta. "Notes for Proteus: Doris Lessing Reads the *Zeitgeist.*" *Doris Lessing: Interrogating the Times.* Ed. Debrah Raschke, Phyllis Sternberg Perrakis, and Sandra Singer. Columbus: The Ohio State UP, 2010. 11–31.

———. *The Novelistic Vision of Doris Lessing: Breaking the Forms of Consciousness.* Urbana: U of Illinois P, 1979.

Russo, Joseph. "A Jungian Analysis of Homer's Odysseus." *The Cambridge Companion to Jung.* Ed. Polly Young-Eisendrath and Terence Dawson. New York: Cambridge UP, 1997. 240–54.

Said, Edward W. *Orientalism.* New York: Vintage, 1979.

Sarma, S. K. "Okonkwo and His *Chi*: Notes towards a Mythological Approach to Achebe's Novels." *Indian Response to African Writing.* Ed. Adapa Ramakrsnaravu and C. R. Visweswara Rao. New Delhi: Prestige, 1993. 66–70.

Sarvan, Charles. "*Disgrace*: A Path to Grace?" *World Literature Today* 78.1 (2004): 26–29. *Biography in Context.* Web. 25 Sept. 2015.

Scheub, Harold. "'When a Man Fails Alone': A Man and His *Chi* in Chinua Achebe's *Things Fall Apart.*" Okpewho 95–122.

Schiller, Friedrich. *Letters Upon the Aesthetic Education of Man.* Internet History Sourcebooks. Fordham University. Web. 17 Apr. 2013.

Schlueter, Paul. *The Novels of Doris Lessing.* Carbondale: Southern Illinois UP, 1969.

Schreiner, Olive. *Olive Schreiner Letters.* Ed. Richard Rive. Vol. 1. New York: Oxford UP, 1988.

———. *The Story of an African Farm.* Ed. Joseph Bristow. New York: Oxford UP, 1992.

———. *Woman and Labour.* London: T. Fisher Unwin, 1911. *California Digital Library.* E-book.

Seidel, Linda. "Death and Transformation in J. M. Coetzee's *Disgrace*." *Journal of Colonialism and Colonial History* 2.3 (2001): n.p.

Seydow, John J. "Francis Macomber's Spurious Masculinity." *Hemingway Review* 1.1 (1981): 33–41.

Shamdasani, Sonu. *C. G. Jung: A Biography in Books*. New York: Norton, 2012.

Shapple, D. L. "Artful Tales of Origination in Olive Schreiner's *The Story of an African Farm*." *Nineteenth-Century Literature* 59.1 (2004): 53–77. *JSTOR*. Web. 10 June 2014.

Sharp, Daryl. *Jung Lexicon: A Primer of Terms & Concepts*. Toronto: Inner City, 1991.

Sheils, Colleen M. "Opera, Byron, and a South African Psyche in J. M. Coetzee's *Disgrace*." *Current Writing: Text and Reception in Southern Africa* 15.1 (2003): 38–50. Web. 5 Oct. 2015.

Shelley, Percy Bysshe. "Alastor; or the Spirit of Solitude." Perkins 1020–29.

——. "A Defence of Poetry." Perkins 1131–46.

Showalter, Elaine. *Sexual Anarchy: Gender and Culture at the* Fin de Siècle. New York: Viking, 1990.

Singleton, Mary Ann. *The City and the Veld: The Fiction of Doris Lessing*. Lewisburg: Bucknell UP, 1977.

Smith, Christopher. "Laurens van der Post." *African Writers*. Ed. C. Brian Cox. Vol. 2. New York: Scribner's, 1997. 879–91.

Smith, Rowland. *Critical Essays on Nadine Gordimer*. Boston: G. K. Hall, 1990.

Snodgrass, Mary Ellen. *Barbara Kingsolver: A Literary Companion*. Jefferson: McFarland, 2004. McFarland Literacy Companions 2.

Soyinka, Wole. *Myth, Literature and the African World*. New York: Cambridge UP, 1976.

Spencer, Herbert. *First Principles*. New York: De Witt Revolving Fund, 1958.

Spencer, Jane. "Aphra Behn's *Oroonoko* and Women's Literary Authority." *Early Women's Writers, 1600–1720*. Ed. Anita Pacheco. London: Longman, 1998. 183–96.

Spenser, Edmund. "Letter to Raleigh." *Edmund Spenser's Poetry*. Ed. Hugh Maclean and Anne Lake Prescott. 3rd ed. New York: Norton, 1993. 1–4.

Sprague, Claire, and Virginia Tiger, eds. *Critical Essays on Doris Lessing*. Boston: G. K. Hall, 1986.

Stevens, Anthony. *Private Myths: Dreams and Dreaming*. Cambridge: Harvard UP, 1995.

——. *The Two Million-Year-Old Self*. College Station: Texas A&M UP, 1993.

Stiebel, Lindy. *Imagining Africa: Landscape in H. Rider Haggard's African Romances*. Westport: Greenwood, 2001.

Stock, A. G. "Yeats and Achebe." Innes and Lindfors 86–91.

Stoltzfus, Ben. "Sartre, *Nada*, and Hemingway's African Stories." Krstovic 217–30.

Stott, Rebecca. *The Fabrication of the Late-Victorian* Femme Fatale*: The Kiss of Death*. London: Macmillan,1992.

——. "'Scaping the Body: Of Cannibal Mothers and Colonial Landscapes." *The New Woman in Fiction and Fact: Fin-de-Siècle Feminisms*. Ed. Angelique Richardson and Chris Willis. New York: Palgrave, 2001. 150–66.

Straton, Florence. *Contemporary African Literature & the Politics of Gender*. London: Routledge, 1994. E-book.

Strychacz, Thomas. *Hemingway's Theaters of Masculinity*. Baton Rouge: Louisiana State UP, 2003.

Sugiyama, Michelle Scalise. "What's Love Got to Do with It? An Evolutionary Analysis of 'The Short Happy Life of Francis Macomber.'" Krstovic 142–51.

Sussman, Charlotte. "The Other Problem with Women: Reproduction and Slave Culture in Aphra Behn's *Oroonoko*." *Rereading Aphra Behn: History, Theory, and Criticism*. Ed. Heidi Hunter. Charlottesville: U of Virginia P, 1993. 212–33.

Sutcliffe, Patricia Casey. "Saying it Right in *Disgrace*: David Lurie, *Faust*, and the Romantic Conception of Language." McDonald 173–201.

Temple-Thurston, Barbara. *Nadine Gordimer Revisited*. New York: Twayne, 1999.

Tennyson, Alfred. "Ulysses." *Victorian Poetry and Prose*. Ed. Lionel Trilling and Harold Bloom. New York: Oxford UP, 1973. 416–18.

Thorpe, Michael. *Doris Lessing*. Ed. Ian Scott-Kilvert. London: F. Mildner, 1973.

Tiger, Virginia. "'Woman of Many Summers': *The Summer before the Dark*." Sprague and Tiger 86–94.

Tocqueville, Alexis de. *Democracy in America*. 1840. Trans. Henry Reeve. 2 vols. *Project Gutenberg*. Web. 16 July 2014.

Todd, Janet. *New Casebooks: Aphra Behn*. London, Macmillan, 1999.

Torgovnick, Marianna. *Primitive Passions: Men, Women, and the Quest for Ecstasy*. New York: Knopf, 1997.

Tucker, Martin. *Africa in Modern Literature: A Survey of Contemporary Writing in English*. New York: Frederick Ungar, 1967.

Van der Berk, Tjeu. *Jung on Art: The Autonomy of the Creative Drive*. New York: Routledge, 2012.

Van der Merwe, Chris N., and Pumla Gobodo-Madikizela. *Narrating Our Healing: Perspectives on Working through Trauma*. Newcastle, UK: Cambridge Scholars, 2007.

Van der Post, Laurens. *The Dark Eye in Africa*. New York: Morrow, 1955.

——. *A Far-Off Place*. New York: Harvest/Harcourt, 1974.

——. *The Heart of the Hunter*. New York: Morrow, 1961.

——. *Jung and the Story of Our Time*. New York: Vintage, 1977.

——. *The Lost World of the Kalahari*. New York: Morrow, 1958.

——. *Man and the Shadow*. London: South Place Ethical Society, 1971.

——. *A Mantis Carol*. Covelo, CA: Island/Morrow, 1975.

——. "Our Mother Which Art in Earth." *Quadrant* 23.2 (1990): 9–19.

——. *A Story like the Wind*. New York: Harvest/Harcourt, 1972.

——. *Venture to the Interior*. New York: Morrow, 1951.

——. *A Walk with a White Bushman*. New York: Morrow, 1986.

Van Wyk Smith, Malvern. "Napoleon and the Giant: Discursive Conflicts in Olive Schreiner's *Story of an African Farm*." *Ariel: A Review of International English Literature* 30.1 (1999): 151–63.

Vermeulen, Pieter. "Wordsworth and the Recollection of South Africa." *J. M. Coetzee in Context and Theory*. Ed. Elleke Boehmer and Robert Eaglestone. London, UK: Continuum, 2009. 47–59.

Vlastos, Marion. "Doris Lessing and R. D. Laing: Psychopolitics and Prophecy." *PMLA* 91.2 (1976): 245–58. *JSTOR*. Web. 15 June 2015.

Virgil. *Aeneid*. Trans. Frederick Ahl. New York: Oxford UP, 2007. E-book.

——. *The Aeneid of Virgil*. Trans. Allen Mandelbaum. New York: Bantam, 1971.

Voeller, Carey. "'He Only Looked Sad the Same Way I Felt': The Textual Confessions of Hemingway's Hunters." Krstovic 230–37.

Von Der Vogelweide, Walter. "Virtue and Charm." *Selected Poems of Walter Von Der Vogelweide, the Minnesinger*. Trans. Walter Alison Phillips. London: Smith, Elder, 1896. 31–32. E-book.

Von Franz, Marie-Louise. *Puer Aeternus: A Psychological Study of the Adult Struggle with the Paradise of Childhood*. 2nd ed. Santa Monica: Sigo, 1970.

Wagner-Martin, Linda. *Barbara Kingsolver's* The Poisonwood Bible*: A Reader's Guide*. New York: Continuum, 2001.

——. *Barbara Kingsolver's World: Nature, Art, and the Twenty-First Century*. New York: Bloomsbury, 2014.

Watkins, Susan. *Doris Lessing*. New York: Manchester UP, 1988.

Watson, James Gray. "'A Sound Basis of Union': Structural and Thematic Balance in 'The Short Happy Life of Francis Macomber.'" *Fitzgerald/Hemingway Annual* (1974): 215–28.

Werness, Hope B. *The Continuum Encyclopedia of Animal Symbolism in Art*. New York: Continuum, 2004.

West, Rinda. *Out of the Shadow: Ecopsychology, Story, and Encounters with the Land*. Charlottesville: U of Virginia P, 2007.

"Western Wind." *Medieval English Literature*. Ed. J. B. Trapp. New York: Oxford UP, 1973. 417.

"What Dreams Reveal: Scientists Come to Kenya to Study Native Mind: Research Among the Bagishu: Psychological Connection Between European and Africa: Primitive Survival in Man." *East African Standard* 19 Nov. 1925: 5.

Whelan, P. T. "H(enry) Rider Haggard." *British Short-Fiction Writers, 1880–1914: The Romantic Tradition*. Ed. William F. Naufftus. *Dictionary of Literary Bibliography*. Vol. 156. Detroit: Gale Research, 1995. *Literature Resource Center*. Web. 16 Aug. 2013.

White, Jeanna Fuston. "The One-Eyed Preacher, His Crooked Daughter, and Villagers Waving Their Stumps: Barbara Kingsolver's Use of Disability in *The Poisonwood Bible*." *South Central Review* 26.3 (2009): 131–44. *JSTOR*. Web. 23 Nov. 2015.

Whittaker, Ruth. *Doris Lessing*. London: Macmillan, 1988.

Wilmsen, Edwin N. "Primitive Politics in Sanctified Landscapes: The Ethnographic Fictions of Laurens van der Post." *Journal of Southern African Studies* 21.2 (1995): 201–23. *JSTOR*. Web. 7 Aug. 2014.

Wolff, Toni. *Structural Forms of the Feminine Psyche*. Trans. Paul Watzlawick. Zurich: Students Association, C. G. Jung Institute, 1956.

Wordsworth, William. "Lines Composed a Few Miles above Tintern Abbey." Perkins 301–03.

——. "My Heart Leaps Up." Perkins 330.

——. "Ode: Intimations of Immortality from Recollections of Early Childhood." Perkins 331–34.

——. *The Prelude*. Perkins 372–423.

Wren, Robert M. *Achebe's World: The Historical and Cultural Context of the Novels*. Washington, DC: Three Continents, 1980.

Wright, Laura. "'Does he have it in him to be the woman?': The Performance of Displacement in J. M. Coetzee's *Disgrace*." *Ariel: A Review of International English Literature* 37.4 (2006): 83–102.

Wright, Laurence. "David Lurie's Learning and the Meaning of J. M. Coetzee's *Disgrace*." *J. M. Coetzee's Austerities*. Ed. Graham Bradshaw and Michael Neill. Farnham, UK: Ashgate, 2010. 147–62.

Yeats, William Butler. "Byzantium." Rosenthal 132–33.

——. "The Second Coming." Rosenthal 91.

Young, Gloria L. "Quest and Discovery: Joseph Conrad's and Carl Jung's African Journeys." *Modern Fiction Studies* 28.4 (1982–1983): 583–89.

Young, Philip. *Ernest Hemingway: A Reconsideration*. University Park: Pennsylvania State UP, 1966.

INDEX